"Never has it been more important to think carefully about the intent of the human creation narrative—to view it through the objective of the narrator as the story was first written down and to seek to understand it through the mind of the audience as it was first heard. . . . Given his many years of teaching experience in evangelical institutions and his remarkable communication skill, perhaps no one is better equipped to guide us through this task than John Walton. *The Lost World of Adam and Eve* is a masterful analysis of authorial intent and contextual understanding of the Genesis narrative in its contemporary Hebrew culture. Walton's years of teaching have enabled him to successfully anticipate all the main questions and to address each in a highly readable fashion."

Darrel Falk, professor of biology, Point Loma Nazarene University, senior advisor for dialog, BioLogos

"Can an interpretation of Genesis 2–3 be true to the biblical text and be supported by the most legitimate claims of science? Can one exegete the accounts of the creation and fall of Adam and Eve in light of all of the partial parallels in other ancient Near Eastern creation literature and still believe in the inerrancy of Scripture? John Walton shows that the answer to both questions is a resounding 'yes.' Whether or not one agrees with every detail of Walton's interpretation, one has to admire the brilliance, clarity and sensibility of his approach. This is a must-read for anyone who thinks one has to choose between faith and science."

Craig L. Blomberg, Distinguished Professor of New Testament, Denver Seminary

"This excellent volume on reading Genesis 2 and 3 will be enormously helpful to Bible readers who wish to take seriously both Scripture and contemporary scientific perspectives on such matters as human origins. Building on previous work, Walton plots an orthodox Christian path through some challenging territory, writing in a highly accessible manner and making great use of example. His extensive knowledge of the ancient Near Eastern world constantly illuminates the text. The reader will not only gain deep insight into the opening chapters of Genesis, but (more generally) will also be helped to think well about what it means to read any ancient text competently."

Iain Provan, Marshall Sheppard Professor of Biblical Studies, Regent College

"John Walton is a gift to the church. In his writing and speaking he has helped Christians to faithfully read the Bible in an environment of competing scientific claims. Now in *The Lost World of Adam and Eve* Walton provides a profoundly evangelical account of how the Bible speaks of Adam and Eve by treating the statements of Scripture in their ancient historical context. This book is the first thing to put in the hands of those wrestling with the perceived tension between the Bible and science."

Timothy Gombis, Grand Rapids Theological Seminary

"I wish every Christian would read this book. John Walton is helping an entire generation of people—believers and skeptics alike—learn how to read Genesis as it was meant to be read. I can't imagine any student of the Bible not being mesmerized by his scholarship. I think this will open up doors of faith and understanding to a vast audience."

John Ortberg, senior pastor of Menlo Park Presbyterian Church, author of *Soul Keeping*

"When strident voices who call the first three chapters of Genesis nothing but myth are met by equally strident voices declaring that the Bible, the gospel and the church will thereby collapse from the inside, we are tempted to take a side and start cheering. Then come the voices of reason that seek an opportunity to calm down the strident voices that often refuse to listen. John Walton is a voice of reason and he has shown time and time again that we must learn to read the Bible as God gave it, not the way we'd like it to be. Here we are treated to more 'propositions' about Adam and Eve that will anchor our faith in the ancient world in such a way that the fresh Spirit of God can blow on those chapters to illuminate all who will listen. Thank God for *The Lost World of Adam and Eve*."

Scot McKnight, professor of New Testament, Northern Seminary

"We who are committed to the authority of Scripture believe it is inerrant in all that it affirms. Determining what it's affirming is the tricky part, and that is precisely what John Walton helps us discern. Armed with a robust knowledge of the Old Testament and its ancient context, Walton equips Christians to read Genesis on its own terms rather than the terms we've inherited from the modern 'science versus faith' narrative of our culture. As a result, Walton opens up new possibilities in the ongoing theological and biblical debate concerning human origins with strong scholarship and Christ-like humility."

Skye Jethani, author of *With*, SkyeJethani.com

"In this ground-breaking work the author places Adam and Eve firmly where they belong—in the cultural and textual world of the ancient Near East. Scholarly and readable, the text seen through ancient Near Eastern eyes provides fascinating new insights into the question of human origins. The fine chapter by N. T. Wright provides the 'icing on the cake.' This book is warmly recommended to all those interested in how the Bible addresses the key question of human uniqueness."

Denis Alexander, emeritus director of the Faraday Institute for Science and Religion, St. Edmund's College, Cambridge, author of *Creation or Evolution: Do We Have to Choose?*

THE
LOST
WORLD
OF
ADAM
AND EVE

Genesis 2 3 and the
Human Origins Debate

JOHN H. WALTON

With a contribution by N. T. Wright

IVP Academic

An imprint of InterVarsity Press
Downers Grove, Illinois

InterVarsity Press
P.O. Box 1400, Downers Grove, IL 60515-1426
ivpress.com
email@ivpress.com

InterVarsity Press® is the book-publishing division of InterVarsity Christian Fellowship/USA®, a movement of students and faculty active on campus at hundreds of universities, colleges and schools of nursing in the United States of America, and a member movement of the International Fellowship of Evangelical Students. For information about local and regional activities, visit intervarsity.org.

Cover design: Cindy Kiple
Interior design: Beth McGill
Images: G. Dagli Orti / Bridgeman Images

ISBN 978-0-8308-2461-8 (print)
ISBN 978-0-8308-9771-1 (digital)

Printed in the United States of America ∞

Library of Congress Cataloging-in-Publication Data

Walton, John H., 1952-
The lost world of Adam and Eve : Genesis 2-3 and the human origins debate / John H. Walton ; with a contribution by N.T.Wright.
     pages cm
  Includes bibliographical references.
  ISBN 978-0-8308-2461-8 (pbk. : alk. paper)
 1. Bible. Genesis, II-III—Criticism, interpretation, etc. 2.
Theological anthropology—Christianity. 3. Adam (Biblical figure) 4.
Eve (Biblical figure) I. Title.
  BS1235.52.W35 2015
  222'.1106--dc23

                                                      2014044466

P	21	20	19	18	17	16	15	14	13	12	11	10	9	8	7	6	5	4	3	2	1
Y	33	32	31	30	29	28	27	26	25	24	23	22	21	20	19	18	17	16	15		

To my student research assistants over the years who have
helped me become a better writer.

Caryn Reeder
Liz Klassen
Melissa Fitzpatrick
Alyssa Walker
Shawn Goodwin
John Treece
Ashley Edewaard
Aubrey Buster
Kathryn Cobb
Kim Carlton
Alexa Marquardt

I am grateful for the careful reading and helpful suggestions provided
by Jonathan Walton, Aubrey Buster and Kim Carlton.

Contents

Introduction

Of the modern controversies currently facing the church, one of the most heated and most prominent concerns the relationship of the Bible to science in general and human origins in particular. Is there an essential, inherent conflict between the claims of the Bible and the current scientific consensus about human origins (a consensus involving biological evolution, common ancestry, comparative genomics, the fossil record and anthropology, just to name a few of the major contributors)?

It is true that science is changing at least in little ways all the time, and, in contrast, it is easy to think of the Bible as static and unchanging. Though the Bible itself does not change, we realize that our interpretation of Scripture is much more dynamic, and the resulting shape of theology consequently subject to constant reassessment (more on the perimeter than in the core). Two millennia of church history have witnessed some dramatic differences in hermeneutics, some deeply ingrained theological controversies (some options cast off as heretical, some bringing major splits and some being retained side by side) and some substantial disagreements about the interpretation of particular passages. The history of interpretation of Genesis 1–3 in particular is anything but monolithic, and neither doctrine nor exegesis is characterized by complete homogeneity. This fact can be observed even in the earliest periods.

> One feature becomes clear from even a cursory study of this period [the first couple of centuries after Christ]: we do not find a univocal reading or a single method. . . . We do, however, find a consistent and coherent pattern of reading, whose theological character is considerably different from the modern mainstream.[1]

This means that Christianity has been forced to be content with a number of alternatives on the table for interpreting the early chapters of Genesis. It is sadly true that some have adopted a view that only their particular parochial reading is legitimate for a "real" Christian. We must confess to our corporate shame that blood has even been shed.

As interpreters of Scripture and as theologians, we are accountable to the biblical text. As important as our theological traditions are, since interpretations and even the hermeneutics by which we interpret have changed over the centuries, we cannot be unflinchingly accountable to tradition at every level. New insights and new information can emerge at any time. Several hundred years ago, renewed access to the original languages had significant impact on biblical interpretation. In recent decades, the availability of documents from the ancient world has provided a remarkable resource for our reading of the biblical text. We dare not neglect these tools when they can contribute so significantly to our interpretation.

On the science side of the equation, the last 150 years have likewise been revolutionary. The development of evolutionary theory was only the beginning, and the exciting information available from the mapping of the human genome is perhaps the most recent advance, but certainly not the last, that provides a basis for investigating what we can learn about human origins. To the dismay of those who take the Bible seriously, the various fields of science are often used to mount attacks against the Bible and against faith. Unfortunately, that has

caused some to become dismissive or antagonistic toward science. This should not be the case for Christians since we affirm the importance of both special revelation (in the Bible and in Jesus) and general revelation (in the world that God has created and that science helps us understand). The fact that some wield science as a weapon against faith is no reason to think that science or scientists are the problem. The philosophy of naturalism is the problem. After all, the same people who use science as a weapon would be just as inclined to use the Bible as a weapon against those who take it as the Word of God. Our response should be simply to try to explain the Bible better and to make it clear to the abusers how they are viewing it wrongly. We can do the same with science.

In this book, I will contend that the perceived threat posed by the current consensus about human origins is overblown. That consensus accepts the principles of common ancestry and evolutionary theory as the explanation for the existence of all life. Though we should not blindly accept the scientific consensus if its results are questionable on scientific principles, we can reach an understanding that regardless of whether the scientific conclusions stand the test of time or not, they pose no threat to biblical belief. Admittedly, however, a perception of conflict is not uncommon.

With that in mind, I will not give very much attention to the question of the legitimacy of the scientific claims. Instead I will be conducting a close reading of the Bible as an ancient document *and* as Scripture to explore the claims that it makes. The focus will be Genesis, but I will bring the full canon under consideration. I will not be trying to isolate *the* right answer or interpretation but will attempt to show that there are faithful readings of Scripture that, while they may differ somewhat from some traditional readings of the past, find support in the text and are compatible with what we find in the context of the ancient Near East as well as with some of the more recent scientific discoveries. At the same time, the broad spectrum of core the-

ology is retained: the authority of Scripture,[2] God's intimate and active role as Creator regardless of the mechanisms he used or the time he took, that material creation was ex nihilo, that we have all been created by God, and that there was a point in time when sin entered the world, therefore necessitating salvation.

We are not compelled to bring the Bible into conformity either with its cultural context or with modern science, but if an interpretation of Genesis, for example, coincides with what we find as characteristic of the ancient world or with what seem to be sound scientific conclusions, all the better. Even in a Bible-first approach (in contrast to a science-first or even extrabiblical-first approach), we can be attentive to the ancient world or to modern science without compromising our convictions about the Bible. Either information from the literature of the ancient world or new insights from scientific investigation may appropriately prompt us to go back to the Bible to reconsider our interpretations. This does not mean that we blindly force the text to conform to demand from other fields. The Bible must retain its autonomy and speak for itself. But that is also true when we hold traditional interpretations up to the Bible. The biblical text must retain its autonomy from tradition. We must always be willing to return to the text and consider it with fresh eyes. That is the goal of this book. I certainly do not have all the answers, but prompted by new information from the ancient world and new insights by modern science, I return to the biblical text to see whether there are options that have been missed or truths that have become submerged under the frozen surface of traditional readings. I have no intention of undermining traditional theology—I work from a firm conviction about the authority of Scripture and those traditions that have been built on interpretation of Scripture. But within our theological framework, there is plenty of room to read the text anew and perhaps even to be surprised by it.

Proposition 1

Genesis Is an Ancient Document

Biblical authority is tied inseparably to the author's intention. God vested his authority in a human author, so we must consider what the human author intended to communicate if we want to understand God's message. Two voices speak, but the human author is our doorway into the room of God's meaning and message. That means that when we read Genesis, we are reading an ancient document and should begin by using only the assumptions that would be appropriate for the ancient world. We must understand how the ancients thought and what ideas underlay their communication.[1]

In one sense, every successful act of communication is accomplished by various degrees of accommodation on the part of the communicator, but only for the sake of the audience that he or she has in mind. Accommodation must bridge the gap if communicator and audience do not share the same language, the same command of language, the same culture or the same experiences, but we do not expect a communicator to accommodate an audience that he or she does not know or anticipate. High-context communication is communication that takes place between insiders in situations in which the communicator and audience share much in common. In such situations, less accommodation is necessary for effective communication to take place, and, therefore, much might be left unsaid that an outsider might need in order to fully understand the communication.

This is illustrated in the traffic reports that we hear constantly in Chicago, where the references to times of travel and locations of problems assume that the listener has intimate knowledge of the highways. As a regular commuter, I find the traffic reports that offer times of travel from various points and identification of stretches where one might encounter congestion to be very meaningful. When it is reported that it is a thirty-eight-minute trip from "the cave" to "the junction" and that it is congested from "the slip to the Nagle curve," I know exactly what to expect. When out-of-town guests visit, however, this information only confuses them. They do not know what the slip or the cave is (nor could they find them on a map), they don't know how far these places are from one another, and they don't know that on a good day one can go from the cave to the junction in about eight minutes.

By contrast, in low-context communication, high levels of accommodation are necessary as an insider attempts communication with an outsider. A low-context traffic report would have to identify local landmarks and normal traffic times between them for out-of-town listeners or inexperienced commuters. These would be much longer reports. If the traffic reporter made the report understandable to the out-of-town visitor, it would seem interminable and annoying to the regular commuter it seeks to serve.

I propose that in the Bible God has accommodated the communicator and immediate audience, employing the communicator in a high-context communication appropriate to the audience. So, for example, a prophet and his audience share a history, a culture, a language and the experiences of their contemporaneous lives. When we read the Bible, we enter the context of that communication as low-context outsiders who need to use all our inferential tools to discern the nature of the communicator's illocution and meaning. We have to use research to fill in all the information that would not have to be said by the prophet in his high-context communication to his audience. This is how we, as modern readers, must interact with an ancient text.

Those who take the Bible seriously believe that God has inspired the locutions (words, whether spoken or written) that the communicator has used to accomplish their joint (divine + human author) illocutions[2] (which lead to an understanding of intentions, claims, affirmations and, ultimately, meaning) but that the foundational locutions are tied to the communicator's world. That is, God has made accommodation to the high-context communication between the implied communicators and their implied audience so as to optimize and facilitate the transmission of meaning via an authoritative illocution. Inspiration is tied to *locutions* (they have their source in God); *illocutions* define the necessary path to meaning that can be defined as characterized by authority.

At times our distance from the ancient communicator might mean that we misunderstand the communication because of elements that are foreign to us, or because we do not share ways of thinking with the communicator. Comparative studies help us to understand more fully the form of the biblical authors' employed genres and the nature of their rhetorical devices so that we do not mistake these elements for something that they never were. Such an exercise does not compromise the authority of Scripture but ascribes authority to that which the communicator was actually communicating. We also need comparative studies in order to recognize the aspects of the communicators' cognitive environment[3] that are foreign to us and to read the text in light of their world and worldview.

Consequently, we are obliged to respect the text by recognizing the sort of text that it is and the nature of the message that it offers. In that regard, we have long recognized that the Bible is not a scientific textbook. That is, God's intention is not to teach science or to reveal science. He *does* reveal his work in the world, but he *doesn't* reveal how the world works.

As an example of the foreign aspects of the cognitive environment, people in the ancient world had no category for what we call *natural laws*. When they thought of cause and effect, even though they could make all the observations that we make (e.g., when you push something it moves; when you drop something it falls), they were more inclined to see the world's operations in terms of divine cause. Everything worked the way that it did because God set it up that way and God maintained the system. They would have viewed the cosmos not as a machine but as a kingdom, and God communicated to them about the world in those terms. His revelation to them was not focused on giving them a more sophisticated understanding of the mechanics of the natural world.

He likewise did not hide information of that sort in the text for later readers to discover. An assumption on our part that he did would have no reliable controls. For example, in the days when we believed in a steady-state universe, people could easily have gone to the Bible to find confirmation of that science. But today we do not believe the steady-state theory to be true. Today we might think we find confirmation of the Big Bang or the expanding universe, but maybe someday we will no longer consider those to be true. Such approaches cannot be adopted within an authority framework.

In the same way, the authority of the text is not respected when statements in the Bible that are part of ancient science are used as if they are God's descriptions of modern scientific understanding. When the text talks about thinking with our hearts or intestines, it is not proposing scientific ideas that we must confirm if we wish to take biblical authority seriously. We need not try to propose ways that our blood-pumping organs or digestive systems are physiologically involved in cognitive processes. This is simply communication in the context of ancient science. In the same way, when the text talks about the water below the vault and the water above the vault (Gen 1:6) we do not have to construct a cosmic system that has waters above and waters below. Everyone in the ancient world believed there were waters above because when it rained water came down. Therefore, when the biblical text talks about "water above" (Gen 1:7), it is not offering authoritative revelation of scientific facts. If we conclude that there are not, strictly speaking, waters above, we have not thereby identified an error in Scripture. Rather, we have recognized that God vests the authority of the text elsewhere. Authority is tied to the message the author intends to communicate as an agent of God's revelation. God has accommodated himself to the world of ancient Israel to initiate that revelation. We therefore recognize that although the Bible is written for us (indeed, for everyone), it is not written to us. In its context, it is not communicated in our language; it is not addressed to our culture; it does not anticipate the questions about the world and its operations that stem from our modern situations and issues.

If we read modern ideas into the text, we skirt the authority of the text and in effect compromise it, arrogating authority to ourselves and our ideas. This is especially true when we interpret the text as if it is making reference to modern science, of which the author and audience had no knowledge. The text cannot mean what it never meant. What the text says may converge with modern science, but the text does not make authoritative claims pertaining to modern science (e.g., some statements may coincide with Big Bang cosmology, but the text does not authoritatively establish Big Bang cosmology). What the author meant and what the audience understood place restrictions on what information has authority. The only way we can move with certainty beyond that which was intended by the Old Testament author is if another authoritative voice (e.g., a New Testament author) gives us that extension of meaning.

I propose instead that our doctrinal affirmations about Scripture (authority, inerrancy, infallibility, etc.) attach to the intended message of the human communicators (as it was given by the divine communicator). This is not to say that we therefore believe everything they believe (they *did* believe that there was a solid sky) but that we express our commitment to the communicative act. Since the form of their message is grounded in their language and culture, it is important to differentiate between what the communicators can be inferred to believe and the focus of their intended teaching.[4] So, for example, it is no surprise that Israel believed in a solid sky and that God accommodated his communication to that model in his communication to Israel. But since the text's message is not an assertion of the true shape of cosmic geography, we can safely reject those details without jeopardizing authority or inerrancy. Such cosmic geography is in the belief set of the communicators but is employed in the framework of their communication, not the content of their message. Beliefs may be discernible specifically in the way they frame their ideas or generally in the communicator's context. Often we judge the author's beliefs about his world as irrelevant or immaterial to the text's message and therefore unrelated to the authority of the text. In the same way, the idea that one thinks with one's entrails is built into the expressions that they use and the beliefs of the biblical communicators, but the revelatory intention is not to make assertions about physiology or anatomy. In these cases, I would contend that cosmic geography and anatomy/physiology are part of the framework of the communication. To set aside such culturally bound ideas does not jeopardize the text's message or authority. Genre is also part of the communication framework and is therefore culturally bound. We have to account for the cultural aspects and shape of the genre before we can properly understand the communicator's intentions.[5] At the other end of the spectrum, having once understood the message, we cannot bypass it to adopt only a generalized application (e.g., "love God and your neighbor and you will do fine") that dismisses as accommodation and potentially erroneous the communicator's genre-encased message.

The authority and inerrancy of the text is, and has traditionally been, attached to what it affirms. Those affirmations are not of a scientific nature. The text does not affirm that we think with our entrails (though it communicates in those terms because that is what the ancient audience believed). The text does not affirm that there are waters above. The question that we must therefore address is whether the text, in its authority, makes any affirmations about material human origins. If the communication of the text adopts the "science" and the ideas that everyone in the ancient world believed (as it did with physiology and the waters above), then we would not consider that authoritative revelation or an affirmation of the text.

So, the question is, is there any new revelation pertaining to science in the Bible? The question does not pertain to statements the Bible makes about historical events that take place in the world, such as the plagues or the parting of the Red Sea. Those historical events involve unusual occurrences that by their very nature are likely beyond the ability of science to explain (not only in the phenomenon, but in the forewarning, timing and selective targeting). The question instead pertains to the regularly occurring events and the normal mechanics and operations of the world around us. Does the Bible give any revised or updated explanations of those? I would contend that it does not. Every aspect of the regular operations of the world as described in the Bible reflects the perspectives and ideas of the ancient world—ideas that Israel along with everyone else in the ancient world already believed. Though the text has much revelation to offer about the nature of God and his character and work, there is not a single incidence of new information being offered by God to the Israelites about the regular operation of the world (what we would call natural science). The text is thoroughly ancient and communicates in that context.

This does not preclude the text from reporting historical events that would have involved science that the ancients did not understand (e.g., the mechanics of the flood). In such cases, the Bible is not *providing* scientific revelation; it is being *silent* on scientific matters. Whatever scientific explanations we might posit would not carry the authority of the text (just as our interpretations do not carry authority). When we apply these insights to the biblical view of human origins, we find that while the text offers theological affirmations (God as active, humans in his image, etc.) and may offer an account of historical events (which will be an issue for genre analysis, discussed later), it does not offer explanations of natural mechanisms. God did it, but the text does not offer a scientific explanation of how he did it. Instead, the text describes origins in ancient-world terms, although informed by correct theology.

We can begin to understand the claims of the text as an ancient document first of all by paying close attention to what the text says and doesn't say. It is too easy to make assumptions that are intrusive based on our own culture, cognitive environment, traditions or questions. It takes a degree of discipline as readers who are outsiders not to assume our modern perspectives and impose them on the text, but often we do not even know we are doing it because our own context is so intrinsic to our thinking and the ancient world is an unknown. The best path to recognizing the distinctions between ancient and modern thinking is to begin paying attention to the ancient world. This is accomplished by immersion in the literature of the ancient world. This would by no means supersede Scripture, but it can be a tool for understanding Scripture. When we are trying to understand the opening chapters of Genesis, our immersion is not limited to the cosmology texts of the ancient world. The clues to cognitive environment can be pieced together from a wide variety of ancient literature. Obviously, not everyone can undertake this task, just as not everyone can devote the time necessary to master Hebrew and Greek. Those who have the gifts, calling and passion for the original languages and the opportunity to study, research and write, use their expertise for the benefit of those who do not. In the same way, those who have the gifts, calling and passion for the study of the ancient world and the opportunity to research and write can use their expertise for the benefit of those who do not.

Such study is not a violation of the clarity ("perspicuity") of Scripture propagated by the Reformers. They were not arguing that every part of Scripture was transparent to any casual reader. If they believed that, they would not have had to write hundreds of volumes trying to explain the complexities of interpretation at both exegetical and theological levels. They were, instead, trying to make the case that there *was* a "plain sense" of Scripture that was not esoteric, mystical or allegorical and could only be spiritually discerned. Everyone could have access to this plain sense.

Throughout most of history, scholars have not had access to the information from the ancient world and therefore could not use it to inform their interpretation. Even the early church fathers were interested in ac cessing the ancient world (as indicated from their frequent reference to Berossus, a Babylonian priest in the third century B.C.) but had very limited resources. However, since the beginning of the massive archaeological undertakings in Iraq in the middle of the nineteenth century, more than one million cuneiform texts have been excavated that expose the ancient literature by which we can gain important new insight into the ancient world. This is what provides the basis for our interpretation of the early chapters of Genesis as an ancient document.

In trying to engage Genesis as ancient literature, we do not want to dismiss the insights of interpreters who have populated the history of the church. At the same time, we recognize that those interpreters have hardly been univocal. It is true that the creeds and councils have offered their conclusions about the key theological issues, and those conclusions have often become the consensus of modern doctrine. Yet it has not been the practice of interpreters to disdain fresh attempts to exegete the early chapters on Genesis just because their forebears had arrived at their various conclusions. Martin Luther begins his chapter on Genesis claiming, "Until now there has not been anyone in the church either who has explained everything in the chapter with adequate skill."[6] We should therefore not be dissuaded from seeking fresh knowledge that may lead to reinterpretation, for when we do so, we are following in the footsteps of those interpreters who have gone before us, even as we stand on their shoulders.

In the Ancient World and the Old Testament, Creating Focuses on Establishing Order by Assigning Roles and Functions

We live in a culture that has assigned high, if not ultimate, value to that which is material. Science has a prominent place in our cognitive environment as the most reliable source of truth, and it stands as *the* authority when it comes to knowledge. Consequently, when we think about the origins of the universe in general or humans in particular, our epistemology (what it means to know something and how we know what we know) has scientific parameters, and our ontology (what it means for something to exist and what constitutes the existence of something) is decidedly material in nature. Many people in our culture are strict materialists and/or naturalists, who acknowledge only that which is empirical or material.

In such a climate, it is no surprise that we think in material terms when we think about origins. If existence is defined materially, then to bring something into existence (i.e., to create) is going to be understood in material terms. This way of thinking has so dominated our culture that we do not even question whether there might be other ways to think. We do not consider other options for ourselves, and the possibility that other cultures in other times or places might think differently is not a consideration. We read the opening chapters of Genesis and assume that since it is discussing creation, it must be focused on the material cosmos. We indiscriminately read the details of the text from our material perspective and believe that we are reading the text literally.

As we discussed in the previous chapter, however, the cognitive environment in the ancient world was very different from ours. Therefore, we must be cautious about reflexively imposing our cultural assumptions on the text. Indeed, to do so risks undermining the authority of the text by attaching it to ideas it was not addressing. As people who take the Bible seriously, we are obligated to read it for what the human communicator conveys to us about what God was revealing. The human communicator is going to do that in the context of his native cognitive environment.

Our procedure, then, is first to set aside our own cultural assumptions as much as we are able and then to try to read the text for what it is saying. Armed with our insights from a study of the text, we then take a look at the broader ancient Near Eastern cultural context to determine in which ways the Bible shows a common understanding and to identify ways in which God's revelation lifted the Israelites out of their familiar ways of thinking with a new vision of reality. We cannot start by asking of the Bible our scientific questions. The Bible is not revealing science, and the biblical authors and audience would be neither aware of nor concerned with our scientific way of thinking. Our questions would not resonate in their minds, and neither would they even have meaning to them. Likewise, we cannot start by seeing how or where the Bible corresponds to scientific thinking that we have today if we have not yet understood the text in its original context. We need to penetrate the ancient text and the ancient world to understand their insider communication and their cognitive environment. We want to know what questions they were answering and what the biblical communicator is affirming from his perspective. It is the Bible's claims that have authority, and our procedures must focus on those claims as they were originally intended.

As we begin, then, we cannot assume that we know what kind of activity *create* conveyed in the ancient world. Some people give value to taking the biblical text "literally," and, although that term can be a little slippery, we can all recognize the value of reading a text for what it intends to say—no more and no less. Having said that, we cannot be content to have the English text be the ultimate focus of that kind of attention because we recognize that the English text is already someone's fallible interpretation. All translation is interpretation, and we have no inspired translations. We have to analyze the Hebrew terms and their nuances as best we can.

If the translation "create" takes us in the right direction (and I believe that it does), we start with the idea that we are dealing with a verb that expresses the transition between nonexistence and existence. Consequently, before we can gain further understanding of the verb translated "create," we must investigate what constituted ultimate existence in the ancient cognitive environment. We cannot assume that they shared our materialistic, naturalistic, scientific perspectives and values or our obsessive focus on the physical world. We must set those aside and read the text afresh.

If creation involves a transition from nonexistence to existence, then a creation or origins account is likely to begin with the description of nonexistence. The way an account describes the initial situation prior to creation can therefore help us to see what it means by nonexistence. With this procedure in mind, we are basically asking the question, what sort of origins account is this? We cannot assume that it is the same kind of account that we would write, and we cannot assume that our intuition will take us the right direction. Intuition is culturally shaped.

The initial situation is described for us in Genesis 1:2 (and again in Gen 2:5-6). In fact, when we consider the many cosmology texts in the ancient world, we find it is commonplace to begin with a description of non-creation—the pre-creation condition. We will return to this after a consideration of the biblical account. The biblical account begins with Genesis 1:1, which is not a description of any actual activity of God.[1] Alternatively, it is widely recognized that Genesis 1:1 serves as a literary introduction to the subject matter that the chapter is going to discuss, stating the activity that God will be involved in. The main supporting evidences for this conclusion are (1) the fact that throughout Genesis sections begin with a literary introduction (Gen 2:4; 5:1; 6:9; etc.) and (2) the literary form of the account, concluding with a statement that on the seventh day God completed his work (Gen 2:2). This work was the work of creating (Gen 2:3, same word as in Gen 1:1), and what was created were the heavens and the earth (Gen 2:1). Thus, God's creating of the heavens and the earth took place *in* the seven days. Genesis 1:1 is outside the seven days, so we know that Genesis 1:1 tells the reader what is going to happen *in* the seven days. So we would read: "In the inaugural period [this is the nature of the Hebrew word 'beginning'], God created the heavens and earth, and this is how he did it." The actual account, therefore, begins in Genesis 1:2, where we find the description of the pre-creation situation.

As Genesis 1:2 opens, we find that material is already present (earth, seas) and that this inchoate world is covered with water and darkness. Again, we know that ancient Near Eastern cosmologies share this characteristic. Darkness and sea are conditions of non-order. But if material is already present, we are immediately prompted by the text to ask why it does not begin with no material if it is going to recount material origins. This should make us curious.

The most important descriptor that is offered in Genesis 1:2 is the Hebrew combination *tōhû wābōhû*, translated in the NIV "formless and empty." The implications are that materiality is generally present but without shape, and that the stage is empty of players. We must investigate whether that is what the Hebrew words actually convey.

The biblical writers left us many books, but a dictionary was not among them! We, therefore, have to try to determine what the words mean. The methodology for such lexical study has been firmly established and is confirmed as sound based on what we all recognize about language and how it works. Words mean what they are used to mean. There is sort of a social contract about how words can be used and what they communicate. Words can be given new meaning for a small group of individuals to use among themselves, or new meanings can develop in response to societal needs. In all of these cases, we can determine what words mean by the contexts in which they are used.[2]

The combination *tōhû* and *bōhû* occurs two other times in the Hebrew Bible (Is 34:11 and Jer 4:23, and *bōhû* never occurs by itself).[3] These uses offer no basis on which to determine that *bōhû* refers to emptiness. Usage is insufficient to establish its meaning. Sadly, then, we have to be content with what we can determine about the meaning of *tōhû*. In its twenty occurrences (more than half in Isaiah), we find that it often describes a wilderness or wasteland (e.g., Deut 32:10; Job 6:18; 12:24; Ps 107:40). It can describe the results of destruction (Jer 4:23). It is used to convey things that have no purpose or meaning (e.g., idols, Is 41:29, and those who make them, Is 44:9). All its uses can be consolidated in the notion of things that are of no purpose or worth. They are lacking order and function.

It now becomes clear that the starting condition in Genesis 1:2, the pre-creation situation that describes nonexistence, is a condition that is not lacking material. Rather, it is a situation that is lacking order and purpose. "Formless" is not a good choice because it still implies that material shape is the focus. It is not. This leads us to the conclusion that for Israel, creation resolves the absence of order and not the absence of material. If this "before" picture conveys "nonexistence," we would deduce that "existence" is not a material category for them; it is a functional category pertaining to an ordered condition.

This conclusion is further confirmed in Egyptian cosmologies, where the desert and the cosmic seas are described as nonexistent. Despite their obvious materiality, they are not considered to exist because they are not fully part of the ordered world. It is also confirmed in Sumerian and Babylonian texts, where the beginning state is described as "negative cosmology" or "denial of existence." The absence of creation is characterized as major gods not living, daylight and moonlight not shining, no vegetation, no priests performing rituals, nothing yet performing its duties. It is a time outside time. This same feature has long been recognized in the opening lines of the most famous Babylonian cosmology, *Enuma Elish*:

> When on high no name was given to heaven,
> Nor below was the netherworld called by name . . .
> When no gods at all had been brought forth,
> None called by names, none destinies ordained.[4]

Such texts express the pre-creation state as one lacking divine agency, a time in which the gods were not yet performing their duties.[5] In Genesis, however, the spirit of God is hovering over the waters—divine agency ready to move into action.

The next step in trying to clarify the nature of the ancient origins account in Genesis is to examine the operative verbs used in the account. The Hebrew verb translated "create" is *bārāʾ* (Gen 1:1, 21; 2:3), and the verb translated "made" is *ʿāśâ* (Gen 1:7, 16, 25, 26; 2:2, 3). The former occurs about fifty times in the Hebrew text, the latter over 2,600 times. Here I will only summarize conclusions since the detailed study has been done elsewhere.[6]

By observing the direct objects of the verb *bārāʾ* throughout Scripture, one can conclude that the verb does not intrinsically pertain to material existence. Although a number of occurrences *could* refer to material creation, many of them cannot. Ones that may refer to material existence only do so if we presuppose that materiality is the focus of the verbal activity. Those that clearly do not refer to materiality easily fit into the category that describes activity bringing order, organization, roles or functions (such as rivers flowing in the desert, Is 41:20; a blacksmith to forge a weapon, Is 54:16). Since the "before" picture deals with the absence of order, it is easy to conclude that *bārāʾ* pertains to bringing about order, as it often demonstrably does.[7] Absence of order describes nonexistence; to *bārāʾ* something brings it into existence by giving it a role and a function in an ordered system. This is not the sort of origins account that we would expect in our modern world, but we are committed to reading the text as an ancient document. In this view, the result of *bārāʾ* is order. The roles and functions are established by separating and naming (in the Bible as well as in the ancient Near East). These are the acts of creation. They are not materialistic in nature, and they are not something that science can explore either to affirm or to deny.

The second verb, *ʿāśâ*, is more complicated. When beginning Hebrew students learn this vocabulary word, they are told that it means "to do, make." But that does not begin to cover the scope of this word's usage. In its more than 2,600 occurrences, it is translated in dozens of different ways. Consequently, one cannot say that the word "literally means 'make.'" Perhaps even more importantly than the six occurrences of the verb in Genesis 1, the verb is used in Exodus 20:11: "In six days the LORD made [*ʿāśâ*] the heavens and the earth, the sea, and all that is in them." This verse figures prominently in discussions of the six days of Genesis 1 and what happened in them.

When we look carefully at the context in Exodus 20:8-11, we learn that for six days people are to "do" (*ʿāśâ*) all their work, and on the seventh day they are not supposed to "do" (*ʿāśâ*) any of their work. We could therefore plausibly conclude that the reason given in the text is that God "did" his work in the six days of Genesis 1. The heavens, earth and sea are his work. In fact, Exodus 20 is alluding to Genesis 2:2-3, where it is indicated that on the seventh day God completed the work (same Hebrew word translated "work" in Ex 20) that he had been "doing" (*ʿāśâ*). Then, most significantly, we are told what that work was in Genesis 2:3: the work of creating (*bārāʾ*) that he had "done" (*ʿāśâ*). In Exodus 20:11, God is doing his work, and that work is the creating described in Genesis 2:3. *Bārāʾ* is what God "does." *Bārāʾ* is associated with order and functions, and this is what God did.

If we substitute the verb "do" into all the verses in Genesis 1 that appear in translations as "make," the result is not a good English idiom ("God did two great lights"). However, other options are readily available. There are numerous places where NIV chooses to translate *ʿāśâ* as "provide" (18x) or "prepare" (46x). Genesis 1 might be read quite differently if we read "God prepared two great lights" or "God provided two great lights." Such renderings would be no less "literal." Perhaps a way to grasp the general sense of *ʿāśâ* is to understand that it reflects some level of causation. (Note, for example, verses like Gen 50:20 and Amos 3:6.)[8] To say it another way, causation at any level can be expressed by this verb.[9]

Other interesting usages of the verb include the following:

- The phrase *ʿāśâ nepeš* can mean "to take people under your care" (Gen 12:5; cf. Eccles 2:8).

- For the midwives who defied pharaoh, God *provided* families (*ʿāśâ bāttîm*, Ex 1:21).

- The Israelites are to *celebrate* the Sabbath from generation to generation (Ex 31:16; cf. Ex 34:22; Num 9:4-14; etc.).

- Responsibilities are *assigned* to the Levites (Num 8:26).

- Priests are *appointed* (1 Kings 12:31).

- The phrase *ʿāśâ šālôm* means "to establish order" (Job 25:2; cf. Is 45:7).

In Genesis 1:26, God determines to "make" (*ʿāśâ*) humankind in his own image. This is an important statement, but we should realize that it does not pertain to what he does uniquely for just the first human(s). The Bible is clear in numerous places that God "makes" (*ʿāśâ*) each one of us (Job 10:8-9; 31:15; Ps 119:73; 139:15; Prov 22:2; Is 27:11; 43:7).

Finally, when we examine the direct objects used with the verb ʿāśâ, we find many examples where they are not material:

- God makes the Israelites (Deut 32:6, 15; Ps 149:2; Hos 8:14) and the nations (Ps 86:9).

- God made (ʿāśâ) the moon to mark seasons (Ps 104:19);[10] cf. lights to govern (Ps 136:7-9).

- God made (ʿāśâ) constellations (Job 9:9; Amos 5:8).

- The wind was established (ʿāśâ) (Job 28:25).

- God makes (ʿāśâ) each day (Ps 118:24).

- God makes (ʿāśâ) lightning to accompany the rain (Ps 135:7; Jer 10:13).

These instances show us that the Hebrew communicators did not have to have a material-manufacturing activity in mind when they used the verb ʿāśâ.

We have looked at only two of the main verbs for the activities of creation. As we look at the wide range of creation statements throughout the Bible, we will discover that the biblical communicators often used words that we tend to think of as referring to material manufacturing for addressing that which is not material, specifically, for cosmic ordering:

- Formed summer and winter (Ps 74:17)

- Created the north and south (Ps 89:12)

- Mountains born; world brought forth (Ps 90:2; mountains are material, but birthing them is not a material description of their origins)

- Planted the cedars of Lebanon (Ps 104:16; trees are material, but planting them is not a material description of their origins)

- Created waters above the skies (Ps 148:4-5; terminology applied to that which we know does not exist)

- Building the house with Wisdom (Prov 8:12, 22-29)

- Forms human spirit (Zech 12:1)

In conclusion, we cannot consider these verbs to intrinsically reflect material production, either because the direct objects are not material or because the verbs do not represent any sort of understanding that we adopt as scientifically viable.

Furthermore, we find that the way God carries out these creation activities (created, made, caused) is at times by "separating" and "naming." To distinguish something from other things is to create it; to name something is to create it. For example, naming a room and giving it a distinct function distinguishes (separates) it from other rooms and represents the "creation" of the room. In our house, a room had previously been used as a dining room by its former owners. We decided we didn't want it to be a dining room so we called it a "den," gave it a function as a den, put in it the furniture of a den and began to use it that way. By its name and function it was distinguished from other rooms in the house, and thus the den was created. And it was good (functioned as it was intended to function). This serves as a good illustration of the role that naming, separating and determining a function have in the creation of a room and its existence as that room. It is important to realize that separating and naming are also prime creation activities in the rest of the ancient Near East. Note, for example, the opening lines of the famous Babylonian creation epic, *Enuma Elish*, quoted earlier (p. 29).

At this stage in the discussion, we should say a brief word about the concept of ex nihilo (from Latin meaning "out of nothing"). An interpretation of Genesis 1 that understands the text as concerned with bringing order and functionality instead of producing material objects would recognize that the activity in the seven days is not creation out of nothing. Ex nihilo is a material category, though that was not always its focus.[11] If Genesis 1 is not an account of material origins, then ex nihilo would not apply. Please note, however, that when God created the material cosmos (and he is the one who did), he did it ex nihilo. Ex nihilo doctrine comes from John 1:3 and Colossians 1:16, not Genesis 1. In both of these New Testament passages, the emphasis is on the authority and status of the Son of God and not on the objects created. In other words, ex nihilo creation is still theologically sound (indeed essential, since God is non-contingent), but literarily it is not under discussion in Genesis 1. The story of material origins is not the story the text is telling here. The authors, under the guidance of the Holy Spirit, have told the part of the story that is most significant to them (the origins of the ordered, functional cosmos) and, arguably, also most theologically significant. God did not just build the cosmos, he made it work in a certain way for a certain reason and sustains its order moment by moment.

Ancient cosmologies had little interest in material origins, though they recognize that the material cosmos is that which is ordered so that the functions can be carried out. I have elsewhere discussed this at length, so I will not repeat the data here.[12] But, before we conclude, we should note the pervasive lack of material focus in the seven-day account in Genesis. This is the third area of evidence (we have already discussed the starting point and the verbs used for the transition from nonexistence to existence) and is the subject of the next chapter.

In conclusion, the concept that Genesis 1 pertains to the establishment of order carries two corollary ideas that we are going to be bringing forward into the chapters that follow. First, in biblical terms, order is related to sacred space. It is God's presence that brings order and establishes sacred space. Sacred space is the center of order as God is the source of order. Therefore, when we talk about the establishment of order, we are, in effect, talking about the establishment of sacred space. We will discuss this in more detail in chapter four.

Second, we should keep in mind that all of this discussion is setting up the real focus of this book: the question of human origins. Just as we are finding that the account of cosmic origins is less material than we may have thought from our reading of Genesis 1, we are also going to find that the discussion of human origins has less interest in the material than we may have thought.

Genesis 1 Is an Account of Functional Origins, Not Material Origins

In the last chapter, I offered evidence that the activity of creation in the ancient world, including the biblical text, was seen largely in terms of bringing order and giving functions and roles. It included naming and separating. This view is also found throughout the ancient Near East. In this chapter, I am going to go the next step to show how the seven-day account focuses on order and function rather than material production.

We saw in the last chapter that the starting point in Genesis 1 was a time when there was no order or function. In the ancient world, that description meant that nothing existed (since existence only pertained to what had been ordered). We are now going to proceed to look at each of the seven days to see whether the emphasis is on material objects or an ordered environment.

DAY ONE

The final result of the activities of day one is the naming of day and night. We note that God does not call the light "light"—he calls the light "day," and the darkness he calls "night." Thus, we can see that the focus is day and night rather than light and darkness. "Day" names a period of light, and "night" names a period of darkness (Gen 1:5). Those periods are "created" when they are separated from each other. This is not a discussion of physics, and the Israelite audience would not have seen anything here that was a material object. Right from the first day, then, the text does not recount anything material coming into existence. Instead, the alternating periods of light/day and darkness/night constitute the origins of time. Time orders our existence. It is a function, not a material object. On day one God creates day and night—time. As this origins account begins, the Israelite audience would not view it as focused on material.

All of it is introduced by God saying "Let there be . . ." This portrays the power of God's spoken word. His decree calls light into existence, but again we have to understand the statement of the text with a recognition of what the Israelite audience considered "existence" to mean.

DAY TWO

Day two begins with another act of separation: the waters above from the waters below. Everyone in the ancient world believed there were waters above (since it sometimes came down) and waters below (since you could dig to find water and since there were springs where the waters emerged). No new scientific information is being given here; the text reflects the ways in which everyone in the ancient world thought about the cosmos and has particular significance for what they believed about the weather. God accomplished this separation by means of the *rāqîaʿ* ("vault, expanse, firmament"). Prior to the mid-second millennium A.D., this term was consistently understood as a solid sky that held back the rain. When it became widely recognized that the sky was not solid, other translations began to be used that focused more on the lower levels of the atmosphere, using nontechnical terms such as *expanse* or *vault*.

Everyone in the ancient world believed in a solid sky, though there were varying opinions about its composition. The Israelites undoubtedly believed in a solid sky, though it is open to question whether *rāqîaʿ* is the word for that solid sky. For many years, I believed that it was.[1] Further reflection and more recent research, however, have led me to a different conclusion as I have encountered another Hebrew term that I believe refers to the solid sky.[2] If this is the case, *rāqîaʿ* refers instead to the space created by the separating of the waters that are held back by the solid sky. That space would be the living space for all creatures. This space is significant in ancient Near Eastern cosmologies, particularly in Egypt, where they associate it with the god Shu. Ancient cosmology is reflected in the Hebrew Bible since the sun and moon are together in this space. But most important for our discussion, we recognize again that we are not being introduced to the manufacture of a material object.[3] In Israelite perception, the space is not material. (We cannot bring in the concept of molecules of hydrogen and oxygen; that is no longer thinking with the text.) The separating of the waters, the existence of a solid sky and the establishment of space for living all pertain to the environment in general and to weather systems specifically (regulation of the upper waters).

Day Three

As we examine the text closely, we realize that even though activities involve components of the material world (waters, dry land, plants), the verbs do not describe God making any of those objects. The seas are gathered, the dry land appears and the plants sprout. This is the work of organization and ordering, not the work of manufacture. The function of plant growth is initiated. This ordering provides the basis for food production.

In days one through three, we find that the discussion centers on the ordering of the world in terms of what could be identified as the major functions of human existence: time, weather and food. These three would be recognized by any culture in any place, as they represent what all humans have recognized as providing a framework in which we exist. Regardless of one's scientific knowledge or sophistication, these communicate the most important understanding of the cosmos. We can see that the text of Genesis is reflecting on these three because after order has been eliminated in the flood, it is reestablished by God. He promises in Genesis 8:22:

> As long as the earth endures,
> seedtime and harvest [food],
> cold and heat,
> summer and winter [weather],
> day and night [time]
> will never cease.

Days one through three, then, deal not with the manufacture of material objects but with ordering and establishing functions.

DAY FOUR

As the first three days addressed major functions in the ordered cosmos, days four through six discuss the functionaries that are provided.[4] If this is not a material account, then we do not expect a sequence of material events to be recounted. It is therefore no problem that we had light referred to on day one though sun, moon and stars are not mentioned until now. The focus of the first day was time, not light, and the functions have been treated separately from the functionaries.

We need to continue our investigation of whether there is also an element of material origins in this discussion of the functionaries. The first important observation to make is that in the ancient world they were not aware that the sun, moon and stars were material objects. In Israel, they believed they were exactly what the text calls them—lights, not material objects that produce light or reflect light. In the rest of the ancient world, they were also considered gods. No one knew that the sun is a burning ball of gas or that the moon is a rock in orbit that reflects the light of the sun. They believed these two lights to be very close (inside the solid sky, Gen 1:17). They are discussed not as being or becoming objects but as having designated functions in the ordered system of humans:

- separating day from night
- signs, celebrations (religious seasons, not weather seasons), days and years
- governing day and night

The stars in the ancient world were thought to be engraved on the underside of the solid sky rather than being suns that were farther away. It is not clear whether the Israelites shared this view.[5] Nevertheless, day four would not have been considered by the Israelites to be focusing on the origins of material objects since they did not realize these *are* material objects. Instead, the account gives attention to the roles assigned by God to these functionaries.

DAY FIVE

As the account of this day begins, we see that God says that the waters should teem with living creatures rather than saying that he made them. Those who have observed that days four through six are involved in filling the world are correct. I would be more inclined to speak of him installing functionaries in the way that furniture fills a room and beautifies it but also carries out the functions of the room. Here, the birds beautify the space established on day two, and the sea creatures beautify the waters below (which are the creatures in the realm of human observation—humans can't see the waters above).

In Genesis 1:21 the text returns for the first time since Genesis 1:1 to the verb *bārā'* ("God *created* the great creatures of the sea"). We saw in the previous chapter that *bārā'* represents the main activity of this account, since Genesis 2:3 indicates that the *'āśâ* activity represented the way in which he accomplished *bārā'*. Interpreters throughout history have wondered about the significance of this distinction. If it is correct to consider *bārāʾ* the act of giving a role and function in an ordered system, then this verse is making a remarkable claim. The creatures of the sea were in a liminal zone in the ancient Near East. After all, the sea was the very embodiment of non-order. Therefore, there would be questions about the functions of the sea creatures (and whether they even had any). Liminal creatures (whether sea dwellers or desert dwellers) were sometimes considered to be representatives of non-order (sometimes referred to as chaos creatures, referred to in Greek as *daimon*; many were later classified as demons). The *tannîn* referred to here (NIV: "great creatures of the sea") are counted among the chaos creatures in the Old Testament (see Job 7:12; Ps 74:13; Is 27:1; 51:9; Ezek 32:2; cf. the Ugaritic chaos creature *tunnanu*). It is remarkable that these creatures are included in the ordered world in Genesis 1, and this is made explicit by virtue of the use of the verb *bārāʾ*. The creation events of this day again focus on order and not on the production of material objects.

The phrase "according to their kinds" is a statement of how order reigns in the ways that creatures reproduce. Sharks give birth to sharks, not to crabs; angelfish give birth to angelfish, not to stingrays. This is the same kind of statement that we saw in day three when God proclaimed that plants bear seed according to their various kinds.

Having discussed how order can be observed, the text now moves to function that is expressed through the blessing of fecundity. As in the blessing here, creation of animals in ancient Near Eastern cosmologies addresses the fecundity of animals.[6] The function of the sea creatures is to furnish and beautify this world that is being prepared for humans in God's image. All the functions and functionaries are discussed in light of that intended purpose—serving human beings. God is putting the cosmos in order not to serve himself but to serve humans. This is very different from what we find in the rest of the ancient world, where the gods set up the cosmos to function for themselves and humans were a utilitarian afterthought.

DAY SIX

Notably, the presentation of day six begins with God commissioning the *land* to produce living creatures. Since this introduces this day, it is logical to infer that this is a description of the intermediate mechanism by which God *made* (*'āśâ*, Gen 1:25) the various classes of animals. This connection does not express any modern scientific view, nor should we expect it to. It does, however, agree with an ancient world perspective.[7] Since many animal births took place in sheltered places (dens, burrows, etc.), the observations of the ancients indicated that the land brought forth the animals (babies emerging from the ground). This would not refer only to the initial round of animals.[8] This brings up an important point: the descriptions in this account focus on what happens all the time, not just on what happened on one initial occasion. Day and night alternate continuously, plants always sprout, the sun always shines, creatures always teem. When we recognize this, we may be inclined to title the account "God and World Order."[9] Such a label would give a new identity to the text and give us a different view of what it is describing.

As in day five, the animals are ordered to reproduce according to their kinds. Interestingly, however, the function is not expressed by the blessing of fecundity as with sea/air creatures and humans. That is, the text does not include a blessing bestowed on land animals to be fruitful and multiply. Consequently, it could not be said that their function is to multiply and fill the world. In fact, Genesis 1:24-25 does not indicate the function of these land creatures, nor does it indicate the process of their material origin. God provided (*'āśâ*) them . . . for what?

Land animals have all sorts of different functions, and God is going to give humans the task of discerning those functions and assigning them. One aspect of this is observable in Genesis 2:19 when God brings the animals to the man "to see what he would name them; and whatever the man called each living creature, that was its name." We will recall that the giving of a name is a creative activity and is related to function. Another aspect, however, can be discerned from the account of the sixth day in Genesis 1. As we know, the report of the sixth day does not end with animals, so the functional order of the sixth day may not yet emerge in Genesis 1:24-25. I would suggest that the functions of the animals and their role in the ordered system are addressed at the end of Genesis 1:26. When humans subdue and rule, they are identifying functions for the animals and determining what role they will play. This is part of the human role—to serve as vice-regents for God in continuing the process of bringing order.

Day six also addresses the roles that people play in the world that was being ordered for them. Here again, we see both *ʿāśâ* (Gen 1:26) and *bārāʾ* (3x in Gen 1:27) being used. At the same time, there is a clear focus on functions, the most important of which is found in the image of God.

The uniquely human abilities that are often associated with the image of God (e.g., self-awareness, consciousness of God) give us the ability to fulfill our role as the image of God, but these abilities do not themselves define the image. These capacities could feasibly develop as neurological advances in our material development. But the image of God is a gift of God, not neurologically or materially defined. The image of God as an Old Testament concept can be understood in four categories.[10] It pertains to the *role and function* that God has given humanity (found, for example, in "subdue" and "rule," Gen 1:28),[11] to the *identity* that he has bequeathed on us (i.e., it is, by definition, who we are as human beings), and to the way that we serve as his *substitute* by representing his presence in the world. When Assyrian kings made images of themselves to be placed in conquered cities or at important borders, they were communicating that they were, in effect, continually present in that place. Finally, it is indicative of the *relationship* that God intends to have with us.

These four aspects of the image of God pertain not only to each individual but, perhaps more importantly, to the corporate species— to the human race. They will be discussed in more detail in chapters nine and twenty-one. For now, it is essential to affirm that all people are in the image of God, regardless of their age, their physical ability or inability, their moral behavior, their ethnic identity, or their gender. The image is not stronger in some than others, and it is something that gives us all the dignity of being specially gifted creatures of God. As God's stewards, we are tasked to do his work in the world; we are to be his assistants in the order-bringing process that he has begun.[12]

Having completed our survey of the six days, we find that most have no material objects produced. The only hint that materiality may be of interest comes in the use of the verb ʿāśâ. Even in some of the verses where a contemporary reader could assume that use, the Israelites are not thinking about that which is material. I have further suggested that the Hebrew verb itself is overparticularized when analyzed as inherently material in nature or only in cases of direct material causation.

At the same time, we have seen that the text is pervaded by an interest in order and function. Not only is this evident in the text of Genesis; it is also the primary way that cosmologies in the ancient world talk about origins. It is the dominant way that people think about existence and origins in the ancient world. It is also arguably a more significant theological assertion to make, and one that all people everywhere can understand regardless of the level of their scientific sophistication. If we ask, why can't it be both material and functional?, the answer is clear enough: it could be, but the material cannot be considered a default interpretation; it must be proved. If the reports of day after day in the text fail to relate God creating material objects, we have to be willing to set aside the culturally determined presupposition that origin accounts are essentially material.

It is interesting that even those who have thought of Genesis 1 as an account of material origins have noted the repeated reference to the efficacy of the spoken word. Some researchers have gone so far as to investigate other ancient cosmologies to conclude that, with the exception of one Egyptian text (the Memphite Theology), creation is never carried out by the spoken word of deity. Unfortunately, this offers too narrow a view. Pervasive throughout the ancient Near East is the idea that the gods issue decrees that determine the destinies of everything in creation (whether initially or on a year-by-year basis).[13]

Though many ancient Near Eastern texts talk about creation as functional in nature,[14] a brief look at the *Instruction of Merikare* will give the reader a good example:

> Well tended is mankind—god's cattle,
> He made sky and earth for their sake,
> He subdues the water monster,
> He made breath for their noses to live.
> They are his images, who came from his body,
> He shines in the sky for their sake;
> He made for them plants and cattle,
> Fowl and fish to feed them. . . .
> He makes daylight for their sake,
> He sails by to see them.
> He has built his shrine around them,
> When they weep he hears.[15]

Here, the text clearly conveys the idea that the god orders the cosmos to function on behalf of people in his image.

In conclusion, I have discovered over the years of presenting this material that people struggle to understand the whole idea of an origins account that is all about functions, role and order rather than about material objects. After all, when we speak only in abstractions (e.g., functional, material), are we not just going back to modern categories? It is therefore desirable to explain by use of an analogy.

When Americans need to move to a new city, they have to seek out a new residence. As a family investigates one location after another, some members of the family might examine the physical structure of the house. Roof, foundation, electricity, plumbing, furnace and general condition are all of immense importance. At the same time, others in the family may be assessing how the house will serve as a home. Domestic traffic patterns and open design are only the beginning. Which room will be used in which way? Where will the furniture fit? The kids are most likely to run upstairs to figure out which rooms will be theirs. In this way, some are considering the house; the others are considering the home.[16]

In the same manner, we could talk about the origins of the house or the origins of the home. When students come over for dinner, they may ask us about the place where we live. They do not want to know about the plumbing or the condition of the roof. They generally do not care about when or how the house was built. They are asking about when and how it became our home.[17]

I have proposed that in the ancient world people were far more interested in the origins of the home than in the origins of the house. It is a question of which story to tell. They were not interested in how the material objects of the house came into being—God did it and that was enough for them.[18] Of much more interest to them was how this house (the cosmos) had become a home for humans but even more importantly how God had made it his own home. The seven-day origins account in Genesis is a "home story"; it is not a "house story." It is a different sort of origins story than we expect in our modern world, but it is not difficult to understand why it should be important.

In John 14:2-3 Jesus says:

> My Father's house has many rooms; if it were not so, would I have told you that I am going there to prepare a place for you? And if I go and prepare a place for you, I will come back and take you to be with me that you also may be where I am.

He is talking about the future, but he is also referencing what he has done in the past. The cosmos was prepared as a place for us with a very specific purpose in mind: that we may be where he is. This has always been God's plan. It is God's presence in the cosmos that is worthy of note. By his presence, he has turned the cosmos into sacred space. That concept will be developed in the next chapter.

In Genesis 1, God Orders the Cosmos as Sacred Space

Genesis 1:1–2:3 contains a seven-day account of origins, not a six-day account. Our frequent reference to a six-day account is at least in part the result of not knowing what to do with the seventh day. What does God resting have to do with creation? Why would God need to rest anyway? What would it mean for God to rest? Perhaps one of the main reasons we face this conundrum is that we have assumed that the account is a material account, and nothing material takes place on day seven. In contrast, I maintain that even though people are the climax of the six days, day seven is the climax of this origins account. In fact, it is the purpose of this origins account, and the other six days do not achieve their full meaning without it. Rest is the objective of creation.

At the end of the last chapter, I offered the illustration contrasting the house and home. We can begin to understand better when we push that analogy to the next level. When a family finally chooses a house to make their home, they pack up all their belongings and move to their new location. On that first rather depressing day, their house is filled with unopened boxes and furniture sitting all over the place. There is no order; the *house* is functioning well enough (plumbing, electricity, roof, foundation), but there is no functioning *home*. So the family begins to spend time, day after day, arranging the furniture, unpacking the boxes, ordering their home. They begin to take stock of all that has been provided for them in the house to help make it a comfortable and functional home.

Why are they ordering their home? For what purpose? That sounds like a silly question. When the task of unpacking is done, they expect to live there. They are not doing all of that work just so they can take a nap when it is done. Nor are they expecting to get it all set up and then leave. They are doing all of this so that they can reside there. When they *rest* from all the ordering work they have done, they do so not by *relaxing* but by functioning in this ordered space. Even as they *cease* the ordering activity (which would be represented by the Hebrew root *šbt*), they begin to enjoy this established equilibrium of order (which would be represented by the Hebrew word *nwḥ*, "rested"; e.g., in Ex 20:11). *Šbt* is the transition; *nwḥ* is the purpose. This concept can be understood both through an analysis of the theology of rest in the Bible and through an analysis of divine rest in the ancient world.

THEOLOGY OF REST IN THE BIBLE

When God tells the Israelites that he is going to give them rest (*nwḥ*) from their enemies (Deut 12:10; Josh 1:13; 21:44; 2 Sam 7:1; 1 Kings 5:4), he is not talking about sleep, relaxation or leisure time. The rest that he offers his people refers to freedom from invasion and conflict so that they can live at peace and conduct their daily lives without interruption. It refers to achieving a state of order in society. Such rest is the goal of all the ordering activities that the Israelites are undertaking to secure their place in the land.

When Jesus invites people to "come to me, all you who are weary and burdened, and I will give you rest" (Mt 11:28), he is not offering a nap or leisure time. He is inviting people to participate in the ordered kingdom of God, where, even though they have a yoke, they will find rest. Furthermore, when the author of Hebrews refers to the rest that remains for the people of God (Heb 4:10-11), he is not referring to relaxation but to security and order in the kingdom of God.

In light of this usage, we can discern that resting pertains to the security and stability found in the equilibrium of an ordered system. When God rests on the seventh day, he is taking up his residence in the ordered system that he has brought about in the previous six days. It is not something that he does only on the seventh day; it is what he does every day thereafter. Furthermore, his rest is not just a matter of having a place of residence—he is exercising his control over this ordered system where he intends to relate to people whom he has placed there and for whom he has made the system function. It is his place of residence, it is a place for relationship, but, beyond those, it is also a place of his rule. Note Psalm 132:7-8, where the temple is identified both as God's dwelling place and as his resting place. Psalm 132:14 goes on to identify this resting place as the place where he sits "enthroned."[1] The temple account in Ezekiel 40–48 also identifies this element clearly: "Son of man, this is the place of my throne and the place for the soles of my feet. This is where I will live among the Israelites forever" (Ezek 43:7).

When Jesus talks about the Sabbath, he makes statements that seem unrelated to rest if we think of it in terms of relaxation. In Matthew 12:8, he is the Lord of the Sabbath. When we realize that the Sabbath has to do with participating in God's ordered system (rather than promoting our own activities as those that bring us order), we can understand how Jesus is Lord of the Sabbath. Throughout his controversies with the Pharisees, Jesus insisted that it was never a violation of the Sabbath to do the work of God on that day. Indeed, he noted that God is continually working (Jn 5:17). The Sabbath is most truly honored when we participate in the work of God (see Is 58:13-14). The work we desist from is that which represents our own attempts to bring our own order to our lives.[2] It is to resist our self-interest, our self-sufficiency and our sense of self-reliance.

ANCIENT NEAR EASTERN CONCEPT OF DIVINE REST

It would not have been difficult for a reader from anywhere in the ancient Near East to take one quick look at the seven-day account and draw the conclusion that it was a temple story.[3] That is because they knew something about the temples in the ancient world that is foreign to us. Divine rest in ancient temples was not a matter of simply residence. As we noted in Psalm 132, the temple was the center of God's rule. In the ancient world, the temple was the command center of the cosmos—it was the control room from where the god maintained order, made decrees and exercised sovereignty. Temple-building accounts often accompanied cosmologies because after the god had established order (the focus of cosmologies in the ancient world), he took control of that ordered system. This is the element that we are sadly missing when we read the Genesis account. God has ordered the cosmos with the purpose of taking up his residence in it and ruling over it. Day seven is the reason for days one through six. It is the fulfillment of God's purpose.

In the ancient world, a god's place in his temple is established so that people can relate to him by meeting his needs (ritually). That is not the case in Israel, where God has no needs. He wants to relate to his people in an entirely different way. Despite this difference, it is the temple that remains the focus of this relationship as elsewhere in the ancient world. When God entered the temple, he established sacred space. Sacred space is the result of divine presence and serves as the center and source of order in the cosmos. In this "home story," God is not only making a home for people; he is making a home for himself, though he has no need of a home for himself. If God does not rest in this ordered space, the six days are without their guiding purpose. The cosmos is not just a house; it is a home.

These ideas are supported not only by biblical theology, by lexical semantics and by comparative study with the ancient Near East; they are supported by the connection to a seven-day period. If this cosmic origins story has to do with the initiation of the cosmos as sacred space, then we should inquire as to how sacred space is typically initiated in the Bible and the ancient world when a temple is involved.

Solomon spent seven years building the house to be used as the temple of God in Jerusalem. When the house was complete, however, all that existed was a structure, not a temple. It was ready to be a temple, but it was not yet functioning like a temple, and God was not dwelling in it. Consequently the temple did not exist even though the structure did. What constituted the transition from a structure that was ready to be a temple to an actual functioning temple? How did the house become a home? This is an important question because there is a comparison to be drawn if Genesis 1 is indeed a temple text.

We find that in both the Bible and the ancient Near East there is an inauguration ceremony that formally and ceremonially marks the transition from physical structure to functioning temple, from house to home. In that inauguration ceremony, the functions of the temple are proclaimed, the functionaries are installed and rituals are begun as God comes down to inhabit the place that has been prepared by his instruction. It is thus no surprise that in Genesis 1 we find the proclamation of functions and the installation of functionaries. More importantly, we should note that in the Bible and the ancient world, the number seven figures prominently in the inauguration of sacred space.[4]

If we therefore ask about the significance of seven days in the account, the biblical and ancient Near Eastern background provides the key. It is not that God decided to build the house in six days and added a Sabbath to make a theological point. We must remember that the audience of this account is Israel, not Adam and Eve. We might imagine a scenario in which Moses communicates to the Israelites in the wilderness (hypothetically, realizing that the book makes no such claims). This shift in our perspective is extremely important. Expanding on that idea, we can imagine not only a setting (Moses communicating to Israelites); we can imagine an event. As a thought experiment, let's consider the scenario of Moses sitting down with the elders of the people on the eve of the tabernacle dedication at the foot of Sinai.

He is trying to help the Israelites understand the gravity of what is about to happen. They are ready to establish sacred space defined by the indwelling presence of God for the first time since Eden. So he explains to them that God had planned for the cosmos to be sacred space with him dwelling in the midst of his people—he had set up the cosmos and ordered it for that very purpose. He was preparing a place for them (cf. Jn 14:3). Sadly, people chose their own way, and sacred space was lost. Now, after all this time, they were going to reestablish God's presence in their midst. In the same way, God had built the cosmos to be sacred space and then put people in that sacred space as a place where he could be in relationship with them. So, the inauguration of the tabernacle over the next seven days was going to accomplish the same thing. It is the story of sacred space established, sacred space lost and sacred space about to be regained. In this way of thinking, the account of Genesis 1–2 is an account of the origins of sacred space rather than an account of the origins of the material cosmos, and Genesis 1–3 forms an inclusio with the last chapters of Exodus.

If the period of seven days is related to the inauguration of the cosmos as sacred space, it represents the period of transition from the material cosmos that has been prepared over the ages to being the place where God is going to relate to his people.[5] It has changed from space to a place. The seven days are related to the home story, not the house story—the ordering and establishing of functions, not the production of material objects.

Many have believed in the past that the seven days related to the age of the earth because they read the chapter as a house story. The age of the earth pertains to that which is material. If this is a home story, however, it has nothing to do with the age of the physical cosmos. A period of seven days does not pertain to how long it took to build the house; it pertains to the process by which the house became a home.

This interpretation finds support both in the biblical text and in the ancient Near Eastern background. If accepted, this would mean that the Bible makes no claims concerning the age of the earth.

This concept of sacred space carries across to Genesis 2. In Genesis 1, we find an account of how God had created sacred space to function on behalf of humans. It does not say where sacred space is centered, only that God has ordered a place for people to call home, even though it is ultimately his place. In Genesis 2, the center of sacred space is identified, explanation is given concerning how humans will function on behalf of sacred space, and we see God interacting with people in this sacred space.[6]

Reading the chapters as a home story allows the emergence of rich theology that is obscured by reading the text as a house story. We learn that, even though God has provided for us, it is not about us. The cosmos is not ours to do with as we please but God's place in which we serve as his co-regents. Our subduing and ruling are carried out in full recognition that we are caretakers. Whatever humanity does, it should be directed toward bringing order out of non-order. Our use of the environment should not impose disorder. This is not just a house that we inhabit; it is our divinely gifted home, and we are accountable for our use of it and work in it.

When God Establishes Functional Order, It Is "Good"

The Hebrew word translated "good" (*ṭôb*) is rendered in dozens of different ways in any given English translation. Many interpretations of the word's implications in Genesis have been identified over the years, often with a proposed or anticipated theological significance; that being, if the word describes the state of creation prior to the fall, it may offer a glimpse of what a pre-fall world would have been like or what the creation ideal would have been. Interpreters have often concluded that in order for that world to be "good," there must have been no pain, no suffering, no death and no predation; everything was pristine and perfect. This view sometimes assumes that new creation in Revelation 21 is a return to this state. It attributes to Adam and Eve a state of righteousness and wisdom that is only surpassed in Christ. In this way of thinking, one can infer what "good" means by drawing a contrast with the state of sin after the fall. The conclusion is that anything that is negative in our experience did not exist in that primeval world. As popular as this view is, in reality the word never carries this sense of unadulterated, pristine perfection.[1]

To reconsider our view, we must engage in lexical and contextual inquiry. In the lexical realm, we explore the ways the word is used

throughout the Old Testament. We find many affirmations that the
Lord is good (e.g., 1 Chron 16:34; 2 Chron 7:3; Ps 25:8; and many more),
but these contexts do not justify the contrasts referred to in the last
paragraph. They indicate that he acts in good ways in his attribute of
goodness. The word is therefore describing the way he carries out his
work in the world and pertains to functions rather than an abstract
quality of perfection. God is perfect and good, but, as a thorough examination of its contexts demonstrates, this word does not convey that
particular idea when describing anything but God.

We also find numerous passages where good is contrasted to evil
(e.g., Job 30:26; Ps 4:6; 52:3), but in these contexts, "good" cannot reflect pristine perfection because we discover that in that regard, people
can still be good today (e.g., Eccles 9:2). Often the word is relative
("better than"), and most commonly it is used to refer to situations and
objects that people experience or perceive as good for them.

A third major semantic category for the word is to indicate that something is functioning the way it is designed to; that is, it has its role in an
ordered system (Ex 18:17, not optimal functioning; 2 Chron 6:27, ordered
[translated "right way" here]; Ps 133:1, well-ordered; Prov 24:23, not optimal functioning; Is 41:7, optimally functioning; and many others).

When many possibilities exist for the meaning of a word, it is not
appropriate to look at the list of possibilities and just choose the one
we like. Instead, we have to try to discern which nuance the context
suggests that the communicator had in mind. That leads us from
lexical inquiry to contextual investigation. Our best way to understand what a particular label ("good") affirms is to ask what its negation would look like. So, in the example above about God, we might
ask what would it look like for God *not* to be good. Likewise, in the
context of Genesis, it would be helpful if we had a way to discover what
"not good" would look like. We might think that the fall (and our
present experience of the world) gives us a picture of "not good," but
the text never makes that connection. Instead, however, it *does* tell us

that something is "not good"—"It is not good for the man to be alone" (Gen 2:18). In this we have a contextually determined direction to follow in the determination of the intended meaning.

From this usage, we would have reason to favor the concept that man's aloneness means that the functionality of the ordered system is not yet complete. Some have wondered about this statement because Genesis 1:31 had said that everything was good. As I will propose in the chapters to follow, however, Genesis 2 is dealing with functionality at a different level.

Based on the semantic categories that are available (and recall that "perfect, pristine" is not among them) and the contextual indicators (specifically a use of a negation), I would conclude that "good" refers to a condition in which something is functioning optimally as it was designed to do in an ordered system—it is working the way God intended. A modern illustration can help clarify the nuances I am suggesting. When pilots are preparing for a flight's departure, they have a checklist to go through to make sure everything is ready to function. All the mechanical operations are checked, and they determine that all the essential contents of the plane (food, luggage, passengers) are on board. We can imagine them going through the checklist ticking things off: "good, good, good." In this way they conclude that the flight is ready to take off—it is all prepared to serve the needs of the passengers on the plane. I would propose that God is doing the same thing in Genesis 1— ascertaining that all systems are go and that everything is in place.

Before we conclude, we must address a few technicalities. Many have noticed that in Genesis 1, day two is not labeled as good. Fewer have noticed that the technicalities of the Masoretic assignment of accents patiently worked out according to their rankings indicate that in day five the great sea creatures (*tannînim*) are not included in the statement that "it was good." It is not easy to decipher the significance of these exclusions. Given my interpretation of the meaning of "good," we might consider the idea that the waters above and below remained part of the non-ordered realm and therefore would not be "good" (i.e., functioning as they were designed to do). What God sets up on day two is the control on the non-ordered world—the living space and the solid sky that exert control over the waters above.

As we recall that day five is parallel to day two, we should not be surprised to find the *tannînim* likewise relegated to the continuing realm of non-order. If the *tannînim* are chaos creatures, they are liminal to the ordered world and do not function on behalf of people. So they are not functioning in the ordered system as they were de-signed to do—they are in the ordered system but not of the ordered system. Returning to the pilot's checklist, these would be the cater-wauling children on the airplane—they are there within the system, but they are not on the checklist.

Those explanations would work very well except for two details in the text. First of all, we would have to account for the fact that, ac-cording to Genesis 1:31, all that God made is considered "very good." On day two, God made the *rāqîaʿ*, "vault." It would have been appro-priate to label that as good in day two. The second detail is that the text explicitly says that on day five, God created (*bārāʾ*) the *tannînim*. Therefore, since *bārāʾ* indicates the defining of a role and function in the ordered system, one might conclude that the *tannînim* must therefore be good. On the other hand, they perhaps don't need to be good just because they are in the ordered system.[2] This issue requires more nuanced investigation.

If this interpretation is correct, it first of all confirms the overall interpretation that I have offered of Genesis 1: that it concerns the setting up of a functional, ordered system—the home story, not the house story. Second, it does not suggest that everything pre-fall is perfect. God has established a modicum of order adequate for our survival and for his plan to unfold. There is still a long way to go before the ultimate order of new creation is achieved. People are supposed to be part of that ordering process as vice-regents. Some non-order remains and will eventually be resolved, but the order that has been established is functional ("good"), and there is not yet disorder (for the distinction between non-order and disorder see chap. 16). This conclusion can be confirmed further by some of the other occurrences of the designation *ṭôb mĕʾōd* ("very good"). For example, the same description is given to the Promised Land (Num 14:7), though it is filled with enemies and wicked inhabitants, not to mention wild animals who are predators.[3]

Consequently, we cannot deduce on the basis of this word alone that the pre-fall world could not have included pain, suffering, predation or death. We could feasibly find reason to draw such conclusions based on other statements of Scripture (and we will explore those in due time), but the mere use of the word *ṭôb* does not warrant these conclusions. To assume otherwise would not be interpreting the text literally. It would be reading into the text that which is not represented in the word the author used. It would be a case of imposing our own meaning on the word with no regard to what the text was communicating. This "good" condition is not necessarily absent of experiences or situations that we perceive as negative, though sin has not yet made its entrance.

Likewise, we cannot deduce that Adam and Eve were specimens of humanity who were perfect in every way. The writings of both the rabbis and the church fathers are filled with expositions of the supreme wisdom and righteousness of these two humans before the fall. But this condition is neither insinuated in the text nor corroborated by the text, and alternative opinions are also pervasive in the history of interpretation.

ʾādām Is Used in Genesis 1–5 in a Variety of Ways

Understanding the varied use of the term ʾādām is essential to sorting out the early chapters of Genesis. But before we even get to that issue, there are two important observations to make. The first is that the word ʾādām is a Hebrew word meaning "human." Regarding this observation, the fact that it is Hebrew indicates that the category designation ("human") is imposed by those who spoke Hebrew. Adam and Eve would not have called each other these names because whatever they spoke, it was not Hebrew. Hebrew does not exist as a language until somewhere in the middle of the second millennium B.C. That means that these names are not just a matter of historical reporting, as if their names just happened to be Adam and Eve like someone else's name is Bill or Mary. Although I believe that Adam and Eve are historical personages—real people in a real past—these cannot be their historical names. The names are Hebrew, and there is no Hebrew at the point in time when Adam and Eve lived.

If these are not *historical* names, then they must be *assigned* names, intended by the Hebrew-speaking users to convey a particular meaning. Such a deduction leads us to the second observation. In English, if we read that someone's name is "Human" and his partner's name is "Life," we quickly develop an impression of what is being communicated (as, for example, in *Pilgrim's Progress,* where characters are named Christian, Faithful and Hopeful). These characters, by virtue of their *assigned* names, are larger than the historical characters to whom they refer. They represent something beyond themselves. Consequently, we can see from the start that interpretation may not be straightforward. More is going on than giving some biographical information about two people in history.

In terms of the variety of uses of these words in Genesis 1–5, we find that, in some cases, *'ādām* refers to human beings as a species, in others it refers to the male individual of the species, and in some it refers to the designation of a particular individual as the equivalent of a personal name.[1] Morphologically (i.e., by form), the single distinction is whether it has a definite article (= "the") attached or not. When it has the definite article, it cannot be understood as a personal name. (Hebrew does not use a definite article on personal names.) Syntactically (i.e., by its role in the sentence), the single distinction is whether it is treated as a corporate plurality or as a singular being. The following data summarize the use of the word *'ādām* in the book of Genesis:

- Twenty-two times with definite article: Genesis 1:27; 2:7 (2x), 8, 15, 16, 18, 19 (2x), 20, 21, 22 (2x), 23, 25; 3:8, 9, 12, 20, 22, 24; 4:1

- Three times with attached preposition: Genesis 2:20; 3:17, 21

- Nine times with no definite article or preposition: Genesis 1:26; 2:5; 4:25; 5:1 (2x), 2, 3, 4, 5

The interpretation of most of these data is largely uncomplicated, but a few difficulties are encountered. The major irregularities are as follows:

It seems unusual that the indefinite form is used in Genesis 1:26, then the definite article is used in Genesis 1:27. This is further complicated when the latter half of the verse refers first to the singular ("he created *him*," Hebrew; NIV "them") and then to the plural ("male and female he created *them*"). Taking our lead from Genesis 2:5, where the context indicates a generic sense, we would understand Genesis 1:26 as generic: "God said, 'Let us make generic humanity (the human species) in our image.'" Note that this coincides with previous creative acts of living beings. God created animals, birds and fish en masse. For humans, this particularly makes sense since the verse proceeds to talk about them in the plural ("they may rule"), indicating that a corporate focus is intended. In Genesis 1:27, the definite article is used because the subject, *ʾādām*, has already been introduced in the last verse. The use of the singular ("created *him*") reflects the collective (which in Hebrew often uses singular modifiers), and the return to the plural ("male and female he created *them*") clarifies that one individual is not both male and female (i.e., hermaphrodite).

• Genesis 4:25 does not have the definite article, though one would expect it because of its presence in the very similar statement in Genesis 4:1. By context, it cannot possibly be generic. The alternative is to take it as a personal name, which is inconsistent (because of Gen 4:1), though not impossible. The editors of the modern critical edition of the Hebrew Bible contend that the article was inadvertently omitted in copying, though no Hebrew manuscripts offer the alternative.

• Genesis 5:1 contains two occurrences without the definite article. The first appears in the title and could be judged as a personal name in keeping with the titles of the same sort that occur throughout the book. The second one, however, seems anomalous. Nevertheless, once we realize that the verse is referring back to Genesis 1:26, the interpretation as a generic usage is logical.

• The three occurrences that feature the attached prepositions are pointed by the Masoretes as indefinite. They do not make sense as indefinite, and the form of the consonants could be either definite or indefinite. Like the modern editors of the critical edition of the Hebrew Bible, I would favor the definite form.[2]

The analysis in figure 1 suggests then that only Genesis 4:1, 25 remain anomalous. The term is generic in Genesis 1:26-27; 2:5; 5:1, 2 and archetypal or representational in all those with the definite article in Genesis 2–3. The use as a personal name is only in the genealogical section, Genesis 5:3-5, and in the title to that section (Gen 5:1).

Generic (some with definite article, some not)	Gen 1:26-27; 2:5; 3:22; 5:1, 2
Archetypal (definite article)	Gen 2:7, 18, 21, 22, 23
Representational agent (definite article)	Gen 2:8, 15, 16, 19, 25; 3:8, 9, 12, 20, 24
Personal name (no definite article)	Gen 5:1, 3-5
Anomalous	Gen 4:1, 25
Preposition attached	Gen 2:20; 3:17, 21

Figure 1. Use of the word *'ādām* in the book of Genesis

Consequently, we can see that the profile of Adam is complex rather than straightforward. These chapters are not just giving biographical information on a man named Adam. Larger statements are being made. When the generic is used, the text is talking about human beings as a species. When the definite article is being used, the referent is an individual serving as a human representative. Such representation could be either as an archetype (all are embodied in the one and counted as having participated in the acts of that one) or as a federal representative (in which one is serving as an elect delegate on behalf of the rest).[3] In either case, the representational role is more important than the individual. Only in the cases where the word is indefinite and by context being used as a substitute for a personal name would the significance be tied to the individual as an individual, historical person.

The text itself gives us what we need to make these determinations. The use of the definite article tells us that *'ādām* is being used to refer to something beyond the person. Then the determination between archetype and federal representative is made based on the circum-stances of the context. If what is being said of *ha'ādām* (the form with the definite article) is true of all humans and not of just this one indi-vidual, then we can conclude that he serves there as an archetype. If, in contrast, the definite article is used and *ha'ādām* is acting as an individual on behalf of others, we can conclude that he serves as federal representative.

The Second Creation Account (Gen 2:4-24) Can Be Viewed as a Sequel Rather Than as a Recapitulation of Day Six in the First Account (Gen 1:1–2:3)

Most people reading Genesis 1–2 believe that Genesis 2:7 begins a more specific account of what happened on day six of Genesis 1—a recapitulation giving more detail. They draw this conclusion because day six reports the creation of humanity, and they see Genesis 2 as a description of how God formed that first human being. That view understands Genesis 2 as doubling back to elaborate on a part of Genesis 1 (day six). We need to examine whether such a conclusion is the only possibility.

While it is easy to see how this conclusion can be drawn, one does not have to read very deeply into the text to detect problems with that reading. First of all, there seem to be some problems in the order that is given for those who are inclined to interpret these texts as representing historical, material sequences. If Genesis 2 is read as a recapitulation, Genesis 2:5-6 is confusing. It says that there were no plants when God created humans, yet plants come on day three and humans on day six in Genesis 1. Another sequence problem is that God created the animals first and then humans on day six. In Genesis 2, Adam is formed before the animals.[1] The second problem exists for those who consider the days to be twenty-four-hour days. That the events of Genesis 2 could all take place in a twenty-four-hour day (among them, naming all the animals, which apparently is completed because no helper was found) stretches credulity.

Given these problems, it is worthwhile to go back and reconsider the question of whether Genesis 2 is detailing day six or an event that comes later. Therefore, we must consider what evidences the text offers and whether it is possible to read these two accounts as sequels. If they are sequels, we do not have to worry about fitting Genesis 2 into day six. But if they are sequels, it means that the people in Genesis 1 may not be Adam and Eve, or at least not only Adam and Eve. The question would then be why we have a forming account like Genesis 2 sometime after the creation of people as reported in Genesis 1.

Furthermore, if Genesis 2 is a sequel, it would mean that there may be other people (in the image of God) in Genesis 2–4, not just Adam and Eve and their family. That has certain advantages when reading Genesis 4. In Genesis 4, Cain has a wife (Gen 4:17). The option that he has married his sister has never been an attractive one, though many have embraced it as seemingly the only possibility. We also find that Cain fears that "whoever finds me will kill me" (Gen 4:14) when he is driven from the LORD's presence. Who he is he afraid of? If he is driven away from the LORD's presence, then he is also being driven away from his family. This suggests that there are people other than his family in the land. Finally, we note that Cain builds a city (Gen 4:17). The term *city* would not be appropriate unless it was a settlement of some size for many people. We would conclude then that the text actually implies that there are other people.[2] We then have to explore how such a reading of Genesis 2 would make sense.[3]

Genesis 2:4 serves as an introduction to the second account: "This is the account [*tōlĕdōt*] of the heavens and the earth when they were created, when the LORD God made the earth and the heavens." The literary formula "this is the account of *x*" occurs here and ten other times in the book of Genesis. It stands as one of the formal characteristics of the book. In all the other occurrences in the book, the *x* is the name of a person. The formula introduces either a narrative of that person's sons or a genealogy of that person's descendants. In other words, it tells about what came after that person (though it sometimes overlaps with the life of the person) and what developed from that person. In Genesis 2:4, it is not a person's name. Using the same logic, we would conclude that the section being introduced is going to talk about what came after the creation of the heavens and the earth reported in the seven-day account and what developed from that. In other words, the nature of the introduction leads us to think of Genesis 2 as a sequel.

That leads us to question what the usual relationship is between the texts on either side of the introductory formula. As can be seen from figure 2, most of the uses of the introduction transition to a sequel account; a few, however, do not.

Reference	Relation	Connection
Genesis 5:1	parallel/sequel	Cain → Seth
Genesis 6:9	sequel	Pre-flood condition → Noah
Genesis 10:1	sequel	Noah and sons → Table of nations
Genesis 11:10	recursive	Table of nations → Shem's descendants
Genesis 11:27	sequel	Shem's descendants → Terah/Abraham
Genesis 25:12	sequel	Abraham → Ishmael
Genesis 25:19	recursive	Ishmael → Isaac/Jacob
Genesis 36:1	sequel	Isaac/Jacob → Esau's family
Genesis 36:9	sequel	Esau's family → Esau's line
Genesis 37:2	recursive	Esau's line → Jacob's family

Figure 2. Uses of the introductory formula in Genesis

One example (Gen 5:1) has parallel genealogies that are joined by the introductory formula. Yet, Genesis 4:25-26 has already returned to Adam, so the introduction technically transitions between Adam and his descendants—a sequel relationship. Three of the examples (Gen 11:10; 25:19; 37:2) can be identified as recursive. In each of these, the section before the transition follows a family line deep into later history. The introductory formula then returns the reader to the other son in the family (the more important one) to tell his story. In these cases, the text does not feature parallel genealogies like the lines of Cain and Seth, and the text does not bring the reader into the middle of the previous story to give a more detailed account. There is no detailed elaboration even though there may be overlapping. The remaining six examples introduce sequel accounts.

When we return to the relationship between Genesis 1 and Genesis 2, we find that there is therefore no precedent by which to conclude that the introductory formula in Genesis 2:4 is bringing the reader back into the middle of the previous account to give a more detailed description of a part of the story that was previously told. Such introductions never do this in the rest of Genesis, and the word *tōlĕdōt* (account) argues against such an understanding. Furthermore, Genesis 2 does not follow the pattern of the recursive examples that follow a genealogy of the unfavored line before returning to the story of the favored line. This evidence then leads us to give strong preference to the view that Genesis 2 is not adding further detail to what happened during the sixth day in Genesis 1. It would therefore also mean that, though Adam and Eve may well be included among the people created in Genesis 1, to think of them as the first couple or the only people in their time is not the only textual option.[4]

Regarding the role of Genesis 2:5-6, we note that the plants referred to in Genesis 2:5 are qualified so as to indicate that they refer to cultivated crops rather than the general vegetation of Genesis 1 available to the gatherer. After all, the land is generally being watered, so we would

infer it is not totally without vegetation. In the discussion of Genesis
1:2 (*tōhû wābōhû*) we examined the concept of an inchoate cosmos.
Here, attention turns to an inchoate terrestrial setting, which is also
well known from ancient Near Eastern cosmologies.[5]

One early-second-millennium text found at Nippur describes this
setting with phrases such as the following:

- "No water was drawn from the deep, nothing was produced"
- "Enlil's great *išib* priest did not yet exist, sacred purification rites
  were not yet performed"
- "The host of heaven was not yet adorned"
- "Daylight did not yet shine, night spread, but Heaven had lit up his
  heavenly abode"
- "The ground could not by itself make vegetation grow long"
- "The gods of Heaven and the gods of earth were not (yet) per-
  forming their duties"[6]

More focus on humankind is seen in a Sumerian text from Ur
dating to about 1600 B.C.:

- The high plain was not being tilled
- Canals, ditches and dikes were not being built
- No ploughing was being done
- Humans were not wearing clothes[7]

Most notable is the description found in the Royal Chronicle of
Lagash in relation to the re-creation after the flood:

> After the flood had swept over and caused destruction of the earth,
> when the permanence of humanity had been assured and its de-
> scendants preserved, when the black-headed people had risen up
> again from their clay, and when, humanity's name having been
> given and government having been established, An and Enlil had

not yet caused kingship, crown of the cities, to come down from heaven, (and) by (?) Ningirsu, they had not yet put in place the spade, the hoe, the basket, nor the plow that turns the soil, for the countless throng of silent people, at that time the human race in its carefree infancy had a hundred years. (But) without the ability to carry out the required work, its numbers decreased, decreased greatly. In the sheepfolds, its sheep and goats died out. At this time, water was short at Lagaš, there was famine at Girsu. Canals were not dug, irrigation ditches were not dredged, vast lands were not irrigated by a shadoof, abundant water was not used to dampen meadows and fields, (because) humanity counted on rainwater. Ašnan did not bring forth dappled barley, no furrow was plowed nor bore fruit! No land was worked nor bore fruit! . . . No one used the plow to work the vast lands.[8]

These texts offer rich information for comparative studies, but, unfortunately, this is not the place for such a detailed study.[9] Suffice it to say that, as always, such a study would have to take careful note of both the similarities and differences. For our purposes, we should note that the kind of description found in Genesis 2:5-6 is of the same sort that is common in cosmological texts of the ancient world when a terrestrial pre-ordering condition is being described. Genesis is featuring the same sorts of discussions known in that world, though it often has a different perspective on them.

We can see in these texts that sometimes an inchoate terrestrial situation is discussed alongside an inchoate cosmic situation. But in other texts the two are not treated together. In Genesis 1:2, an inchoate cosmos is described, whereas an inchoate earth is described in Genesis 2:5-6. This is another reason to locate Genesis 2 chronologically after the seven days rather than in day six.

Applying this interpretation to Genesis 1–2 would result in a number of conclusions:

- Genesis 1 recounts the creation of all humanity in God's image as it presents the idea that God has ordered sacred space to function on behalf of humanity.

- Genesis 1 pertains to generic humanity, as indicated by the indefinite term used. This coincides well with the common way of reporting the creation of humans in the ancient world, so it is no surprise that generic humanity is the referent.

- Genesis 1 does not report the mechanisms or processes used in that creative act—indicating only that it is an act of God.

- Just as Genesis 1 began with a state of non-order in the larger cosmos, Genesis 2 begins with a state of non order in the terrestrial realm.

- Genesis 2 explains how humans function in sacred space and on its behalf (in contrast to Genesis 1, which addressed how sacred space functioned for humanity).

- Genesis 2 locates the center of sacred space (the garden) in contrast to Genesis 1, which only indicated that the cosmos was set up to be sacred space.

The question remains as to the significance of Genesis 2 if Genesis 1 had already told about the creation of humanity. If Genesis 2 comes sometime later, or even represents a different process (e.g., individual focus vs. corporate focus), why do we have forming accounts that could easily look like they describe the unique formation of the first human beings? These are the questions that we will take up in the next several chapters of the book.

"Forming from Dust" and "Building from Rib" Are Archetypal Claims and Not Claims of Material Origins

When people first become acquainted with my view of Genesis 1 as an account of origins connected with order rather than material (summarized in the first several chapters), it is not long before they ask, "But what about Genesis 2?" They go on to state what to them seems obvious: that "forming" is transparently a material term and that "dust" is a material ingredient. It is therefore easy for the reader to conclude that even if Genesis 1 is focused on order, at least here in Genesis 2 we have an account of *material* human origins.

Certainly if the Bible is here making a claim about the mechanisms and process of material human origins, we would insist on taking that seriously. If we read Genesis 2 as an account of God making human beings in a quick and complete process, not developed materially from any previously existing species, we would be affirming a de novo creation of humans (and I will use that terminology throughout the rest of the book).[1] The alternative to de novo is creation that features material continuity between species.[2]

In this book, we are not going to be suggesting a scientific explanation of what happened. We are focusing our attention on what the Bible claims or does not claim. Even if we should discover that the Bible does not claim a de novo creation of humans, the scientific question would not be settled. We would still have to explore the options or explanations that science has to offer and consider them on their own merit. But if the Bible does not make a clear de novo claim, and thus does not rule out material continuity, then the Bible would not be inherently contradictory to scientific models that are based on material continuity. In other words, we could not reject the idea of material continuity by saying that the Bible rules it out by a competing theory that constitutes a mutually exclusive claim.

FORMING

We will first address the assumption that the word translated "formed" (Hebrew *yṣr*) necessarily implies a material act. The simple fact is that it does not, as usage demonstrates. One of the clearest examples is found in Zechariah 12:1, "The LORD, who stretches out the heavens, who lays the foundation of the earth, and who forms [*yṣr*] the human spirit within a person." Here the direct object of the verb is the human spirit, which is categorically not material. This demonstrates that "forming" is not essentially or necessarily a material act. This is not an isolated incident. In the forty-two occurrences of the verb in the Hebrew Bible,[3] it is used in a variety of nonmaterial ways:

- God speaks of events that are taking place as having been *formed* (NIV: "planned") long ago (2 Kings 19:25//Is 37:26; cf. Is 22:11; 46:11; Jer 18:11).[4]

- When God *forms* the heart, the statement is not referring to the blood pump but to thoughts and inclinations (Ps 33:15).

- God *formed* summer and winter (Ps 74:17).

- A corrupt administration *forms* (NIV: "brings on") misery for the people through its decrees (Ps 94:20).

- Our days are *formed* (NIV: "ordained") by God (Ps 139:16).

- Israel is *formed* by God (Is 43:1, 21; 44:2, 21, 24; 45:11; Jer 10:16; 51:19) as a people; therefore not a material act.

- God *forms* light and creates darkness (Is 45:7).[5]

- Servant (having been identified as Cyrus) is *formed* by God in the womb (Is 49:5; cf. Jer 1:5) though he is born through a normal human process.

- God *forms* (NIV: "prepares") a swarm of locusts (Amos 7:1).

More than half of the occurrences are shown by context to be unrelated to material. Many of the occurrences listed above communicate how God ordains or decrees phenomena, events, destinies and roles. Most of the occurrences not listed here could easily be translated by alternatives like "prepare," "ordain" or "decree." This understanding corresponds precisely with the perspective of functional origins proposed in Genesis 1. We therefore discover that our predisposition to understand "form" as a material act has more to do with the English translation than with the Hebrew original. Even those committed to literal interpretation must recognize that any literal reading must be based on Hebrew, not English.

DUST

The other element that often leads us to think that Genesis 2:7 is speaking in material terms is the reference to dust, presumed by many to be a material ingredient. By now, however, we have learned that we must think this through before jumping to conclusions.

The most basic way to think about dust would be to view it as part of the chemical composition of the human body. That approach immediately has several drawbacks. First, the Israelites would not be inclined to thinking in terms of chemistry. They would have no means to do that, and therefore they had something else in mind as they considered this detail. Second, we would have to consider it flawed chemistry from our vantage point, in that dust could hardly be considered the primary ingredient of the human body.

A common alternative to thinking in terms of chemistry is to understand the statement in the text as referring to craftsmanship. In this way of thinking, the imagery is of a "hands-on" God who has fashioned his creature with loving care and then bestowed on him the breath of life. The major problem with this is that the ingredient chosen would not make sense if the main idea were craftsmanship. One shapes clay, not dust. The latter is impervious to being shaped by its very nature.[6]

Therefore, we must look for another alternative, and there is no place better to look than in the text itself. We find the decisive clue in Genesis 3:19: "For dust you are and to dust you will return." Here we discover that dust refers to mortality. This association would make sense to an Israelite reader who was well acquainted with the idea of a corpse that was laid out on the slab in the family tomb and deteriorating to merely a pile of bones and the dust of the desiccated flesh within a year.

Nevertheless, some have been reluctant to adopt this view because of a sense that other scriptural passages contradict it. Specifically, many have concluded that since Paul states that "death [came] through sin, and in this way death came to all people, because all sinned" (Rom 5:12), people were created immortal. We must carefully consider whether this is what Paul is saying. Besides the likelihood that Genesis 3:19 suggests people were created mortal, another piece of evidence in Genesis offers even stronger evidence. In the garden, God provided a tree of life. Immortal people have no need for a tree of life. The provision of one suggests that they were mortal.[7]

Now, lest we think that Paul's statement might be out of sync with Genesis, we ought to look more carefully at what he is affirming. In Genesis, we find that people are cast from God's presence when they sin and that a cherub is posted by the entry to the garden to prevent access to the tree of life (Gen 3:24). If people were created mortal, the tree of life would have provided a remedy, an antidote to their mortality. When they sinned, they lost access to the antidote and therefore were left with no remedy and were doomed to die (i.e., subject to their natural mortality). In this case, Paul is saying only that all of us are subject to death because of sin: sin cost us the solution to mortality, and so we are trapped in our mortality. He is therefore not affirming that people were created immortal and is precisely in line with the information from Genesis.

Some have objected that it would not be possible for God to say that creation was good if people were created mortal and there was death all around. As I have proposed previously (chap. 5), there is no sound reason to understand the "good" creation in that way. So we return to the proposition that dust in Genesis 2:7 has the significance of indicating that people were created mortal.[8] This interpretation stands in contrast to the all-too-facile modern presupposition that we must believe that "formed from dust" has scientific implications in order to take the text literally. Yet, it is perhaps odd that those same interpreters often do not apply the same understanding to Genesis 2:19, where the animals are "formed out of the ground." More importantly, they rarely read scientific implications into Genesis 1:24, "Let the land produce living creatures."

ADAM AND THE REST OF US

The next question to consider is whether this statement about Adam pertains to him uniquely or to all of us. The core proposal of this book is that the forming accounts of Adam and Eve should be understood archetypally rather than as accounts of how those two individuals were uniquely formed. When I use the word *archetype*, I am not referring to the way that literature uses *archetypes*. I am referring to the simple concept that an archetype embodies all others in the group. An archetype in the Bible can well be an individual and usually is. I am quite prepared to affirm the idea that Adam is an individual—a real person in a real past. Nevertheless, we have seen in the usage of the term *'ādām* that the use of the definite article tends toward an understanding of Adam as a representative of some sort, and an archetype is one form of representation.

Paul treats Adam as an archetype when he indicates that all sinned in Adam (Rom 5:12). In this way, all are embodied in the one and counted as having participated in the acts of that one. In order to determine whether the treatment of Adam in the text focuses on him primarily as an archetype or as an individual, we can ask a simple question: is the text describing something that is uniquely true of Adam, or is it describing something that is true of all of us? If only Adam is formed from dust, then it is treating him as a discrete and unique individual. If God only breathes the breath of life into Adam, he is thereby distinct from the rest of us. If Eve's formation conveys a truth about her that is true of her alone, then it is the history of an individual. If, however, any or all of these are true of all of us, it would cease being a reference to a unique, individual event and would have to be interpreted more broadly to capture its intended sense.

When we begin to examine the evidence with these questions in mind, our findings may surprise us. First, we discover that all of us have the breath of life and that it comes from God (Job 27:3; 32:8; 33:4; 34:14-15; Is 42:5). Then we discover that all creatures have the breath of life, presumably given by God (Gen 7:22). But this is neither surprising nor controversial and has little to do with the question of human origins.

More significantly, as we examine the biblical evidence, we must conclude that we are all formed from dust. Psalm 103:14 states,

> for he knows how we are formed,
>   he remembers that we are dust.

The vocabulary here (formed, dust) is the same as in Genesis 2:7.[9] Paul alludes to this universality when he contrasts the first man of dust and the second man of heaven, then indicates that all of us on earth share that "dust" identity:

> The first man was of the dust of the earth; the second man is of heaven. As was the earthly man, so are those who are of the earth; and as is the heavenly man, so also are those who are of heaven. (1 Cor 15:47-48)

On the basis of biblical evidence, we must therefore conclude that all people are formed from dust (see also Eccles 3:20). This is confirmed when we learn in Genesis 3:19 that dust is an expression of mortality—dust we are and to dust we will return. All of us share that mortality. We thus discover that Adam's formation from dust does not pertain uniquely to him; it pertains to all humans. Further evidence can be found in Job 10:9:

> Remember that you molded me like clay.
>   Will you now turn me to dust again?

Here Job sees *himself* as molded by God, which is not a claim that he was not born of woman like everyone else. When the text reports Adam being formed from dust, it is not expressing something by which we can identify how Adam is different from all the rest of us. Rather, it conveys how we can identify that he is the same as all of us. Being formed from dust is a statement about our essence and identity, not our substance. In this, Adam is an archetype, not just a prototype.

If we are all formed from dust, yet at the same time we are born of a mother through a normal birth process, we can see that being formed from dust, while true of each of us, is not a statement about each of our material origins. One can be born of a woman yet still be formed from dust; all of us are. That means that even though Adam is formed from dust, he could still have been born of a woman.[10] "Formed from dust" is not a statement of material origins for any of us, and there is no reason to think that it is a statement of Adam's material origins. For Adam, as for all of us, that we are formed from dust makes a statement about our identity as mortals. Since it pertains to all of us, it is archetypal.

Special attention to Adam's forming is best connected to his role. In Egyptian iconography, we see reliefs of the pharaoh being formed on the potter's wheel by the god Khnum as part of the pharaoh's coronation. The gods have formed him *to be king*. In Jeremiah 1:5, we read that the prophet had been formed in the womb for a particular role—"appointed . . . as a prophet to the nations." These statements have to do with one's destiny and identity, not one's material origin. All the evidence points to understanding Genesis 2:7 in the same way. Adam's significance pertains to his role in the garden and what happened there. Given this reasoning, we have other alternatives beyond thinking that this is an account of material origins, and in these other options, Genesis would not be offering a competing claim to the scientific account of human origins. That does not mean the science is right; it means only that the Bible does not offer a competing claim. The Bible's claim is that whatever happened, God did it. He is the one responsible for our human existence and our human identity regardless of the mechanisms or the time period. The Bible does not say clearly how he did it. Consequently, the Bible does not necessarily make a de novo claim for human origins, though it *does* make a claim that God is the ultimate cause of human origins.

"Rib"

The first question to ask is whether the text suggests that Adam thought of Eve as having been built from his rib. The text gives us the answer: he did not. The first words out of his mouth were: "This is now bone of my bones and flesh of my flesh" (Gen 2:23). More than a rib is involved here because she is not only "bone of his bone" but also "flesh of his flesh."

This leads us to ask then about the meaning of Genesis 2:21, which NIV translates, "He took one of the man's ribs and then closed up the place with flesh." Adam's statement leads us to inquire whether the translation

"rib" is appropriate for the Hebrew word ṣēlāʿ. The word is used about
forty times in the Hebrew Bible but is not an anatomical term in any
other passage. Outside of Genesis 2, with the exception of 2 Samuel 16:13
(referring to the other side of the hill), the word is only used architec-
turally in the tabernacle/temple passages (Ex 25–38; 1 Kings 6–7; Ezek 41).
It can refer to planks or beams in these passages, but more often it refers
to one side or the other, typically when there are two sides (rings along
two sides of the ark; rooms on two sides of the temple, the north or south
side; etc.). On the basis of Adam's statement, combined with these data
on usage, we would have to conclude that God took one of Adam's sides—
likely meaning he cut Adam in half and from one side built the woman.

When we investigate the Hebrew word and the way that it has been
handled throughout history, we discover much supporting evidence
for this reading. Beginning with the way that the cognate ṣēlu is used
in Akkadian (Assyrian and Babylonian), we find that the word has a
certain ambiguity. Rarely, it refers to a single rib. Most times it refers
to the entire side or to the entire rib cage. This is comparable to our
English use when we talk about a "side of beef."

When we turn our attention to early translations, we find that the
Aramaic translation in the Targums (Aramaic: ʿilʿ) can refer to either
rib or side, and the same is true of the word chosen by the translators
of the Septuagint (Greek *pleura* can be either rib or side). In the Latin
Vulgate, Jerome used the Latin word *costis*, which can be either rib or
side. One of the earliest discussions found in the rabbinic literature is
in the comments in *Midrash Rabbah* by Rabbi Samuel ben Nahmani,[11]
who was already arguing the use of "side" instead of "rib."

By the time we finally get to the period of English translations, the
interpretation "rib" has become entrenched (Wycliffe Bible, Geneva
Bible, Great Bible and King James Version). Based on the lexical information above, however, we can see that this is an interpretation from
a word that in Hebrew, Aramaic, Greek and Latin could mean either

"side" or "rib." Adam's own statement and the more dominant use of the word both suggest that "side" would be the better choice.

This conclusion poses a conundrum for us. If God cut Adam in half, that is pretty radical surgery. Certainly God can do whatever he wants, but would Israelites naturally think in terms of surgery? Would they think that Adam was anesthetized when God put Adam in a deep sleep? Israelites knew nothing of the use of anesthesia, and, if God were going to perform such a profound miracle, he could simply make Adam impervious to pain. In fact, many would claim that there was no pain before the fall, thereby rendering anesthesia unnecessary.

The text, however, leads us in another direction. We need to examine the word "deep sleep" (*tardēmâ*, from *rdm*). The noun occurs seven times and the verbal root from which it is drawn another seven times.[12] We find that the sleep the word describes could be used in three different sorts of circumstances.

1. When someone is unresponsive to circumstances in the human realm induced by something in the human realm (Sisera's exhaustion and warm milk, Judg 4:19, 21; horse and charioteer in the sleep of death, Ps 76:6; sloth brought on by laziness, Prov 19:15; cf. Prov 10:5)

2. When someone is unresponsive to circumstances in the human realm and equally unresponsive to deity (Saul, 1 Sam 26:12; faithless Israel, Is 29:10; Jonah, Jon 1:5-6)

3. When someone has become unresponsive to the human realm in order to receive communication from the divine realm (Abraham, Gen 15:12; Eliphaz, Job 4:13; Daniel, Dan 8:18; 10:9; cf. Job 33:15)

Michael Fox adds the insight that the word pertains to "untimely sleep or stupefaction, not to normal sleep at night."[13] In all three categories, this sleep blocks all perception in the human realm.[14] In each of these passages there is either danger in the human realm of which the sleeper is unaware, or there is insight in the visionary realm to be gained. Pertaining to the latter possibility, it is of interest that the Septuagint translators chose to use the Greek word *ekstasis* in Genesis 2:21. This word is the same as the one they used in Genesis 15:12, suggesting an understanding related to visions, trances and ecstasy (cf. the use of this Greek word in Acts 10:10; 11:5; 22:17 [NIV: "trance"]). This interpretation is also evident among the church fathers (Ephrem, Tertullian).[15] For the Vulgate, Jerome chose the Latin word *sopor*, which refers to any sort of abnormal sleep, including that which comes about in trances.

From these data it is easy to conclude that Adam's sleep has prepared him for a visionary experience rather than for a surgical procedure. The description of himself being cut in half and the woman being built from the other half (Gen 2:21-22) would refer not to something he physically experienced but to something that he saw in a vision. It would therefore not describe a material event but would give him an understanding of an important reality, which he expresses eloquently in Genesis 2:23. Consequently, we would then be able to conclude that the text does not describe the material origin of Eve. The vision would concern her identity as ontologically related to the man. The text would therefore have no claim to make about the material origin of woman.

Furthermore, once we see that gender identity is under discussion, we conclude that the text is not expressing something that is true about Eve alone; it is true of all womankind. This interpretation is confirmed in Genesis 2:24, where the text offers an observation that is true of all mankind and all womankind. Again the archetypal element is clear because what has transpired pertains to all, not just uniquely to Adam and Eve. All womankind is "from the side" of all mankind. Marriage is being rejoined and recovering humanity's original state. This should not be mistaken to infer that someone who does not marry is less than a whole person or that there is a particular spouse that is your other half. The text is referring generically to the corporate human race that is ontologically gendered.

Genesis 2:24 is responding to the question of why a person would leave the closest biological relationship (parents to children) in order to forge a relationship with a biological outsider. The answer offered is that marriage goes beyond biology to recover an original state, for humanity is ontologically gendered. Ontology trumps biology. This has shown Adam that the woman is not just a reproductive mating partner. Her identity is that she is his ally, his other half.

We can now see that Genesis 2:24 makes more of a statement than we had envisioned. Becoming one flesh is not just a reference to the sexual act. The sexual act may be the one that rejoins them, but it is the rejoining that is the focus. When Man and Woman become one flesh, they are returning to their original state.[16]

Previously in this chapter, we found reason to conclude that "formed from dust" was archetypal rather than a description pertaining to Adam alone. We have also seen reason to believe that "rib" should be understood as "side." Furthermore, we have suggested that Adam has seen Eve's formation in a vision but that the vision conveys an ontological truth with Eve serving as an archetype. In both cases, the archetypal interpretation offers the reader significant theology about the identity of mankind and womankind. As such, it does not, however, make definitive claims about the material origins of either Adam or Eve. If Genesis 2 makes no claims about material human origins, one would find no other statement in the Bible to offer details beyond the fact that we are all God's creatures. If, on the basis of scientific evidence, some conclude that God was not involved in human origins (which, of course, is illegitimate since that issue is not in the purview of science to determine), we would have a biblical and theological basis on which to disagree. But if scientific evidence suggests that human beings were not created de novo, we could not necessarily claim that the Bible contested that evidence. That does not mean that we would necessarily accept the current scientific explanation. It would only mean that we would have to judge the science on its own merits rather than dismiss it based on a biblical claim.

Proposition 9

Forming of Humans in Ancient Near Eastern Accounts Is Archetypal, So It Would Not Be Unusual for Israelites to Think in Those Terms

In the preceding chapters, evidence has been presented in support of the interpretation that the forming accounts of Adam and Eve in Genesis 2 concern archetypal humanity rather than offering an account of the material origins that are unique to them as individuals. The evidence has been developed from the text itself rather than from predetermined scientific conclusions. Furthermore, that evidence is not the result of ancient Near Eastern ideas being imposed on the biblical text. At this juncture, however, it is reasonable to ask whether an archetypal view of human origins is consonant with how people in the rest of the ancient Near East thought, or if it is unique to the biblical text. In other words, was there an inclination to think about human origins in archetypal terms in the ancient world? The short answer is yes, but the data will be presented in the remainder of this chapter.[1]

Eleven literary works scattered through Sumerian, Akkadian and Egyptian texts make reference to human origins. Most are brief, but two (*Enki and Ninmaḫ* and *Atraḫasis*) extend over several dozen lines.

SUMERIAN

- *Song of the Hoe:*[2] As a result of Enlil's work with a hoe and a brick mold, people sprout from the earth. After a model of a person is built, people are mass-produced and begin their work: "[Enlil] had [the hoe] place the first model of mankind in the brickmold. And (according to this model) his people started to break through the soil towards Enlil."[3] Nothing is said of this first model and where it came from. The material they used to make them is not mentioned, but clay can be inferred as the source because of the mention of the brick mold. The account is, however, more interested in all the things that the hoe does than in what humans do. Though no archetypal being is identified here, the ingredient, clay, is considered the material from which all are made.

- *Hymn to E-engura:*[4] In a passing comment reminiscent of the *Song of the Hoe,* this temple hymn mentions only that humans "broke through the earth's surface like plants."

- *Enki and Ninmaḫ:*[5] The gods complain about their hard life, and Enki is finally aroused to respond. Instigated by Nammu, who conceived of the idea, and aided by a number of birth goddesses (Ninmaḫ foremost among them), people are created from clay, the archetypal ingredient. Several stages are involved in the creation process: Nammu has the idea and mixes Enki's blood[6] with the clay on top of the Abzu, the house of the subterranean cosmic waters, Enki's realm. Then, the birth goddesses pinch off pieces of clay to form people, who are then given the work of the gods as their destiny. The account ends with Enki and Ninmaḫ in a drunken contest, creating human archetypes that are defective to see whether functions can be found for them.

- *KAR 4:*[7] Available in both Sumerian and Akkadian, this account provides some details not available elsewhere in the literature. Here, people are created from the blood of some slaughtered gods (the gods are not rebels in this story) to do the work of the gods. This work includes not only irrigation (working *in place of* the gods) but also building and maintaining temples and performing the rituals (working *to serve* the gods). As in some of the other Sumerian accounts, humans spring forth from the earth once the prototype has been designed. It is possible that in this work we have the only known reference to initial individuals, though the issue remains controversial.[8] Again, the named ingredient is archetypal (pertaining to all, not just the initial beings).

- *Founding of Eridu:*[9] In this bilingual (Sumerian and Akkadian) text, only two lines are given to the creation of humans. Marduk creates "the seed of mankind" with the help of Aruru. No ingredients are mentioned. The text proceeds to report the creation of animals, creation of the Tigris and Euphrates, and assigning of names.

AKKADIAN

- *Atraḫasis:*[10] The epic of *Atraḫasis* contains the most detailed account of human creation in ancient literature. The topic begins about halfway through column 1 and takes up more than 150 lines, though some portions of these lines are broken. The process is introduced through the character of Mami (otherwise known as Belet-ili and Nintu), the mother-goddess, and contains many of the elements known from other accounts (e.g., humans take on themselves the drudgery of the gods). The most important, unique feature of the creation portion of this epic is that people are created from a combination of the blood of the deity who was the ringleader of the rebellion and the clay that has been spat upon by the gods.[11] Mami, aided by Enki, creates seven human pairs (though unfortunate breaks in the text obscure the details), who mature and then begin to reproduce.[12]

- *Enuma Elish:*[13] In tablet VI, Marduk envisions humankind as composed of blood and bones and names them, giving them the task of relieving the burden of the gods. Ea carries out Marduk's vision, using Kingu's blood in the process; there is, however, no mention of clay. The entire account takes up slightly more than thirty-five lines.

- *Neo-Babylonian Creation Account*:[14] In this text, the creatrix, Belet-ili ("mistress of the gods"), pinches off clay in order to form a clay figure on whom to impose the labor of the gods because hostility has broken out. It is considered an act of creation (*banu*). This section of the text is badly broken, so many of the details cannot be recovered at this time. It appears that she brings the model before the gods for their approval. It is likely that this is an archetypal model because it is unlikely that all the labor for all the gods would be put on one human. He is called *lullu*-man—a whole category of humans—common folk. Next, she creates the archetypal king:

> Belet-ili, you are the mistress of the great gods.
> You have created *lullu*-man:
> Form now the king, the thinking-deciding man!
> With excellence cover his whole form,
> Form his features in harmony, make his whole body
>   beautiful!
> Then Belet-ili fulfilled her commission with the major gods
>   contributing specific attributes.
> The great gods gave the king the battle.
> Anu gave him the crown, Ellil ga[ve him the throne],
> Nergal gave him the weapons, Ninurta ga[ve him shining
>   splendor],
> Belet-ili gave [him a handsome appea]rance.
> Nusku gave instruction, imparted counsel and sto[od by
>   him in service]

In this description, we can see all the archetypal characteristics of the king spoken of as built into a singular individual. As with Adam in

Genesis 2, these characteristics are true of everyone in the class, not just of one individual, so we can identify the description as archetypal.

EGYPTIAN

- Coffin Texts[15] (spell 80, CT II:43): In this spell, there is only a passing reference to breath being put in the throats of human beings, along with all other creatures.[16]

- Coffin Texts (spell 1130): This spell includes references to a few functions in society, but it only offers an etymological play on words in regard to human origins: people have their origin in the tears of the eye of the creator god.[17]

- *Instruction of Merikare*: This piece of wisdom literature contains the most important and extensive treatment concerning human origins and roles:[18]

   > Provide for people, the cattle of God, for he made heaven and earth for their liking. He repelled the greed of the waters; he made the winds in order that their nostrils might breathe; [for] they are likenesses of him that came forth from his flesh. He shines in the sky for their liking; he has made vegetation, small cattle, and fish for them to nourish them. He has killed his enemies and destroyed his own children, because they planned to make rebellion. He makes daylight for their liking, and he sails around in order to see them. He has raised up a shrine behind them, and when they weep he hears. He has made them rulers even from the egg, a lifter to lift [the load] from the back of the weak man. He has made for them magic to be weapons to oppose what may happen.[19]

- Here, the station of people in the cosmos and their relationship to the gods are addressed. Other elements of the cosmos are identified as functioning for the sake of human beings (sky and earth, sun, daylight, as we saw also in Gen 1). Human beings are provisioned by deity with food, leadership and magic (the first two addressed in Gen 2). Deity disciplines rebellion and guards people from traitors. The text adds a reference to the provision of a shrine to house the god so that he can hear the people's weeping.

- A variety of texts allude to people being fashioned by Khnum on a potter's wheel. Some scholars have identified these allusions as early as the Pyramid Texts, but the references become more obvious in the Coffin Texts and in pictorial representations.[20] It is important to recognize that it is the king whose image is on the potter's wheel and that his formation is more directed to his role as king than to his existence as a human being. In other words, this is not about his material origins as much as about his function.

Neither Egyptian nor Sumerian accounts put human origins in the context of conflict among the gods, unlike the Akkadian accounts, though two of the Sumerian accounts (*Enki and Ninmaḫ* and *KAR 4*) specify that people are to take over the work of the gods.[21] The accounts typically mention the process involved, the materials used in creation, and the roles or functions assigned to humankind. In Egypt, there is no reference to humans taking up the labor that the gods had previously been doing: people are cattle who are cared for, not slaves who are driven. Similarly, no hint of a prior scenario or circumstance that led to humans being made is cited in Egyptian literature.

As can be seen from the examples above, very little commonality exists between the Egyptian accounts and Mesopotamian accounts of human origins, with the exception that clay as a source ingredient is mentioned in specific texts from both cultures. The variety of materials used in the creation of humanity reflects differences in the archetypal elements that each account wishes to emphasize and for which an explanation is provided. The commonality in the cognitive environment, therefore, is that people are conventionally portrayed as being created out of elements that will explain the archetypal roles assigned to the people (clay, blood, spit or tears).

HUMAN FUNCTIONS

In this section, we are not concerned with addressing all the different functions that humans could serve in the cosmos; instead, we want to focus specifically on functions that they are said to have been created to fulfill and roles that they were given at creation. These roles are typically not assigned to a single human, couple or even group. Accounts of human creation focus on the functions that all humans have. There are three major aspects of the role and function of humanity that are identified in the texts. Human beings are created in order to

- take over the drudgework of the gods

- serve the gods through the performance of rituals and through provisioning the deities in the temples

- be in the image of deity

The first of these roles has already been treated above and is attested only in Sumerian and Akkadian sources. The second is demonstrated in the context of the decreeing of destinies in Mesopotamian literature[22] and can be seen throughout Egyptian literature.[23] These two roles together compose what I would like to call the Great Symbiosis. The foundation of religion in Mesopotamia is that humanity has been created to serve the gods by meeting their needs for food (sacrifices), housing (temples) and clothing and generally giving them worship and privacy so that those gods can do the work of running the cosmos. The other side of the symbiosis is that the gods will protect their investment by protecting their worshipers and providing for them. Humans thus find dignity in the role that they have in this symbiosis to aid the gods (through their rituals) in running the cosmos.

EXCURSUS: IMAGE OF GOD

The image of God is not mentioned in Genesis 2–3 and therefore is not applied directly to Adam and Eve. Nevertheless, in the view that I have proposed, Genesis 1 and 2 are a continuum, and what applies to all people in Genesis 1 applies to Adam and Eve in Genesis 2. This is not the place for a substantial treatment, but a few brief comments are in order.[24]

1. Unlike in the rest of the ancient Near East, the image of God in the Bible applies to all humanity, not just the king (the only exceptions are brief comments in a few pieces of Egyptian wisdom literature: *Instruction of Merikare*; *Instruction of Ani*).

2. In Mesopotamia, the image of the king serves as a substitute through representation.

3. In the Bible as well as in Mesopotamia, the king, as the image of God, is considered to be the son of God and functions on behalf of God.

4. In Egypt, images of the deities were thought to contain the essence (*ba*) of the deity and to manifest the presence of the deity.

It is evident in all of these that the image of God is also an element of function (not material) that pertains to all people (not just an initial group or pair). In this way, we continue to confirm the functional interests of the text.

SUMMARY CONCLUSION REGARDING THE ROLE OF HUMANITY

The role of humanity is not an independent topic; in the ancient Near Eastern cognitive environment, it can only be understood in relationship to the role of deity. All of the ideology concerning the role of humanity in the cosmos—whether it addresses the circumstances under which people were created, the materials of which they were

made (i.e., their composition), their functions or their propagation—
associates them with deity.

The conception of humanity focuses on two roles:

1. humanity's role with regard to its place or station in the cosmos

2. humanity's role with regard to its functions in the cosmos

The place or station assigned to humanity in the first role is often addressed through the material ingredients used in creation. Thus, the place of archetypal humanity in the cosmos is expressed in material terms: the tears of the god, the blood of the god, clay or dust. The *Instruction of Merikare* also addresses the place of humanity although in broader terms. Most of the Egyptian texts that concern the creation of humanity focus on this first role: humanity's place in the cosmos.

The second category, humanity's function in the cosmos, is evident in Mesopotamian accounts in which people are created to carry out functions *for* the gods and in the process replace the gods by doing the menial tasks that the gods previously did to care for themselves. It later became part of royal ideology throughout the ancient Near East that select individuals carried out the functions *of* the gods, in this case pertaining primarily to rulership. A variety of functions is evident in texts and can be summarized in the following categories:

- Function *in place of* the gods (menial labor; Mesopotamia only)

- Function *in service to* the gods (performance of ritual, supply of temple; Mesopotamia, Egypt and Gen 2:15)

- Function *on behalf of* the gods (rule, either over nonhuman creation or over other people; role of the image in Mesopotamia, Egypt and Gen 1)

We can therefore conclude that in the general ancient Near Eastern cognitive environment, the interest of all of the accounts currently available to us is to elucidate the role of humanity through archetypal depictions that fall into the few paradigmatic categories we have listed above. Notable as the most radical departure from this general perspective is the contention in *Merikare* that creation was for the sake of humankind.[25] Though this text deals with the station of humanity, as do other accounts, it nonetheless offers a unique perspective on humankind's place. This exceptional case notwithstanding, the most common interest in humanity has to do with its role and function in the cosmos (animate or inanimate), not merely biological existence.[26]

- Accounts of human origins focus on their role in the cosmos, whether in terms of station or function.

- Materials mentioned in the creation of humans have archetypal significance, not material significance, and are characteristic of all humanity.

- Similarly, the image of god concerns role and is mostly found in royal ideology in the political/bureaucratic model, confirming that the king has divine functions.

- People and gods work together to ensure the preservation of order in the cosmos and its smooth operation (Great Symbiosis).

These help us to appreciate the ways in which the Bible takes its departure from the rest of the ancient Near Eastern literature yet, at the same time, remains rooted in the same cognitive environment.

The New Testament Is More Interested in Adam and Eve as Archetypes Than as Biological Progenitors

Various passages in the New Testament will be treated in several parts through the remainder of the book in chapters dealing with the questions of archetypes, historical Adam, theology of the fall, Adam and Jesus, and interpretation of these passages. In this chapter, we treat only the first of these.

In previous chapters we have proposed and supported the idea that the *forming* accounts in Genesis 2 are more interested in Adam and Eve as archetypes than as individuals since the details of the forming accounts apply to all of us, not just to them. We have also demonstrated that human origins in the ancient Near East were typically addressed through the use of archetypes. Now, we seek to determine whether the New Testament offers support for this treatment. As in Genesis, here we will seek to determine whether the New Testament is using Adam and Eve archetypally based on whether what the New Testament authors are saying about Adam and Eve is true only of them or is true of everyone.

Five passages in the New Testament name Adam and Eve specifically (though several more allude to them). The first, the genealogy of Jesus in Luke 3, treats Adam individually but says nothing about him except that he is the beginning of this particular human line of descent. This passage will be part of our discussion of the historical Adam, but it offers no information about material human origins or the fall.

The rest of the passages are Pauline. Paul indicates in Romans 5 that sin and death entered the world through one man (Rom 5:12), thereby talking about Adam's role as an individual (cf. Rom 5:16-17, one sin, the sin of that one man). He then proceeds to observe that "death came to all people, because all sinned." Here he switches to an archetypal observation—when Adam sinned, everyone sinned. This is not true of Adam alone, so Paul is treating him as more than an individual. When Paul moves to the assertion that death reigned from the time of Adam to the time of Moses, we are again talking about an individual. By the end of Romans 5:14 he has added a third perspective: Adam as a pattern or antitype. We can see then that Paul uses Adam on a number of levels in Romans 5, but one of them is as an archetype. Nevertheless, here the archetypal use is connected to the fall, not to his forming.

First Corinthians 15 is the other most extensive treatment of Adam by Paul. In 1 Corinthians 15:21 Paul observes that death came through a man and, in so doing, addresses Adam as an individual who is acting. But in 1 Corinthians 15:22 he expands his vision to the archetypal level: "as in Adam all die, so in Christ will all be made alive." Our status as being "in Adam" treats Adam as an archetype, though still a historical figure. We are all "in Adam." We are not all "in Christ," but those who are also experience life in that identity.

Paul returns to discussion of Adam in 1 Corinthians 15:45-49 as he compares and contrasts "the first man" (also called the "earthly man") Adam to "the last Adam" (also called "the second man" and "the heavenly man"). From the variations that are used, we can see that "second" is the same as "last" and therefore does not focus on actual numeration value.

That is, Jesus was neither the second man in time and history, nor was he the last man in time and history. First Corinthians 15:48-49 brings the discussion to the point Paul has been making throughout the passage: both Adam and Jesus are archetypes with whom we are identified. These verses also must be discussed with regard to historicity and human origins, but those are topics for other chapters to investigate. In 1 Corinthians 15, then, we can see that Paul is treating Adam as an archetype representing mortal humanity. This use is similar to what was proposed for Genesis 2 since the archetypal connection to dust was human mortality. Paul has followed the lead of Genesis here.

In Paul's second letter to the Corinthians, it is not Adam to whom Paul refers, but Eve: "Just as Eve was deceived by the serpent's cunning, your minds may somehow be led astray" (2 Cor 11:3). Paul is not suggesting here that all the Corinthians are archetypally represented by Eve. Instead, she serves as an illustration of what Paul wants to avoid happening at Corinth. She is neither archetype nor antitype. Furthermore, Paul's use does not suggest that Eve was ontologically deceivable, only that she serves as an exemplar—a warning for the people at Corinth and for all of us.

In Paul's letter to Timothy, we encounter one of the most complicated treatments of Adam and Eve. In 1 Timothy 2:13-15, Paul refers to the order of creation as being the opposite of the order of deception: Adam was created first; Eve was deceived first. We are only interested here in the question of the role that Adam and Eve are being given. Unlike Paul's use of Eve in 2 Corinthians, where the fact that she was deceived served as an illustration for all, her situation is now applied to the women of Ephesus. Likewise, Adam is used to make a comment about the role of the men at Ephesus.

Three main options present themselves for understanding Paul's use of Adam and Eve in the point he is making about Ephesus: (1) archetypal, (2) ontological and (3) illustrative. If his comments were archetypal, he would be saying that all men were formed first as Adam was formed first, and all women were deceived in Eve even as she was deceived. Nothing in the passage, in Paul's thinking or in logical assessment suggests this is true. The ontological view could be seen as an extension of the archetypal. If this is what Paul is doing, he is suggesting that man by his created nature is first, and woman by her created nature is deceivable. Therefore, men not only should be first, but it is their nature to be so. Women are inherently deceivable, and cautions should therefore be taken. This is an extreme position, but it is not without adherents in the history of interpretation. Numerous arguments can and should be raised against it, not least of which is that Paul would not have denied that Adam was also deceived (Genesis is clear enough)—he is only making a point of who was deceived first. All of us are therefore susceptible to deception—that vulnerability is not ontological to only one gender. The third option, that Paul is using Adam and Eve as illustrations for the Ephesians, suits the passage well and accomplishes Paul's aims.

In summarizing the New Testament use of Adam and Eve, we find the humans used for a wide variety of affirmations. For now, the most important observation to make is that archetypal is among those options (both in Rom 5 and in 1 Cor 15). Consequently, we see that treating Adam and Eve as archetypal in Genesis does not run against the grain of larger canonical, theological and literary usage. Archetypal use is supported in the context of Genesis, in the cultural context of the ancient Near East and in the canonical context of Scripture. At the same time, it is not the forming accounts that are treated archetypally in the New Testament. Rather, it is the accounts of the fall. The one exception is in 1 Corinthians 15:47-48, where Paul makes the same point made in Genesis 3 and Psalm 103, that all of us are formed from dust just as Adam was formed from dust. Overall, however, it should also be noted that the New Testament gives little attention to the question of human origins one way or another. We will return to that point in chapters eighteen and nineteen.

Though Some of the Biblical Interest in Adam and Eve Is Archetypal, They Are Real People Who Existed in a Real Past

We have already seen in the last chapter that the New Testament treats Adam and Eve in a variety of ways: archetypal, illustrative and historical. Consequently, to contend that some treatment of Adam (in Genesis or anywhere else) is archetypal is not to suggest that he is not historical. Jesus is also treated archetypally by Paul, yet he is historical. Before we proceed to an investigation of Adam and Eve, it will be instructive for us to consider the example of Melchizedek to see how various perspectives about someone can weave together various aspects in a combination of historical, literary, traditional and archetypal elements.

HERMENEUTICAL COMPLEXITY

Melchizedek appears in Scripture only in Genesis 14, Psalm 110 and Hebrews 5:6–7:28. We will examine each text independently and then all together. If we had only Genesis 14, we could easily conclude that Melchizedek was no more than a king in the land of Canaan (whether Canaanite, Amorite or Jebusite). As a prominent force in the region, he welcomes Abram back from his successful campaign, offers refreshment and congratulations, and receives a tithe that indicates the recognition of his suzerainty over Abram. Like most kings in the ancient world, Melchizedek is also a priest. Specifically, he is a priest of "El Elyon," which is a generic identification of deity as best we can tell. It is left to Abram to affirm that, in his opinion, Yahweh is El Elyon—Melchizedek makes no such claim.

In Psalm 110, the very brief allusion uses the priest/king combination (true of most kings in the ancient world) and Melchizedek's location in Jerusalem to provide precedent for a priest/king combination in the ideal Davidic king that eventually develops into a messianic theology. As John Hilber has demonstrated, Psalm 110 is a prophetic oracle that shares many similarities with Assyrian prophecies.[1] As is well established, priesthood in Israel was connected to the line of Levi, not the line of Judah. Here, however, priestly prerogatives for the king are drawn from the historic precedents in Jerusalem rather than from the Torah structures laid out in the Pentateuch. Presumably, it would not give the kings the right to usurp Levitical prerogatives but would give them some additional (unspecified) priestly prerogatives.[2]

The treatment of Melchizedek in Hebrews 5–7 offers an opportunity to explore the complex ways that intertextuality can work. Even a casual reader can detect that there are characteristics attributed to Melchizedek in Hebrews that clearly do not derive from Genesis or Psalms. When we investigate what precursors Hebrews might be drawing from, our attention begins to focus on the intertestamental literature of Second Temple Judaism.

The Hasmoneans, seeking to establish a messianic dimension to their rule, justified their priestly-royal prerogatives by reference to Melchizedek. This practice was continued by the Sadducees.[3] In the Dead Sea Scrolls, 11QMelchizedek and 4QAmran both show that Melchizedek has become the subject of much speculative interpretation. The former assigns him a judging function in heaven and associates Psalms 7:8-9; 82:1 with him. 4QAmran identifies him as Michael and calls him the Prince of Light. He is depicted as a heavenly redeemer figure, a leader of the forces of light who brings release to the captives and reigns during the messianic age. He is the heavenly high priest to whom archangels make expiation for the sins of ignorance of the righteous.[4] In the Talmud (*Nedarim* 32b) and *Targum Neofiti*, Melchizedek is identified as Shem. The former attributes irreverence to him and thereby transfers his priesthood to Abraham. In the later apologetic works of Justin Martyr (*Dialogue with Trypho* 19 and 33), Melchizedek is portrayed as a representative of the Gentiles who is seen as superior to the Jewish representative, Abraham. Philo of Alexandria (*Legum allegoriae* 3.79-82) considers him the eternal Logos.[5]

By the time we get to Hebrews 7, these Jewish traditions are mixed into the consideration of Melchizedek. The author of Hebrews is not drawing his information on Melchizedek solely from the Old Testament; he is also interacting with the traditions known to his audience. It is the Jewish profile of Melchizedek, not just the canonical profile, that informs his comparison. The author has all along been addressing his audience on their own level and in relationship to their own beliefs. He need not accept their beliefs, but he is demonstrating that Christ's position is superior to the position in which they have placed others. He therefore relates not only to the Melchizedek of history but to the Melchizedek of Jewish imagination. In some ways this would be like speaking to a Buddhist about how Christ is superior to Buddha. There is both a historical Buddha and the Buddha that has become the central focus in the traditions of Buddhism. The point for the author of Hebrews is not to argue the validity of his audience's belief one way or another but to use their beliefs for a comparison to Christ. There is no attempt to establish that Jesus is superior to the image cast of Melchizedek, only that the priesthood represented by Jesus on the basis of Melchizedek's precedent (Ps 110) is superior to the Levitical priesthood.[6]

As a result, there is nothing in Hebrews or anywhere else to suggest that we need to believe that Melchizedek was anything other than the Canaanite king depicted in Genesis 14. The profile in Hebrews combines the biblical information about the historical Melchizedek from Genesis 14, the theological-political prototype of Jerusalem-based royal priesthood that finds its precedent in Melchizedek, and the literary-traditional view of Melchizedek evident in Jewish speculative theology. These three strands are inextricably woven together with no roadmap given to the audience to allow them to distinguish the strands. All three are legitimate for the inspired author of Hebrews to use, even though they are not of the same nature.

If the author of Hebrews can employ such strands in sophisticated and complex ways, we must inquire whether Paul could do the same with Adam and Eve. As would be expected, such analysis requires a very sensitive hermeneutic rather than wholesale application that happens to coincide with someone's predetermined outcome. Hebrews offer a comparison between Melchizedek and Christ just as Paul offers a comparison between Adam and Christ. Likewise, both Melchizedek and Adam/Eve have substantial "afterlives" in Hellenistic Jewish literature. But that is where the similarities cease.

In the case of Melchizedek, we identified the literary/traditional elements by observing statements in Hebrews that had no foundation in the Old Testament. In this approach we affirm as historical that he was a priest/king, was from Salem, was associated with El Elyon and had the encounter with Abram (Heb 7:1-2). In contrast, Hebrews is picking up traditional elements in the description of Melchizedek as without father or mother and without beginning or end (Heb 7:3). The comparison that the author of Hebrews draws is not dependent on the factuality of the information in Hebrews 7:3. In fact, the author notes that Melchizedek was "without genealogy," whereas he makes the explicit point that Jesus is "descended from Judah" (Heb 7:14). The comparison is based on Melchizedek's royal priesthood (independent of Levitical priesthood) and on the tithe that Abram gave to Melchizedek.

It is not important what the author of Hebrews or his audience actually believes about the profile of Melchizedek. What matters are the affirmations that he makes as a foundation of his teaching.

When we turn our attention to Paul's use of Adam and Eve, we first ask whether there are points that Paul makes that he did not get from the Old Testament and that do find expression in the traditions developed in Hellenistic Jewish literature. Paul's points about Adam and Eve include:

1. Sin and death entered through Adam (Rom 5:12).

2. Adam was of the dust of the earth (1 Cor 15:47).

3. Eve was deceived (2 Cor 11:3; 1 Tim 2:14).

Though these find significant elaboration in the Jewish traditional literature, they all have their rooting in the Old Testament text. As a result, they cannot be dismissed as simply reflecting Jewish tradition with which Paul is interacting.

Alternatively, some might claim Paul is simply referring to well-known literary details and that doing so does not necessitate that the details be affirmed as historically factual. They would distinguish between literary factuality (yes, this is how the familiar story goes) and that which is historically factual (yes, this is what really happened in time and space). This is the path typically followed in the interpretation of Jude 14: "Enoch, the seventh from Adam, prophesied about them." Even very conservative interpreters consider this a reflection of a literary truth, not a historical truth. None of them seriously considers the Enoch from the book of Genesis to be the author of the intertestamental book of *Enoch*.

We still have to deal with taking a hermeneutically realistic view of what the author is doing with the material he cites. The argument of the author of Hebrews would not work if Abram did not give a tithe to Melchizedek. In the same way, I would contend that Paul's argument would not work if there was not a historical moment when sin entered the world (points 1 and 3 in the list above). His whole approach to the presence of sin, the need for redemption and the role of Christ to bring such redemption is based on these details.

The conclusion of this analysis is that a mix of historical and traditional elements is possible within the framework of biblical authority, as the treatment of Melchizedek in Hebrews attests. At this time, however, I would contend that Paul's information about Adam is not in the same category, so we cannot treat Adam the same way. Nevertheless, we see that Paul's affirmations about historical Adam pertain primarily to sin and the fall. This is sufficient to defend a historical Adam, but it does not yet decide questions concerning Adam being the first human being, the only human being or the ancestor of all humans today. Those issues will be discussed in chapter twenty. As with Melchizedek, it is not significant what Paul and his audience may believe about Adam and Eve; what matters are the elements Paul makes the foundation of his teaching. After all, Paul would have believed in a geocentric universe like everyone else around him, but if that does not become a foundation of his teaching, it makes no difference.

WHY BELIEVE IN A HISTORICAL ADAM AND EVE?

When we identify Adam and Eve as historical figures, we mean that they are real people involved in real events in a real past. They are not inherently mythological or legendary, though their roles may contribute to them being treated that way in some of the reception history. Likewise they are not fictional. At the same time, there may be some elements in their profile that are not intended to convey historical elements. I have already noted (chap. 6) that their names are not their historical names. Likewise, if the forming accounts are archetypal, those are presenting truths about the identity of Adam and Eve rather than historical events. Despite these qualifications and caveats, I believe the textual information leads to the conclusion that Adam and Eve should be considered real people in a real past for several important reasons.

Genealogies. The genre of genealogy can function differently in different cultures.[7] We cannot assume therefore that any genealogy we encounter in another culture's literature is governed by the rules that govern ours or that the genealogy will function in the same way and serve the same purpose.[8] So the question that we must ask is whether there is evidence that lists of ancestors in Israel or in the ancient world could contain characters that do not represent actual individuals who lived in the past. This is important because Adam is included in ancestor lists in Genesis 5, 1 Chronicles 1 and Luke 3.[9]

As we explore the genealogies from the ancient world, we are interested in whether they include in their list any who are not human individuals. Deviations might be that they would include gods,[10] legendary characters[11] or toponyms.[12] Studies in the ancient world have concluded that genealogies typically are more interested in political unity than in lineage ties, but as such their objectives would not be achieved if imaginary or legendary characters were used. Future discoveries may yet provide an example that could lead to a different conclusion, but based on the information currently available, genealogies from the ancient world contain the names of real people who inhabited a real past.[13] Consequently there would be no precedent for thinking of the biblical genealogies differently. By putting Adam in ancestor lists, the authors of Scripture are treating him as a historical person.

Fall. The Old Testament as a whole does not give retrospective information about what we call "the fall." Once the events are reported in Genesis 3, no further reference is made to those events or to their ramifications. If we were working from the Old Testament alone, there would be a lot of flexibility concerning how we thought about the entrance and spread of sin.

The New Testament, however, particularly the discussion of the impact of the work of Christ, places many more demands on our theological interpretation. The New Testament views the reality of sin and its resulting need for redemption as having entered at a single point in time (punctiliar) through a specific event in time and space. Furthermore, Paul correlates that punctiliar event with a corresponding act of redemption: the death of Christ with its resulting atonement—also a punctiliar event. The details of this will be discussed in chapter nineteen (in the excursus by N. T. Wright), but for now we observe that the punctiliar nature of the redemptive act is compared to the punctiliar nature of the fall, which therefore requires a historical event played out by historical people.

In conclusion, then, both a textual element (genealogies) and a theological element (sin and redemption) argue strongly for a historical Adam and Eve. At the same time, it must be observed that for them to play these historical roles does not necessarily require them to be the first human beings, the only human beings or the universal ancestors of all human beings (biologically/genetically). In other words, the question of the historical Adam has more to do with sin's origins than with material human origins. These have not often been separated in the past, perhaps because there has been no impetus to do so. In light of the developments that have come about, particularly with regard to the human genome (see chaps. 17 and 20), it has become more important to ask whether questions of historical Adam on the one hand and material human origins on the other always track together. I have suggested that one can accept the historical Adam without thereby making a decision about material human origins. This has the advantage of separating scientific elements (material human origins) from exegetical/theological elements, with the result that conflict between the claims of science and the claims of Scripture is minimized without compromise. This reading of the biblical text has not been imposed on it by the demands of science, but science has prompted a more careful examination of precisely what the text is claiming.

Adam Is Assigned as Priest in Sacred Space, with Eve to Help

The garden into which Adam was placed would be a familiar setting for sacred space in the ancient world. The image of fertile waters flowing from the sacred space of God's presence is one of the most common in the iconography of the ancient Near East (more on this in the next chapter). Given this background, we can see that the Garden of Eden is not simply beautiful green space (though it is) to provide people with food (which it does). Far more than anything else, it is sacred space that reflects the fact that God is dwelling there (notice that Ezek 28:13 refers to Eden as the "garden of God"; cf. Ezek 31:8). We learned in Genesis 1 that God was coming to dwell in the cosmos, thus making it sacred space.[1] But we were not told where the center of sacred space would be. In Genesis 2, that is clarified. Since the seven days of Genesis 1 have been associated with temple inauguration, it would be logical to assume that the terrestrial location of the center of sacred space, the temple concept inherent in the garden, takes place in close time proximity to Genesis 1. Despite the continuity that this concept has with the ancient world, there are also some sharp contrasts. For example, rather than the produce of the garden providing food for the resident god, this garden was planted by God to provide food for people.

When we understand the garden as sacred space and see that the presence of God (and all that he has to offer) is the main point, we can begin to comprehend that the account in Genesis 2 is not essentially about material human origins. God reveals to Adam that he (Adam) is mortal, but then sets up sacred space (the garden) where relationship to God can bring the remedy, life. God puts Adam into this sacred space, commissioned to serve there.

I have proposed that the terms "serve" and "keep" convey priestly tasks rather than landscaping and agrarian responsibilities.[2] In Genesis 2:15, God places Adam in the garden and commissions him "to work it and take care of it."

Important information can be derived from semantic study of these words. The verbs *'bd* and *šmr* (NIV: "work" and "take care of") are terms most frequently encountered in discussions of human service to God rather than descriptions of agricultural tasks. The verb *'bd* certainly can refer to farming activity (e.g., Gen 2:5; 3:23), but in those contexts the nuance of the verb is conditioned by its direct object (the ground). When the verb does not take a direct object, it often refers to the work connected with one's vocation (e.g., Ex 20:9). The broader sense of the word is often connected to religious service deemed worship (e.g., Ex 3:12) or to priestly functionaries serving in the sanctuary precinct (e.g., Num 3:7-10). In these cases, the object of the verb usually makes reference to what or who is being worshiped (e.g., Ex 4:23; 23:33).

Here, then, is a succinct statement of the problem in deciding whether *'bd* is referring to agricultural tasks or sacred service. *If* the object of the verb is the garden (and we cannot be certain that it is), we have a bit of an anomaly. The verb will usually take dirt/soil/ground objects when it refers to agricultural work, and it will usually take personal objects (God, Baal, Egypt) when sacred service or servitude is the point. *Garden* could be in either category, depending on whether it is understood as a place where things grow or a place where God dwells. We will then have to look to its contextual partner, *šmr*, to take us one direction or another.

The verb *šmr* is used in the contexts of the Levitical responsibility of guarding sacred space, as well as in the sense of observing religious commands and responsibilities. This verb is only used in agricultural contexts when crops are being guarded from those people or animals who would destroy or steal. When the verb applies to Levitical activity, it could involve control of access to the sacred precinct, although it is often applied more generally to performing duties on the grounds.

To conclude, then, I would propose the following line of logic: *Since* there are a couple of contexts in which *šmr* is used for Levitical service along with *ʿbd* (e.g., Num 3:8-9), and

1. the contextual use of *šmr* here favors sacred service, and *ʿbd* is as likely to refer to sacred service as to agricultural tasks, and

2. there are other indications that the garden is being portrayed as sacred space,

then it is likely that the tasks given to Adam are of a priestly nature: caring for sacred space.[3] In ancient thinking, caring for sacred space was a way of upholding creation. By preserving order, non-order was held at bay.[4] As J. Martin Plumley describes it in Egyptian thinking, so it was throughout the ancient world, including Israel at many points:

> But whatever wise men might think about the purpose of creation and whatever might be the official doctrines about the way in which the creation came into being, there was the universal belief that what had been achieved in the beginning of time must be maintained. For mortal men the most essential task of earthly life was to ensure that the fabric of the Universe was sustained. The ancient cosmogonies were in agreement that obscure forces of chaos had existed before the world was created, and that, although in the act of creation they had been cast away to the outer

edges of the world, they nevertheless continued to threaten to encroach into the world. The possibility of such a catastrophe could only be averted by the actions of gods and men, both working together to maintain the world order. That order which embraced the notions of an equilibrium of the universe, the harmonious co-existence of all its elements and its essential cohesion for the maintenance of all created forms was summed up in the word Ma'at.[5]

If the priestly vocabulary in Genesis 2:15 indicates the same kind of thinking, the point of caring for sacred space should be seen as much more than landscaping or even priestly duties. Maintaining order made one a participant with God in the ongoing task of sustaining the equilibrium God had established in the cosmos.[6] Egyptian thinking attached this not only to the role of priests as they maintained the sacred space in the temples but also to the king, whose task was "to complete what was unfinished, and to preserve the existent, not as a status quo but in a continuing, dynamic, even revolutionary process of remodeling and improvement."[7] This combines the subduing and ruling of Genesis 1 with the ʿbd and šmr of this chapter.

Having said all of that, once we have identified the primary role as a priestly one in sacred space, we may find that we can fold other caretaking tasks back into the priestly profile. When garden-parks are associated with sacred space in the ancient world, caring for the trees in the park is a sacred task performed by priests. In Egypt and Mesopotamia, there would likewise be herds and flocks of animals that were the property of the temple and would be cared for by priests. When priests take care of garden-parks and animals associated with the parks, they are engaged in ordering sacred space and in subduing and ruling.

On the basis of this priestly understanding of the verbs that describe Adam's commissioning, I would conclude that the specific point that Genesis 2 contributes to the book is not in relation to Adam's unique material origins or to human origins in general, but rather to Adam's elect role in sacred space. This is not a new idea. In early interpretation, the book of *Jubilees* presents Adam as offering incense when he leaves Eden, thereby supporting both the priestly role of Adam and the identification of Eden as sacred space.[8] In early Christian interpretation, Origen portrays Adam as high priest.[9]

In the account of his origins Adam served as an archetype with all humanity represented *in* him. In his priestly role he serves as a representational agent serving on behalf of humanity; all humans are represented *by* him.

Adam's role must then be understood in light of the role of the priests in the ancient world. When we read the Bible, we often think of priests as ritual experts and as those instructing the people in the ways of the Lord and the law. That is true, but those tasks fit into a larger picture. The main task of the priest was the preservation of sacred space.[10] They preserved sacred space by

- instructing people regarding what sacred space requires of them (purity standards for each zone of sacred space, behavior appropriate to sacred space) so that its sanctity can be maintained

- offering sacrifices in the appropriate ways at the appropriate times and with appropriate gifts so that sanctity will be preserved

- guarding sacred space and the sacred objects found therein so that their sanctity is preserved

- keeping out anything that would compromise or corrupt the sanctity of sacred space

- serving as mediators who make the benefits of sacred space available to the people (thereby extending sacred space) and who assure that the gifts of the people get to God

Sacred space existed because of the manifest presence of God. Adam was given access to this sacred space as a priest in order to be involved in preserving its sanctity and mediating its benefits. Sacred space was also the center of order, because order emanates from God. The idea that people would "subdue" and "rule" is based on the idea that they would have a continuing role as God's vice-regents (in his image) to preserve order and to extend it under God. He is given access to (the tree of) life but (the tree of) wisdom is withheld, presumably pending a process of mentoring by God. We may discuss which of the roles in the list above would be necessary for Adam to do in Eden, but regardless of the conclusions we might draw, we can understand that the listening or reading Israelite audience would have thought of these sorts of activities when the text speaks of Adam's priestly roles.

This was a huge task, and God therefore observes that it is not good for man to be alone. This does not suggest that no other people exist, only that Adam alone had been given the task of carrying out this commission in sacred space—formed for the role as discussed in connection to that verb above.[11] Neither should we assume that the comment has to do with loneliness versus companionship and the psychological need for a "soul partner." Likewise, we cannot import the idea resident in the statement of the blessing of the last chapter and conclude that Adam is in need of a reproduction partner. That is not under discussion in Genesis 2, and he would not be looking among the animals to resolve this. Rather, God is stating that the task is too large for him to do on his own—he needs an ally to help him in sacred space.[12]

Because of the nature of the task of serving in sacred space, the only appropriate ally would be one that is Adam's ontological equal. One of the potentially confusing elements in the text is how the animals fit into what the text is conveying. They would have little connection to the concept of sacred space or priestly roles. In light of the position I am proposing, God brings the animals to Adam, and as he reflects on their roles and functions and names them, he finds that none of them is his ontological equal. God then shows Adam in a vision that woman *is* his ontological equal, and when he awakes she is brought to him and he recognizes that fact: bone of my bone and flesh of my flesh—she is comparable to man. The text then explains that, because of this ontological pairing, man will routinely leave the close biological relationship with parents to reforge what is an ontologically rooted relationship (Gen 2:24).

We might note in passing that in the *Gilgamesh Epic*, Enkidu also discovers that woman, not animals, is his ontological equal. Enkidu, a primitive man, was created individually by the gods from clay and full-grown, inhabiting the wild, unclothed, and keeping company with animals (1:99-112). He eventually finds a woman as his companion (she seduces him) and learns that he cannot continue to enjoy companionship among the animals. He is not a beast of the wild.

In this sense, the scene in Genesis 2 indicates that Adam is not Enkidu—he finds no companion among the animals, but, like Enkidu, he learns that he is not a beast. Many of the elements in Genesis 2–3 find points of contact in the descriptions of Enkidu in the *Gilgamesh Epic*, but none of them works the same. In this way, we could say that Genesis 2–3 is engaged in discussing some of the same topics as the *Gilgamesh Epic* but stands in juxtaposition to it at nearly every point. At one level, then, it is no surprise that Genesis 2 brings up man's relationships with the animals for discussion.

In the *Gilgamesh Epic*, the woman (Shamḫat) seduces Enkidu, with the result that he becomes civilized. Though the mechanism was sexual experience, the focus was the civilizing of a wild man. He gains reason and understanding (1:202), and Shamḫat then leads him to sacred space (1:209-10). In Genesis, the awareness of woman as a companion and ally comes first, and the sexual experience is constant reestablishment of an ontological whole. Again, Genesis turns the discussion upside down. Genesis is thus using common literary motifs to convey the truths about humanity that are the familiar topics of the conversation in the ancient world. They are operating in the same room of discourse, but Genesis has rearranged all the furniture. Adam shows some similarity to Enkidu, and, in other parts of the epic, even to Gilgamesh himself, but he is very different from both of them and is usually portrayed in sharp contradistinction. In this way Genesis 2–3 may be seen as making cultural allusions. See figure 3.

	Humanity	Genesis 2–3	*Gilgamesh Epic*
STATUS	Composition	Man formed from dust (Gen 2:7)	Enkidu formed from clay
	Innocence	Man and woman naked and unaware	Enkidu naked and unaware
M/F	Male/female relationships	Woman shown to be ontological match	Woman provides sexual experience that civilizes Enkidu
ANIMALS	Relations to animals	Man names animals	Enkidu companion of animals
	Distinct from animals	Animals not suitable allies— man is not a beast	Animals reject Enkidu—he is not a beast
	Clothing provision	Man and woman clothed by God	Enkidu clothed by Shamhat to civilize
DIVINE RELATIONS	Connection to God through sacred space	Man and woman serve as priests in sacred space	Shamhat serves in sacred space and takes Enkidu back to sacred space[13]
	Acquisition of wisdom	Man and woman gain knowledge of good and evil	Enkidu gains reason and understanding
	Similarity to divine	Man and woman become like God in wisdom	Enkidu becomes handsome like a god

Figure 3. Observations about humanity in Gilgamesh and Genesis 2–3: Literary touchpoints highlighting comparison and contrast

In class, when I make a cultural allusion, its significance is lost if the class is not familiar with the movie, song or video game to which I am alluding. The line becomes a source of confusion to them because they are unaware of the connection I am referencing. Likewise, if Genesis is making allusions to the literary world of the ancient Near East (as observable in literature such as the *Gilgamesh Epic*) and we as readers have no knowledge of that literary world, we will miss the significance of the allusion.

Through the account in Genesis 2, it is shown that woman was not just another creature but was like the man, in fact, his other half sharing his nature, and was therefore suitable as his ally. She joined him as guardian and mediator with the task of preserving, protecting and expanding sacred space. It was not unusual in the ancient world for women to serve in priestly roles (despite the recognized hazard of their monthly impurity). Israel, however, was an exception to this, as only men served as priests. It may seem odd, therefore, that Genesis 2 presents a woman as a colaborer within sacred space along with the man—especially if the narrative scenario is an Israelite authority figure (such as Moses) talking to an Israelite audience.[14]

The priestesses in the ancient world were sometimes involved as administrators of sacred space, but these roles are seen mostly in the late third and early second millennia B.C.[15] In the Bible, we do find women serving in sacred space (Ex 38:8; 1 Sam 2:22), though not as priestesses, and there are differences of opinions about what their role was. In the ancient world, sexual or magical roles were more associated with women serving in sacred space as time went on. To the extent that such was the case, Israelite practice may have featured only men in priestly roles in order to establish a distinction between themselves and their neighbors and to keep sexual rituals out of the sacred precinct.[16] Whatever explanations might be found, they are not sufficient to discount the idea that in Genesis 2 the woman is seen as the ally to man in service in sacred space. As an ally, she would not have to have the same roles as man, but little more can be said given the lack of information provided in the text. The text comments only on her ontological identity as man's other half rather than delineating her role in sacred space.

Returning to the priestly roles of Adam and Eve, we will gain more insight if we look to the larger paradigm offered by the identification of Israel as a "kingdom of priests" (Ex 19:6, the very context of communication about constructing sacred space, the tabernacle, at Sinai).[17] Israel's priestly role is found neither in the offering of rituals on behalf of the rest of the nations nor in servicing sacred space for them. Their role is to mediate knowledge of God, and their end goal is ultimately not to restrict access to the presence of God but to mediate access through instruction.[18] The role of Adam and Eve in the garden, I would propose, has less to do with how the priests operated within Israel and more to do with Israel's role (and later, that of believers, 1 Pet 2:9) as priests to the world. In such a view, we need not be concerned about the lack of women priests in Israel.

We previously spoke of Adam and Eve as archetypal representatives. Here we find that they are also priestly representatives. These two types of representation should be distinguished from each other. In the first, their individuality is submerged in their archetypal significance. In the second, they serve as individuals on behalf of a group (as priests always did). In that priestly role, they are mediators, and their actions have implications and at times real impact on the entire group they represent.

Before concluding this chapter it is relevant to remark on an anecdotally parallel passage in the *Gilgamesh Epic* that could shed some light on Genesis 2. In tablet XI, the flood hero, Uta-napishti, disembarks from the ark to be met by a group of the gods discussing how he was spared, whether he should have been spared and what they were to do with him now. In lines 203-6 the decision is made and a blessing conferred:

> "In the past Uta-napishti was one of mankind,
> But now Uta-napishti and his woman shall be like us gods!
> Uta-napishti shall dwell far away, at the mouth of the rivers!"
> They took[19] me and settled me far away, at the mouth of the
>   rivers.[20]

The setting to which the flood hero is "taken" is an Edenic setting ("at the mouth of the rivers") where he will have an existence "like [the] gods." It is not a dwelling *with* the gods, but it is removed from the strictly mortal realm. Note that Gilgamesh had to cross the ocean and the "Waters of Death" to get there.[21] Uta-napishti's being "taken" is seen as a blessing. This sort of understanding would also make sense for Enoch in Genesis 5, where the same verb is used.

Not only is Adam "taken" as Uta-napishti is (Gen 2:15); he is also situated at the source of the rivers (Gen 2:10). In Gilgamesh, Uta-napishti is "settled"[22] there, whereas the word used for the placement of Adam is even more significant, since it is the causative form of the verb "to rest" (*nwḥ*). In God's presence, Adam finds rest—an important allusion to what characterizes sacred space. Both Adam and Uta-napishti are placed in sacred space, where they have access to life.

Despite these similarities, we must not neglect the significant differences. Though both Adam and Uta-napishti are in sacred space, Adam is there in a special relationship with God. In contrast, Uta-napishti's situation has no connection to the realm of the gods, nor does it anticipate relationship with them. Adam and Eve become "like the gods" when they seize wisdom for themselves; Uta-napishti's becoming like the gods is a promotion—a boon granted to him. Uta-napishti is unique, not archetypal or priestly in any way; no particular role for him is identified. Unlike Adam and Eve, Uta-napishti and his wife are neither guardians nor mediators of sacred space—they are simply privileged denizens.

The benefit of comparing Genesis 5 and Gilgamesh tablet XI is the understanding that Adam, the archetypal human, is being removed from the everyday realm of human existence and placed in a specially prepared place (the source of the rivers) as a blessing with access to life.[23] Interestingly, Uta-napishti's name refers to him as one who found life,[24] and in finding Eve, Adam has found the "mother of all the living" (Gen 3:20), as he names her.

In conclusion, rather than understanding Scripture as necessitating the view that Adam and Eve are the first humans, in light of their specific role concerned with access to God in sacred space and relationship with him, we might alternatively consider the possibility that they are the first *significant* humans. As with Abram, who was given a significant role as the ancestor of Israel (though not the first ancestor of Israel), Adam and Eve would be viewed as established as significant by their election. This would be true whether or not other people were around. Their election is to a priestly role, the first to be placed in sacred space. The forming accounts give them insight into the nature of humanity, but they also become the first significant humans because of their role in bringing sin into the world (for fuller discussion see chap. 15). Adam was the "first" man, given the opportunity to bring life, but he failed to achieve that goal. Christ, as the "last" man, succeeded as he provided life and access to the presence of God for all as our great high priest (see 1 Cor 15:45).

The role of Adam and Eve as priests in sacred space is what sets them apart, not their genetic role. If Genesis 1 features the inauguration of sacred space and God taking up his rest, the presence of a center of that sacred space (i.e., a temple) is implied. If the Garden of Eden serves that temple function, then Genesis 2 must be viewed as taking place in the same general time, though it can come after the seven days rather than within it. In such a scenario, Adam and Eve should likely be considered part of that initial human creation in Genesis 1, though since only corporate humanity is mentioned, the text does not explicitly rule out the idea that there were others. According to my analysis of the *tōlĕdōt* (account), I would suggest that Genesis 2 is not recursively recounting what happened *on* day six but is talking about what happened in the *aftermath* of day six.

The Garden Is an Ancient Near Eastern Motif for Sacred Space, and the Trees Are Related to God as the Source of Life and Wisdom

Issues that need to be addressed in this chapter include the literary nature of the text, the theological significance of the chapter and the ancient Near Eastern background that gives it shape. In the process we need to discuss the two central trees and the question of the nature and location of the garden.

From the start it is important to recognize that the garden, the trees and the serpent are symbols. By that, I do not mean to suggest that they are not real.[1] We must simply recognize that they stand for something beyond themselves. That symbolized reality is transcendent and far more important than the physical realities, however one might assess the latter.

GARDEN OF EDEN

When we consider the Garden of Eden in its ancient context, we find that it is more *sacred space* than *green space*. It is the center of order, not perfection, and its significance has more to do with divine presence than human paradise.[2]

In the textual description, it features rivers that bring fertility and an arboretum of sorts. This parklike environment is well known in the ancient world. The motif of flowing rivers (four is common) is connected to sacred space early and often. The same motif can be seen in Ezekiel 47, and there are allusions to it throughout the Psalms and the Prophets. Gardens were constructed adjoining sacred space as evidence of the fertility that resulted from the presence of God. They were not vegetable gardens or fields of crops; they were beautifully landscaped parks. They provided fruit that was offered to the god. Kings also built gardens adjoining their own palaces where they would receive (and impress) visitors. Thus, the text of Genesis can be seen to describe a garden, a park landscaped with exotic trees and stocked with wildlife. These were common accoutrements to temples and palaces in the ancient world.[3]

I suggested that in Genesis 1 the cosmos was being designated as sacred space. But no information was given there about where the center of sacred space was located, though it was designed to function on behalf of people. In Genesis 2, the center of sacred space is located for us, and people are placed there.[4] If Eden is the center of sacred space, it bears some resemblance to the holy of holies in the tabernacle/temple. We are not surprised, then, that scholars have long recognized Eden symbolism in the temple.[5] Elizabeth Bloch-Smith refers to the temple as a "virtual garden of Eden."[6] Victor Hurowitz similarly concludes, "The decorations in the Temple and their distribution were significant and logical. It seems as if the Temple was not merely Yhwh's residence, but a divine garden on earth."[7] This interpretation of Eden is found in the earliest interpretation outside the Bible, the book of *Jubilees* (second century B.C.), though it is subtle. In the interpretation of *Jubilees,* Adam and Eve have relations right after Eve is brought to Adam, and at that time they are outside the garden. Then they have to purify themselves before entering the garden, which then by implication is considered sacred space.[8] Among early Christian interpreters,

Ephrem (fourth century) gave extensive treatment to the ways in which the Garden of Eden was similar to the tabernacle.[9]

Iconography amply supports this relationship between garden/rivers and temples, but most of the archaeological evidence relates to palaces rather than temples.[10] It is no surprise that kings replicated for themselves the perquisites that the gods enjoyed. Archaeologists have discovered a temple near Assur with many rows of tree pits in the courtyard.[11] In Egypt a divine grove at times was associated with a temple.[12] Artificial pools, exotic trees and plants, fish and water fowl, and produce grown for the provision of the gods were all features of these temple gardens. Their fertility and ordered arrangement symbolized order in the cosmos.

Besides the iconographical and archaeological data, texts inform our understanding of the Garden of Eden. Even though there is no precedent in the ancient Near Eastern literature that would serve as a parallel to the full profile of Genesis 2, there are a number of texts that touch on various parts of it. I referred to a number of the associations with the *Gilgamesh Epic* in the last chapter. There is no paradise myth in the *Gilgamesh Epic* or in the following pieces that we will examine. In fact, there is no paradise myth in any of our extant ancient Near Eastern literature. Nevertheless, we find some of the motifs that are familiar to us from Genesis 2–3, although they are in a very different sort of context.

ENKI AND NINḤURSAG (DILMUN)

Among the features that this myth[13] shares with Genesis is that the setting is described in "not yet" terms, as is also found in Genesis 2:5-6. The land of Dilmun is described in terms of the absence of normal behavior at various levels (lines 11-28). In the animal world, birds were not making their sounds. Predators were not killing for their food, but neither were other animals aware of what they should eat (pigs did not know of grain). Other habitual animal behaviors pertaining to caring for young or sleeping were not yet practiced. There were no diseases,

and no one was growing old. There was no darkness. Human behaviors had likewise not been initiated: no heralds, no mourning.

Dilmun, located at the mouth of the waters, is the place to which
Uta-napishti was taken in the *Gilgamesh Epic*. It is of a place of cultic
purity, and in that sense is sacred space, though it is not being set up
as such in this myth—it is already that. Differences include the absence of the concept of a garden of God for human and divine interaction.[14] There is a garden in the myth, featuring a number of trees,
which the god Enki identifies—he decrees their destinies as he eats
from them. Ninhursag curses Enki because she had planted the trees.
So, there is a garden on Dilmun, but Dilmun itself is not a garden.
Furthermore, this garden is neither a site of divine-human interaction
nor a place for human dwelling. Dilmun is certainly not a paradise but
an inchoate scenario in which destinies have not yet been decreed
(order has not yet been established).[15]

As the myth closes, Ninhursag is asking Enki what parts of him hurt.
He identifies several (head, hair, nose, mouth, throat, arm, ribs and
sides), and for each one Ninhursag gives birth to a deity, and each of
them is then assigned a different role. Scholars have paid particular attention to the one given birth because Enki's ribs hurt: Ninti (lady of the
ribs). When roles are assigned, Ninti is identified as "lady of the month."
The context, however, shows that there is no parallel here of any sort. All
the characters are gods, not humans. Ninti is only one in a series of
deities associated with various parts of the body, and the goddesses are
given birth, not formed. Ninti has no continuing association with Enki.
This is not even close enough to be considered a parallel motif. We can
see that this myth provides us very little for evaluating or understanding
Genesis 2–3. The inclusion of "rib" is incidental.

JEWEL GARDEN OF GILGAMESH

In the Neo-Assyrian version of the *Gilgamesh Epic*, Gilgamesh encounters a jewel garden near the end of his quest for Uta-Napishti, the

Babylonian flood hero.[16] It is located where Shamash, the sun god, enters and exits each day. Scholars are divided about whether the jewels metaphorically refer to fruit or whether the trees actually grow jewels. While there is no indication of divine presence and no prohibitions or trespass, the motif of jewels in the garden of God is found in Ezekiel 28.

TREES AND FRUIT

We now turn our attention specifically to the trees in the garden and that which they confer. Despite some general points of contact, no direct parallel exists in the ancient world for the two special trees in the center of the garden, the tree of life and the tree of the knowledge of good and evil (= tree of wisdom[17]). First we will summarize what information does exist in the ancient world and then proceed to a discussion of the biblical material.

Adapa. In the tale of Adapa, we find the main character playing an archetypal role, as has been suggested for Adam and Eve. Here, however, the archetype does not concern human origins and nature but particular human roles. Adapa was one of the first antediluvian sages (the *apkallus* of whom there were seven) and the most famous. These beings were storied as having emerged from the sea and were credited with teaching the arts of civilization. This character is known as late as the Hellenistic compilation of traditions by the Babylonian priest, Berossus.

In the tale known as *Adapa and the South Wind*,[18] Adapa has an encounter with Anu in heaven, where he is offered food of life and water of life. He has been warned by another god, Ea (for whom he is a priest), that this offer is insincere and accepting it will bring his doom. But in that warning he has been deceived, and by declining the offer he, and apparently all of humanity with him, actually loses the chance for eternal life.[19] The text of the Adapa tale is not clear on this issue, but one factor that would suggest that all of humanity is affected by Adapa's choice is Anu's exclamation—"Alas for inferior humanity!"[20]—after Adapa refuses the food.

The most important element of the tale of Adapa for our study of Genesis 2–3 is that, by virtue of his priestly position, his actions have ramifications for all of humanity. In a further comparison to Adam, Adapa is perhaps the most famous of the ancient sages, so he already has wisdom; he nevertheless lacks immortality. In contrast, Adam and Eve in Genesis have access to immortality (tree of life) but lack wisdom (associated with the forbidden tree of the knowledge of good and evil).

We can see that Genesis is interested in the same issues as the tale of Adapa, and both of them discuss these issues in terms of representatives of humanity. This is no reason to think that the literary pieces are related in any way or that one is derivative from another. It simply shows us how Genesis is presenting its material in the context of the conversations that occurred in the second millennium B.C.[21]

Cosmic tree in Eridu. In a Neo-Assyrian text from Ashurbanipal's library that features interlinear text in Sumerian and Akkadian, CT 16.46, we encounter a number of motifs that are familiar from Genesis 2–3, as is immediately evident from this translation of the pertinent lines:[22]

> In Eridu grows the dark *giš-kin* tree, shining in a pure place (183),
> Its brilliance is that of lapis-lazuli, it rises from the underground water-*apsu* (185),
> When Enki walks about Eridu, it is filled with abundance (187),
> Its foundation is the opening of the underworld (189).
> Its bed is the sanctuary of Nammu (191).
> From its pure temple, a grove where no one enters, the dark tree rises (193),
> Inside are the gods Shamash and Tammuz (195),
> At the mouth/confluence of two rivers (197),

The *giš-kin* tree[23] here is not a tree whose fruit has special qualities, but a "cosmic tree," an important feature of cosmology in the ancient cultures.[24] As can be seen here, it has its roots in the netherworld, it is associated with fertile waters, and it is located in a grove associated with a temple housing Shamash (sun god) and Tammuz (netherworld deity). It binds together heaven, earth and the netherworld.[25] Description of this tree can also be seen in Ezekiel 31, where it is compared to the trees of Eden (Ezek 31:18, see also Dan 4).[26] We can therefore see that the cosmic tree motif has some overlap with the trees in Genesis 2–3.

Ancient Near Eastern literature has no obvious parallel to a tree of wisdom, but scholars speak often of a "tree of life" motif. Before turning to that, we should note the plant of life (named "plant of the heart beat" and designated "Old man becomes young") that Gilgamesh plucks from the *Apsu* (subterranean waters in the cosmological realm of the god Ea). Unfortunately, the plant was subsequently stolen by a serpent.[27] It is also a plant of life (u_2 nam-til$_3$-la) that sustains Lugalbanda when he has been abandoned by friends in the wilderness because of his sickness.[28] We have already noted the food of life (*akal balati;* here, not specifically a plant) that is offered to Adapa. These three examples have in common that something is ingested that leads to the enhancement of life in some way (respectively, rejuvenation, healing sustenance and immortality).[29] Even though the details vary, the conversation provided by Genesis 2–3 is similar: ingestion is the mode, and enhanced life (unspecified, though presumably immortality as inferred from Gen 3:22) is the objective. The concerns represented in the texts are similar, as are the direction taken by the answers, but the literary contexts vary, as do the beliefs and assertions that emerge. Yet, we can see that it makes sense against the backdrop of the ancient world for the Israelites to formulate the literature the way that they do.[30]

Besides these literary occurrences of the motif (something that one eats to gain life), much has been made of the iconography, especially from the Neo-Assyrian period, of what is commonly referred to as the "tree of life" or, preferably, the "sacred tree."[31] The motif of a sacred tree occurs throughout the ancient Near East across the spectrum of both time and culture.[32] When the tree can be identified botanically, it is typically either a pomegranate or date palm.[33] It is often flanked by winged genies (in Assyria) or some variety of caprids (in the Levant).[34] A winged disk at times appears over the tree. In the Assyrian motif, the genies on either side are often thought to be holding date-palm flower clusters for the purpose of pollination and thus represent fertility.[35] The tree itself is generally understood to represent a god or the king (for the latter, note Dan 4 and Zech 4). No ancient Near Eastern texts offer explanation of the symbolism. If art historians, however, are on the right track, the tree represents *order* more than *life* (seen in the "cosmic tree" motif that we *do* know of in the ancient literature) and would therefore be more comparable in its properties to the tree of wisdom in the garden (given the close association of wisdom and order throughout the Old Testament and the ancient world).

> The Neo-Assyrian flanked tree (and its antecedent and subsequent versions) seems often to have figured in imagery of the world order as maintained by some deity. Such symbolism seems to be derivative from the tree as a symbol of cosmic well-being and of the good life in general.[36]

The properties of this sacred tree make it the source of wisdom and order rather than the source of life. Simo Parpola suggests that the tree can represent "man as a microcosm, the ideal man created in the image of God."[37]

Genesis 2–3. As we found in the previous discussion of the tale of Adapa, comparison with CT 16.46 shows that the motifs and themes used in Genesis 2–3 are hardly arbitrary. Instead, the story includes concepts familiar to people in the ancient world. In light of this observation, we have to keep in mind that Genesis 2–3 is the form that the account took in Israelite traditions. The inspired storyteller is speaking to Israel and is prompted by the Spirit to use imagery that would communicate clearly in that world dealing with issues that were current in that society. We do not have an account that is portrayed as being conveyed to Adam and Eve. It is an account about Adam and Eve being conveyed to Israelites. If it were given to Adam and Eve, we could not meaningfully talk about ancient Near Eastern backgrounds since Adam and Eve did not have such a background. In this Israelite telling, however, it is clear that the broader cognitive environment of which ancient Israel is a part is reflected in the shaping of the account (sacred garden, special trees, involvement of serpent, concerns about wisdom and immortality), even though the Israelite account is characterized by deep differences and has points to make that are unique in the ancient world.

In Genesis, the trees are understood best in the context of sacred space rather than as isolated trees that happen to be in a garden. Whether interpreters consider them real, physical, floral specimens with the ability to bestow benefits to those who partake, figurative symbols of divine gifts, mythological motifs, or anything else, we must not miss the theological and textual significance that they have. Whether they confer or represent, they provide what is only God's to give. He is the source of life, which is given by him and found in his presence (Deut 30:11-20). He is the center of order, and wisdom is the ability to discern order. Relationship with God is the beginning of wisdom (Job 28:28; Prov 1:7). Consequently, we make a mistake to think that this is simply about magical trees in a garden paradise. It is about the presence of God on earth and what relationship with him makes available.[38]

At one level, we can simply say they are whatever the Bible considers them to be (even if we cannot decide for certain), because whether they are literal or not, we know their significance. In this way, we commit to taking the Bible seriously and fulfilling the demands of our commitment to the truthfulness of Scripture. If the text chooses to use metaphorical symbols, it is free to do so, and we would be remiss to read them any other way. Alternatively, if God chose to endow fruit trees with the wherewithal to confer the life and wisdom that comes from him, we cannot say that it is impossible. God chose Samson's hair to provide him with strength, but strength came from God, not from hair. Whether the trees are literal or figurative, the basic point remains: life is gained in the presence of God, and wisdom is his gift (not to be taken on one's own). God is the source and center of wisdom—not us. Regardless of our literary interpretation, the theology must be maintained: life and wisdom are the gifts of God, and human representatives incurred guilt for all of us by grasping the latter illegitimately and therefore losing the former. As discussed in chapter eleven, I believe that the biblical material makes the most sense when sin's entry is seen as punctiliar rather than the result of a gradual process.

Conclusions

As we step back to draw some conclusions from this chapter, we have to discuss whether Eden in Genesis 2–3 is central or peripheral in the cosmos. In the ancient Near East, both Dilmun and the jewel garden in Gilgamesh are peripheral. In contrast, the "sacred tree" imagery presents a cosmic tree that is central. This sacred tree is symbolic of divine presence (according to Parpola) whereas none of the peripheral garden possibilities in the ancient Near East is a place of divine presence. The central garden that contains the sacred tree in CT 16.46 does feature the presence of gods. When the fertile waters are thought of as sources, they are located in the center; the mouth of waters motif (e.g., Dilmun) is peripheral.[39] From this information we might conclude that a central location would be identified as sacred space whereas a peripheral location would be more appropriately labeled numinous space.

In the Bible, evidences of centrality would include the use in Ezekiel as it seems associated with the mountain of God and a cosmic tree, as well as the location in Genesis at the source of the rivers. Yet, in Genesis, there is no indication that the trees are considered cosmic trees. The fact that Adam and Eve are sent out of the garden and dwell "to the east" also suggests centrality because when the garden is peripheral, it is as far to the east as one can go.

Evidences that the Genesis garden should be considered peripheral
are fewer.[40] Aside from the comment that Adam was "taken" and
settled in the garden (the same wording used for the peripheral relo-
cation of Uta-napishti), there is not much support. Two of the four
rivers named in Genesis 2 are real rivers in the real world. It is true
that the few gardens featured in the mythology of the ancient world
are peripheral, but the differences that we have noted between them
and the Garden of Eden make that insufficient to construe Eden in the
same way. Evidence heavily favors the central location of the Garden
of Eden. The presence of God, the source of the rivers (known rivers
at that) and the possibility that the tree of wisdom is comparable to
the cosmic tree all argue for its centrality. If God is the center, then
humans are driven out to the liminal/periphery—instead of humans
being at the center and the divine/numinal realm on the periphery.

Yet even as we understand the case for Eden's centrality, we recognize a sense in which it is removed from easy access (if not numi-
nously peripheral). As noted, two of the rivers are known rivers, but
their sources are at the edges of the known world—a region eventually
known as Urartu, where the "mountains of Ararat" in the flood narrative are located as well. Though the Tigris and Euphrates are well
known, the identities of the Gihon and Pishon have long been debated.
One well-supported theory now identifies the Pishon as the Halys
River that flows from the region of Urartu around central Asia Minor
and into the Black Sea. In this theory, the Gihon is identified as the
Aras River flowing eastward from Urartu and into the Caspian Sea.[41]
This would place the Garden of Eden in a high mountain valley near
Lake Van, and thus explain how Eden is sometimes viewed as being
on a mountain (e.g., Ezek 28:14). This region was populated early by
the Hurrians, some of whom eventually settled in Canaan and were
encountered by the Israelites and their ancestors. The cosmic center
can still be located in this remote region far removed from Israel. We

therefore might conclude that the garden is considered cosmically central though at the outskirts of the known world.

In the ancient Near East, life and wisdom are the prerogatives of the gods that they are reluctant to grant as they try to maintain distance between themselves and humanity. In the Bible, life and wisdom are possessed by God, and they are made available to humans as they are in relationship to him. The trouble comes when humans try to seize wisdom on their own terms. They are told that the fruit will make them like God, but unfortunately this is as independent agents rather than in relationship to him. In this way, the Bible has a very different read on these issues than its ancient Near Eastern counterparts.

The Serpent Would Have Been Viewed as a Chaos Creature from the Non-ordered Realm, Promoting Disorder

Christian readers of Genesis have at times been confused by the serpent. Why did God allow such a creature to infiltrate the garden? How could this creature be in a "good" world? Based on New Testament references, the serpent is easily identified as Satan (Rom 16:20; Rev 12:9; 20:2), raising questions about where he came from and what he is doing in this account.

If we are going to understand Genesis as an ancient document, however, we have to read the text first in ancient terms. That means that we cannot immediately jump to the eventual conclusion that the serpent is associated with Satan, for there is no indication that the serpent was so identified during Old Testament times. Before considering the implications of later biblical interpretation, we should understand the ancient text on its own terms. Furthermore, we cannot read the text as if it is communicating in the world of Adam and Eve's knowledge because, as mentioned in previous chapters, we have an Israelite storyteller communicating to an Israelite audience. That audience would have made certain associations with the serpent imagery that are not necessarily natural to us.

Serpent symbolism was rich in the ancient Near East. We have already made reference to the serpent who stole the plant of life from Gilgamesh, but that is only the beginning. We have discussed the *Tale of Adapa* but have not yet referred to the serpent figure there. In that narrative, the serpent is not involved in any temptation and is not a main character. When Adapa responds to Anu's invitation to meet with him, one of the guardians of Anu's palace is Gizzida (= Ningishzida, "Lord of the Productive Tree"), who has the shape of a serpent and is accompanied by horned serpents (*bašmu*). He is known as the guardian of demons who live in the netherworld.[1]

In Egypt, we find serpents everywhere from the crown of Pharaoh to pictures on painted sarcophagi, as well as in the Book of the Dead (as deadly enemies along the path to the afterlife). These creatures are associated with both wisdom and death. Apophis was a serpent of chaos who tried to swallow the sun as it rose every morning.[2] Other elements can be found in the Egyptian Book of the Dead that connect to ideas that are evident in the Genesis account, including crawling on the belly, eating dust, a crushing head and striking a heel. The following entries drawn from the *Zondervan Illustrated Bible Backgrounds Commentary: Old Testament* address some of the details in Genesis:[3]

> **Crawl on your belly (3:14).** The Egyptian Pyramid Texts were designed to aid the pharaohs of the Old Kingdom (end of the third millennium) on their journey to the afterlife. Among the over 700 utterances are several dozen spells and curses on snakes that may impede the king's progress. These utterances contain phrases that are reminiscent of the curse on the serpent in Genesis 3. For instance, the biblical statement that the serpent will "crawl on your belly" is paralleled by frequent spells that call on the snake to lie down, fall down, get down, or crawl away

(Pyramid Text 226, 233, 234, 298, 386).[4] Another says that he should "go with [his] face on the path" (PT 288).

These suggest that when God tells the serpent that he will crawl on his belly, there is no suggestion that the serpent had legs that he now loses. Instead, he is going to be docile rather than in an attack position. The serpent on its belly is nonthreatening, while the one reared up is protecting or attacking. Notice that on the Pharaoh's crown, the serpent (*uraeus*) is pictured as upright and in an attack position. Nevertheless, I should also note that there are occasional depictions of serpent creatures with legs.[5] There is no indication, however, of an occasion in which serpents lost their legs.

Eat dust (3:14). Eating dust is not a comment about the actual diet of a snake. It is more likely a reference to their habitat. Again the Pyramid Texts show some similarity as they attempt to banish the serpent to the dust.[6] The serpent is a creature of the netherworld (that is why the pharaoh encounters it on his journey), and denizens of the netherworld were typically portrayed as eating dust. So in the Descent of Ishtar, the netherworld is described as a place where their food is dust and their bread is clay.[7]

Crush your head (3:15). Treading on the serpent is used in Pyramid Texts 299 as an expression of overcoming or defeating it. Specific statements indicate that the "Sandal of Horus tramples the snake underfoot" (PT 378), and "Horus has shattered [the snake's] mouth with the sole of his foot" (PT 388). This reflects a potentially mortal blow to this deadly enemy. There is no suggestion that the Israelites are borrowing from the Pyramid Texts, only that these texts help us to determine how someone in the ancient Near East might understand such words and phrases.

Strike his heel (3:15). It is true that the ancients were aware that many snakes were not poisonous.[8] But since harmless snakes usually were not seen as aggressive, if someone were bitten by a snake, it was assumed that the snake might be poisonous. Thus the strike to the heel is a potentially mortal blow.

As an example of several of these items, see the Pyramid Texts, utterance 378:

> O Snake in the sky! O Centipede on earth! The Sandal of Horus is what tramples the *nhi*-snake underfoot. . . . It is dangerous for me so I have trodden on you; be wise about me (?) and I will not tread on you, for you are the mysterious and invisible one of whom the gods speak; because you are the one who has no legs, because you are the one who has no arms, with which you could walk after your brethren the gods . . . beware of me and I will beware of you.[9]

In the above examples, we can see how information about the serpent in the Genesis account can be documented in various ways in the ancient Near East. A separate direction of inquiry could comb the ancient Near East for serpent symbolism, interpret it and then try to bring those elements into an understanding of the Bible without biblical precedent. Unfortunately, such attempts are bound to produce unsatisfactory results because there are just too many different aspects to serpent symbolism. We would have no way to conclude confidently which ones the Israelites would prefer or which would be significant in any given context. Serpent symbolism has been connected to fertility, sexuality, protection, life, death and numerous other important attributes.[10]

While many of these motifs may well have been familiar to the mind of an Israelite, especially one who had been recently in Egypt, we want to explore the question of the nature of the serpent in Genesis 3. If the Israelites would not have thought of the serpent as Satan (and there is no evidence that they did—in fact, they have a far less developed idea of Satan than what we find in the New Testament[11]), then what would they have thought?

We can begin with the description that is given in Genesis 3. The main adjective used there identifies the serpent as *'ārûm*, variously translated as "subtle," "wily," "cunning," "shrewd," "prudent" or "clever." It is an adjective that operates primarily in reference to wisdom and is inherently neutral (that is, it is a quality that can be used well—Prov 1:4; 8:5—or in questionable ways—Ex 21:14; Josh 9:4).[12] Ziony Zevit offers a helpful profile of someone who is *'ārûm:*

> [They] conceal what they feel and what they know (Prov 12:16; 23). They esteem knowledge and plan how to use it in achieving their objectives (Prov 13:16; 14:8, 18); they do not believe everything that they hear (Prov 14:15); and they know how to avoid trouble and punishment (Prov 22:3; 27:12). In sum they are shrewd and calculating, willing to bend and torture the limits of acceptable behavior but not to cross the line into illegalities. They may be unpleasant and purposely misleading in speech but are not out-and-out liars (Josh 9:4; 1 Sam 23:22). They know how to read people and situations and how to turn their readings to advantage. A keen wit and a rapier tongue are their tools.[13]

Ultimately, such a descriptor does not aid us in determining the creature's nature. Other than that, we can only identify the serpent as one of "the wild animals the LORD God had made" (Gen 3:1). At the same time, we should notice that the serpent is not described as "evil." This devious creature does not become associated with evil until much later.[14]

Recent study has focused attention on the serpent as a chaos creature. Chaos creatures in the ancient world were typically composite creatures that belonged to the sphere of the divine yet were not deified.[15] Their composite features gave them a combination of attributes. In the ancient world the chaos creatures are not thought of as evil. They are amoral but can be mischievous or destructive. They cause problems if left unchecked but can be domesticated and become associates of gods. Demons also function much like chaos creatures, as do liminal creatures (e.g., coyote, screech owl).[16]

It is true that the Hebrew word for the serpent, *nāḥāš*, is one of the normal ways to designate a common snake. Furthermore, the snake in Genesis 3 is identified as among the creatures of the field that God created, and nothing in the text suggests it is a composite creature. Nevertheless, all creatures in the Hebrew Bible, including chaos creatures, are created by God (Gen 1:21; Job 40:15-19; Ps 104:26). That *nāḥāš* can also designate a chaos creature is evident from its usage in Isaiah 27:1, where it describes Leviathan.[17] Such an understanding is confirmed finally in the apocalypse of John in which the serpent, now Satan, is described as a great dragon (Rev 12:9)—the chaos creature par excellence.[18] We could therefore conclude that the serpent in Genesis 3 is a chaos creature on the basis of its role in the story and other supporting contexts.[19]

Richard Averbeck is then correct to observe that this is not just a snake story. "The Israelites would have seen a great deal more in Genesis 3 than a simple tale about snakes and mankind. . . . From their point of view, this would have been the very beginning of a cosmic battle that they were feeling the effects of in their own personal experience and their national history."[20] Though I am not ready to go as far as he does to conclude that this also represents the fall of Satan, I believe that entering the text from the ancient Israelite viewpoint should lead us to think of the serpent in terms of a chaos creature.

What is the result of such an approach?

- An Israelite reader would not identify the serpent as Satan. The consequences are far more significant in the account than the agent. The serpent is the catalyst more than the cause.

- An Israelite reader would recognize the deleterious effects of the temptation but would not necessarily consider the serpent to be morally evil or bent on the destruction of humankind. An Israelite would not give any unique status to this serpent—he is just one of any number of chaos creatures rather than a spiritual, cosmic power of some sort.

- The Israelite reader would have thought of the serpent as a sort of disruptive free agent with less of a thought-out agenda. The Old Testament does not give the serpent an ongoing role. Like the serpent in the *Gilgamesh Epic* who did what its nature led it to do and then disappeared from the scene, no continuing role or place is recognized for the serpent in the Old Testament, though the consequences of the human act remain in place (again as in *Gilgamesh*).

- The serpent's insertion of doubt and his nuanced denial of the woman's understanding of the consequences stated by God would not be interpreted any differently than in our traditional understanding. Deception, misdirection and troublemaking are all within the purview of chaos creatures. It is important to note the syntactical subtlety that is evident in the serpent's words. He does not say "you will not die." Instead the placement of the negation results in something more like "don't think that death is such an immediate threat."[21] God told the truth: when they ate from the tree, they were doomed to die. The words God used did not suggest immediate death (the syntactical expression that he uses, "on the day that," is simply the Hebrew idiom for "when"), but the penalty was carried out by removing their access to the tree of life. They were therefore immediately doomed to die (the force of the verbal construction). The woman was not as careful in her wording, and the serpent therefore told the truth when he picked up on the discrepancy and contradicted *her* (not God) by saying that death was not an immediate threat. In this way the serpent's deception came in exploiting a misrepresentation by the woman and telling her of a benefit to eating the fruit without likewise including the deleterious effects. Notice that the serpent does not suggest outright that Eve eat the fruit or that she should disobey.[22]

- At the same time there is no room for the suggestion that it was the serpent who told the truth (you will not die, you shall be like gods) and God who was wrong (in the day that you eat from it you will surely die).[23] God's statement did not indicate immediate death ("in the day" is the Hebrew way of saying "when"). The construction often translated "surely die" expresses only that they will at that time be doomed to die,[24] which is exactly what happened when the way to the tree of life was barred.

- The Israelite reader would understand that the result of the serpent's role was that evil took root among humanity. This is clear from Genesis 3:15, where an ongoing battle is portrayed between humans (generation to generation) on one side, and the "seed" or "offspring" of the serpent, which does not refer to future generations of serpents but to the evil that had resulted, on the other side. The fact that the two verbs in the verse that describe the antagonistic actions are from the same root (despite the fact that many translations render them differently) shows that the verse does not indicate who the victor will be. Instead it indicates that there will be the ongoing exchange of potentially mortal blows.

- We might well ask what a chaos creature was doing in the garden (the center of order in the cosmos). Surprisingly, when we examine the text closely, we discover that the text never suggests that the serpent *was* in the garden (let alone in the tree). If we inquire how then Adam and Eve would have encountered the creature, we must note that Adam and Eve's tasks in the garden do not necessitate their constant presence. Priests serving in sacred space do not live in sacred space. While the placing of Adam in the garden may suggest a more permanent residence, we would have to ask whether that meant he would never leave. Much is unspecified in the text.

- As a chaos creature, the serpent would be more closely associated
  with non-order than with disorder. Non-order has a certain neu-
  trality to it, whereas disorder is evil in nature and intent. We might
  describe an earthquake or a cancer as forces of non-order with evil
  consequences. But they are not inherently evil. We do not control
  them, and therefore they can have disastrous effects. If the serpent
  truly is in the category of chaos creature, neither his contradiction
  of God's statement nor his deception about the consequences are
  part of an evil agenda. They are simply the disruptive, ad hoc behavior that chaos creatures engage in. More complete understanding is offered in intertestamental literature and New Testament theology, but if we limit our analysis to the ancient context
  of the Old Testament, things look very different.

EXCURSUS: MYTH/MYTHOLOGY

I remain uncomfortable applying the genre label "myth/mythology" to
these biblical narratives. The designation has too many definitions, and
therefore the words lose their ability to communicate clearly. Furthermore, we have so thoroughly adapted these terms to Western culture
that their application to ancient culture becomes inevitably anachro-
nistic.[25] But the issue goes beyond the labeling of a genre of literature; it
concerns the process by which literature of any genre is conceived and
composed. The ancients think differently; they perceive the world in different ways, with different categories and priorities than we do.

In our culture, we think "scientifically." We are primarily concerned
with causation, composition and systematization. In the ancient world
they are more likely to think of the world in terms of symbols and to
express their understanding by means of imagery. We are primarily
interested in events and material realia whereas they are more interested in ideas and their representation.[26]

Some might suggest that the Israelites who crafted the early chapters of Genesis are historicizing myth (as can potentially be seen in Is 27:1), that is, presenting real events using imagery as a rhetorical means to capture the full range of truth as it is commonly conveyed in the world in which they live. Since the concept of myth (mythic/mythical/mytho-logical), however, is so volatile and diversely understood, we need to use it in connection with other qualifying terms. The word group *image/imagery/imagination/imaginative* would work well (though *imaginary* would be incorrect). A rhetoric using mythical imagery is easily discernible in biblical poetry (e.g., "from the heavens the stars fought" or "crushed the heads of Leviathan" [Ps 74:14]), and it becomes formalized in the genre of apocalyptic. Nevertheless, it is not absent from prose. To describe this sort of thinking, I would like to adapt the term *imagistic*.[27] It offers a distinction that is easy to understand in today's culture as we find that students are increasingly visual learners—a fact that compels us to be more imagistic in our teaching and communication.

Rather than attempting to define it, in accordance with true imagistic thinking, I will instead describe it by illustrations. Imagistic thinking and representation would stand in contrast to scientific or analytical thinking. We can see the difference if we compare two visual representations of the night sky—one taken by the Hubble telescope, the other presented by Vincent van Gogh's *The Starry Night*. People would never consider doing astronomy from the van Gogh and could not do so even if they wanted to; the image contains nothing of the composition or position of stars. At the same time, we would not say that it is a false depiction of the night sky. Visual artists depict the world imagistically, and we recognize that this depiction is independent of science but not independent of truth. The ancients apply this same imagistic conception to all genres of literature, including those that we cannot conceive of as anything other than scientific. Imagistic history, like that preserved in Genesis, is to history as *The Starry Night* is to a Hubble photograph.

As another example, we would not try to reconstruct historically the bombardment of Fort McHenry in the war of 1812 by a detailed analysis of "The Star-Spangled Banner." Note how our national anthem is set in a historical context but uses the rhetoric of imagery and the power of symbol (the flag) in an artistic way to convey an enduring truth and value that reaches far beyond the War of 1812.

A modern-day example of terminology that offers an alternative to scientific/historical thinking would be what Lutherans today refer to as "sacramental" thinking, a highly controversial term that includes the mystical aspects of the sacraments but goes beyond it into the wider realm of religious thought. In such a context, they find it quite a natural way of thinking. In those traditions people realize that such thinking is not subject to scientific verification, and historicity is simply not a category that would have any meaning. People who are used to sacramental thinking (however defined) find it very hard to describe it (or defend it) to those who are not so inclined. The fact that this seems like a new and unfamiliar way of thinking to some readers who are not Lutheran (or connected with other traditions at home with sacramental thinking) demonstrates the point I am making.

Imagistic thinking presents similar difficulties. Israelites found no problems thinking about Ezekiel's vision of Egypt as a cosmic tree (Ezek 31). This does not warrant labeling the literature mythology, nor does it concern questions of reality or truth. Some might consider the trees, the garden and the snake to be examples of imagistic thinking without thereby denying reality and truth to the account. The author understands *trees* in a way that does not simply indicate a botanical species of flora with remarkable chemical properties.[28] When we put these elements in their ancient Near Eastern context and recognize the Israelite capacity, and even propensity, to think in imagistic terms,[29] we may find that we gain a deeper understanding of important theological realities.

Some scholars today believe that Israel was in the habit of borrowing other people's myths and transforming them into a mythology of their own. I do not share that perspective. What is sometimes perceived as a shared mythology is more often a shared propensity to think imagistically about the same issues using a shared symbolic vocabulary. Nicolas Wyatt distinguishes between those who use the oral discourse of story to represent reality and those who analyze the observed world and formulate hypothetical paradigms to explain that which is observed.[30] Imagistic thinking is not only to be contrasted with causation analysis. It also stands in contrast to metaphysics, which, though not a science, is a product of scientific thinking in that it is also interested in intermediate causation and systematization. These are varying ways to communicate ideas about identity and coherence.

This discussion quickly becomes very esoteric and is both out of my area of expertise and out of the range of this book. I have raised this issue not to solve the questions it entails but to elevate our consciousness of yet another way in which we think quite differently from how people in the ancient world thought. This generates the repeated warning that we have to take care not to impose our categories of thinking on the literature that was more at home in the ancient world than in ours.

Adam and Eve Chose to Make Themselves the Center of Order and Source of Wisdom, Thereby Admitting Disorder into the Cosmos

This is not the place to offer a full analysis of the nature of sin, law, accountability, guilt and punishment. These are matters of theology and would require a trained theologian to provide a credible treatment. The issues are complex, and the debate about the particulars can be traced throughout the entire history of the church.

The focus of this book is neither on the systematic theology of the church nor on trying to sort out the distinctions between, for example, Augustine and Pelagius or Irenaeus. Instead, we are exploring how Genesis 3 might have been understood against the backdrop of the ancient world and what claims are being made in this context. It is certainly important to eventually factor in what Paul has to say on the matter and to form our theology in deep interaction with the church fathers. But our starting point needs to be the text of Genesis itself in its cultural, literary and theological context.

As Mark Biddle points out, one of the most common ways that people think about sin today is as a crime, a view that Biddle considers to be inadequate biblically and theologically.[1] In another book, *Sin: A History,* Gary Anderson investigates the competing paradigms of sin as a "burden to be borne" and sin as a "debt to be repaid."[2] The former metaphor, he contends, is the view supported by the idioms found in the Old Testament ("bearing sin/guilt/punishment," as early as Cain's statement in Gen 4:13). The latter imagery of debt becomes more prominent in the Second Temple period.[3] These paradigms speak eloquently to the consequences of sin (burden, debt) and point the way to its resolution.

A second way that one could analyze sin is by the various Hebrew words that are used to express it.[4] Here some caution is advisable. For example, it is not uncommon to encounter the statement that sin in the Old Testament means "missing the mark." This kind of statement, unfortunately, exposes a misunderstanding of how semantics work. It is true that the verb *ḥṭʾ* can refer to failing to achieve an objective (Prov 8:36; Is 65:20) and is even used once for slingers who do not miss their target (Judg 20:16).[5] There is no reason, however, to think of these uses as reflecting the "original" meaning of the word that is translated "sin." The meanings of words are derived from their use, not from their etymology,[6] and this verb simply means "to sin." It is not necessarily limited to the idea of missing a mark or failing to achieve an objective.[7] The words for sin can help us to recognize its various guises (rebellion, transgression, iniquity, guilt), but such semantic analysis can only take us so far.

In a third approach, others might talk about what sin *does* rather than what sin *is.* In this sort of investigation, sin can be seen as a threat to relationship with God—it results in alienation.[8] This differs from the direction represented in the discussion of the paradigms above in that they addressed the consequences primarily with regard to us (burden, debt), whereas alienation addresses more particularly the consequences pertaining to our relationship with God. The concept of alienation is well recognized in the Old Testament, whether in the banishment of Adam and Eve from the garden or the exile of Israel from the land. It is built into the ideas surrounding sacred space in which holiness must be maintained for the presence of God lest he be driven away. Sin is therefore disruptive to the relationship with God that is the deepest desire of humans. Relationship was God's intention in creation of human beings. It was lost in Genesis 3, and the rest of Scripture documents the stages of its being re-established. Another way to express this is in terms of the disequilibrium caused by sin.

> The biblical model sees sin as the disequilibrium pervasive in a system in disarray. . . . Authentic human existence . . . aspires to realize its full potential of godlikeness while consistently acknowledging its creatureliness and limitations. Sin is disequilibrium in this aspiration: humanity failing to reflect its divine calling, humanity forgetting its limitations.[9]

These approaches are not mutually exclusive, and though the first two have their validity and make a contribution to our understanding, it is the alienation/disequilibrium model that will serve as the focus for the discussion of this chapter. This is a significant theological trajectory that is often neglected or not even recognized. If Genesis 1 is about order and sacred space, the disorder aspect of sin takes on new importance.[10] Disequilibrium (disorder) has disturbed equilibrium (order) that God had set in place. Systematic theology eventually develops other trajectories and gives them high priority, but in the Old Testament, this view takes account of how sin is introduced in these early chapters of Genesis where order and its antitheses are so important.

The Old Testament never refers to the event of Genesis 3 as "the fall" and does not talk about people or the world as "fallen."[11] This is logical enough terminology since biblical language does refer to "falling into temptation," etc., but we should be cautious about giving the concept too large a role in our discussion of the biblical text. The Old Testament does not speak of Adam's sin bringing sin on everyone, though the effects of sin are seen to be pervasive throughout the Old Testament. One of the earliest uses of "the fall" is found in the pseudepigraphal book of 2 *Esdras* 7:118:

> O Adam, what have you done?
> For though it was you who sinned,
> The fall was not yours alone,
> But ours also who are your descendants.[12]

With that disclaimer, I will continue to use the term throughout the chapter for convenience and because it has traditionally been used to encapsulate the problem of sin.

As we consider the Old Testament information, we should be clear that the fall is not just disobedience or eating forbidden fruit. These actions could be considered crimes, but they were crimes that were simply the expressions of the fall.[13] The fall was the decision to be like God, conveyed by the serpent's words (Gen 3:5), the woman's response (Gen 3:6), God's assessment (Gen 3:22) and the reason for the banishment (Gen 3:23). The way in which the man and woman have become like God is qualified in relation to what the tree represented. No suggestion is made that they have become omniscient or omnipotent. I propose that, by disobediently taking the fruit, they were trying to be like God by positing themselves as the center and source of order.

God is, by definition, the source of wisdom, and his presence therefore establishes a center of wisdom. The fear of God is the beginning of wisdom. Wisdom in its biblical focus concerns seeking order in all categories of life (speech, family, government, interpersonal relations, relationship with God, decision making, etc.). Wisdom is the result when we perceive order, pursue it, preserve it, promote it, procure it and practice it. True wisdom finds its source and center in God, not in oneself specifically or humankind in general.

In taking from the tree, Adam and Eve were trying to set themselves up as a satellite center of wisdom apart from God. It is a childish sort of

response: "I can do it myself!" or "I want to do it my way!" These are not
a rejection of authority per se but an insistence on independence. The
act is an assertion that "it's all about *me*," and it is one that has characterized humanity (individually and corporately) since this first act. With
people as the source and center of wisdom, the result was not order
centered on them but disorder. This disorder extended to all people of
all time as well as to the cosmos, and life in God's presence was forfeited.
We will discuss this in more depth in the next chapter.

Wisdom is good, and we can therefore safely assume that God did
not intend to withhold it from humanity. But true wisdom must be
acquired through a process, generally from instruction by those who
are wise. The fall is defined by the fact that Adam and Eve acquired
wisdom illegitimately (Gen 3:22), thus trying to take God's role for
themselves rather than eventually joining God in his role as they were
taught wisdom and became the fully functional vice-regents of God
involved in the process of bringing order.[14] If humans are to work
alongside of God in extending order ("subdue" and "rule" [Gen 1:28]),
they need to attain wisdom, but as endowment from God, not by
seizing it for autonomous use. Given this interpretation, I would disagree with those who see the fall as disobedience to an arbitrarily
chosen test case. I refer to the view that the trees had no inherent
properties but just served to provide an opportunity for obedience
(knowledge of good) or disobedience (knowledge of evil). In this view
God could just as easily have said that they shouldn't walk on the
beach. Instead, I maintain that *what* was taken (wisdom) is not arbitrary and that it is more important than *that it was* taken (failed a test).

If, as proposed earlier (proposition 8), a legitimate option is that
from the start people were mortal, and pain and suffering were already
a part of a not yet fully ordered cosmos, we cannot think of death and
suffering as having been foisted on us by Adam and Eve's malfeasance.
Many have thought it unfair that all of us should suffer the consequences of their offense. Instead, we can have a much more charitable

attitude toward Adam and Eve when we realize that it is not that they initiated a situation that was not already there; it is that they failed to achieve a solution to that situation that was in their reach. Their choices resulted in their failure to acquire relief on our behalf. Their failure meant that we are doomed to death and a disordered world full of sin. These are profoundly significant consequences for what was a serious offense. In contrast, Christ was able to achieve the desired result where Adam and Eve failed. We are all doomed to die because when they sinned we lost access to the tree of life. We are therefore subject to death because of sin. Christ succeeded and actually provided the remedy to sin and death.

Some would follow this same line of reasoning to suggest that what we call original sin is the result of our ancestors "pulling out of the program" prematurely. James Gaffney identifies these approaches as involving a view that our human condition is underdeveloped, failing to achieve the intended goal because we wanted to do it our way—"not paradise lost, but, as it were, paradise ungained."[15] I would go a step further. We did not lose paradise as much as we forfeited sacred space and the relationship it offered, thereby damaging our ability to be in relationship with God and marring his creation with our own underdeveloped ability to bring order on our own in our own wisdom. Yoda laments similarly about Luke Skywalker in the Star Wars movie *The Empire Strikes Back* that he is not yet ready because his training is not complete ("Reckless is he . . . now things are worse").

Thus far, the treatment in this chapter has been trying to recover an Old Testament perspective on these issues. In that way, the lost world we seek to recover is being revealed from analysis inside the biblical text. We can now turn our attention briefly to the ancient world outside the biblical text.

There is nothing like the fall in ancient Near Eastern literature because there is no idealized primeval scenario. In Mesopotamian thinking, civilization in the urban environment was the ideal and the "world outside" was populated by "wild animals, primeval monsters, demons, drifting souls, and nomads."[16] That "world outside" picture was also the description of primeval times. There is no original pair, no sacred space, no disobedience of a command, no grasping for wisdom to become like God.

Even discussion of sin is problematic in an ancient Near Eastern context. They certainly understood the concept of offending a deity and suffering for it. But the gods had not made their expectations known. As described in chapter nine (p. 88), the Great Symbiosis in the ancient world is that the responsibility of humans is to meet the needs of the gods. This mostly involved ritual performance, but it also included ethical behavior insofar as it was recognized that the gods desired sufficient justice in order to ensure a smoothly operating society. A lawless society would be a less productive society, and people would not be able to grow their crops, raise their herds and make their gifts to the gods.

In both the ancient Near East and the Old Testament, sin was often objectified; that is, it was seen as something almost physical to be carried and could be lifted off a person. It was realized in physical consequences (illness especially). But as mentioned earlier, these deal with the consequences of sin. Both contexts may have dealt with sin as objectified, but when we ask what constituted sin, strong differences emerge.

Though ethical behavior was essential in the ancient Near East, a moral imperative based on a discernment of God's nature, as is found in Israel, was lacking. The gods had not revealed themselves, and they were not known to be consistent in character.[17] Consequently, we find many of the same ethical expectations in the ancient world at large as we find in Israel,[18] but the source of such norms in Israelite thinking (God instead of society), the reasoning behind them (holiness for retaining the presence of God) and their objectives (being godlike) are all very different. The ethical norms of the ancient Near East are most concerned with order versus disorder in society whereas in Israel the main focus is on relationship with deity and what is right or wrong as one seeks to live in accordance with the holiness of God. We likewise find similar ritual performances, but, again, they are driven by a very different ideology.

For these reasons, we expect nothing like the fall in ancient Near Eastern thinking. The people of the ancient Near East had to have seen themselves in relationship with God for that relationship to be broken. Neither the gods nor the people desired relationship outside the confines of the great symbiosis. What we find in the Old Testament is a reflection of the revelation of God that resulted in a theology uniquely Israelite. The lost world then needs to be recovered not by learning more about the ancient Near East but by getting back to the Old Testament texts in their ancient context before taking into account the way the interpretation of those texts unfolded in the New Testament and the articulation of theological understanding throughout church history.[19] That does not mean rejection of the later developments, but for the purposes of understanding the Old Testament text in its context, it is important to see the issues that frame the text in their ancient setting.

In conclusion, Genesis 3 is more about the encroachment of disorder (brought about by sin) into a world in the process of being ordered than it is about the first sin. It is about how humanity lost access to the presence of God when its representatives tragically declared their independence from their Creator. It is more focused literarily and theologically on how corporate humanity is therefore distanced from God—alienation—than on the sinful state of each human being (with no intention of diminishing the latter fact).

A similar reflection of the differences of perspective can also be seen in how we think about theological anthropology. We are used to talking about the body, soul and spirit as we discuss who we are as individuals and what parts will continue to define us in eternity. Egyptians talked about the human person in teleological terms, also showing an interest in the afterlife (terms such as *ba* and *ka*). In contrast, Babylonians were more inclined to think of humanity in terms of protology—that is, human beginnings as defining us. In Israel, the terms they used (*nepeš, rûaḥ,* often translated, respectively, as "soul" and "spirit") are terms that help define our relationship to God.

Nepeš is given by God (Gen 2:7) and departs when a human being dies (Gen 35:18). Interestingly enough, God is also characterized by a *nepeš*. *Nepeš* is not something that people have; it is something that they are. It is life, and it is associated with the blood (Lev 17:11). In contrast, *rûaḥ* energizes and is related to consciousness and vitality. Each person has God's *rûaḥ*, and it returns to him when the person dies. God's *rûaḥ* sustains human life. In this way, we might understand their viewpoint as relational and theological rather than psychological components.[20] Neither *nepeš* nor *rûaḥ* is considered to exist in the afterlife.

What difference does all this make? It does not disagree with the traditional ideas that sin entered the world at a point in time because of choices made by real people in a real past and that those choices have affected us all. Viewing Adam and Eve as priestly representatives in sacred space who brought the alienation of humanity from God's presence may lead us to frame differently our questions about our current status in the present. This will be explored in the next chapter. At the same time, it changes nothing about the need we have for salvation and the importance of the work of Christ on our behalf. Perhaps, however, it will help us to remind ourselves that salvation is more importantly about what we are saved *to* (renewed access to the presence of God and relationship with him) than what we are saved *from*. This point is significant because too many Christians find it too easy to think only that they are saved, forgiven and on their way to heaven instead of taking seriously the idea that we are to be in deepening relationship with God day by day here and now.

We Currently Live in a World with Non-order, Order and Disorder

In Genesis 1:2, the state of the cosmos at the beginning of the story is that nothing is yet functioning as it should (for full discussion see chap. 2). This non-ordered state serves as the canvas for the creative acts that bring a semblance of order to the cosmos. It contains traditional descriptors of non-order that were typical in ancient Near Eastern thinking: sea and darkness. It also features the spirit (or wind) of God prepared to go into action.[1] In some of the Egyptian cosmologies, the wind, a manifestation of the god Amun, also plays a role at the beginning in the initiation of creation.[2]

Into this non-ordered state, God begins to establish order by decree. In the ancient Near East, one Egyptian text (*The Memphite Theology* on the Shabako stone) features creation by the spoken word. More importantly, however, throughout Sumerian and Babylonian sources, the gods bring order (both initially as well as year by year) by orally decreeing the destinies of members of the cosmos. To decree the destiny of something is to assign it a role and a function.[3] This is an act of creation as order is established. Consequently, the efficacy of the spoken word in creation is commonplace in the ancient world.

God's creative work is defined as bringing order to this non-ordered existence. This will be carried out in stages through a process. Even as God brought order, there were aspects of non-order that remained. There was still a sea (though its borders had been set); there was still darkness. There was an outside the garden that was less ordered than inside the garden. The order that God brought focused on people in his image to join with him in the continuing process of bringing order, but more importantly on ordering the cosmos as sacred space. Yet, this was just the beginning.

This initial ordering would not have eliminated natural disasters, pain or death. We do not have to think of these as part of the ordered world, though they are not beyond God's control, and often they can be identified with positive results.[4] All non-order will not be resolved until new creation. In Revelation 21 we are told that there will be "no longer any sea" (Rev 21:1), no pain or death (Rev 21:4) and no darkness (Rev 21:23-25). There is no temple because God's presence will pervade all of it (Rev 21:3, 22), not just concentric circles radiating through zones of diminishing sacredness. God will be with humanity and be their God (Rev 21:3). Relationship is conveyed through the imagery of husband and wife (Rev 21:2). This is not a restoration of Eden or the return to a pre-fall condition. New creation is characterized by a level of order that has never before existed.

In this sort of thinking, pain and death do not have to be considered part of what is "good" (= ordered; see chap. 5). These are aspects that have not yet been finally resolved into a fully ordered world. The world before the fall was a combination of order and non-order with a strategy launched to continue bringing order. That progress toward order, however, was set back by the entrance of disorder. The serpent, as a chaos creature, was part of the non-ordered world. Its interference, however, launched disorder when people decided they themselves desired to be the source and center of wisdom and order.

This sort of understanding now offers explanation of the statement made in the last chapter. With people as the source and center of wisdom, the result was not order centered on them but disorder in which sin reigned. They were incapable of establishing order on their own with themselves as the center. The disorder this introduced extended to all people of all time, as well as to the cosmos, and life in God's presence was forfeited.

Therefore, first of all, we now live in a world characterized in part by non-order because it remains in process of being ordered—a process that is hampered because humans have not filled the role for which they were created. This non-order is reflected in natural disasters, disease and pain, among many other things. Sin is not the cause of all of these aspects of our current situation, but they demonstrate human inability to enforce order within creation.[5] I would additionally be inclined to place at least some demon activity in this category, insofar as they may be amoral and nonvolitional spiritual forces that are part of the non-ordered world and bring non-order. This matches the profile that they have in the Gospels.

Second, we also live in a world characterized by order, because that is what creation established. We enjoy not only the benefits of the order that God brought and continues to bring but the benefits of kingdom order established through the work of Christ. Furthermore, humans have brought the benefits of order throughout history through discovery and invention, technology, and industry. These very same human advances that bring order, however, often also bring disorder because we too often proceed with our own selfish ends guiding us (ourselves as the center of order) rather than recognizing that we are stewards of sacred space.

Consequently, and third, we also live in a world characterized by disorder. This disorder is found in the ways that we harm the environment, the ways that we harm one another and the ways that we harm ourselves. Disorder is the result of sin, and it continues to reflect our inability to be as good as we were designed to be. Among its many deleterious effects, sin has made us low-functioning creatures, and the paltry order that we manage to bring is a caricature of what God has intended us for. All of creation groans (Rom 8:19-22) in this state of delayed order and rampant disorder, the latter being the result of sin. That sin is most basically manifested in the idea that we thought we could do better than God—a delusion that still plagues all of us.

All People Are Subject to Sin and Death Because of the Disorder in the World, Not Because of Genetics

We all agree that theologically, biblically and experientially, sin is particular to each of us, universal to all of us corporately and radical in its extent, not just behavioral. As such, sin is in need of a remedy. Less clear in Scripture is how we are infected by it. Neither science nor exegesis provides the answer, though they each can potentially identify problems with proposed answers. In the end, we will inevitably see a variety of possible explanations that are not ruled out by the Bible. We are then left to try to determine which is the best fit.

ORIGINAL SIN

Why/how did all become subject to sin and death? This is not the place to delve into the intricacies of original sin, how sin spread to all humans and how sin affected the cosmos, though some comments will be offered. These issues have been debated throughout the history of the church, and a few caveats can help launch our brief discussion.

1. It is important to differentiate between what we experience nega-
   tively from a not fully ordered world that God still works to perfect
   and what we experience from the disorder brought into the world
   by humanity (see discussion in the previous chapter).

2. It is important to recognize that there are categories of evil, and
   not all of them are connected to sin (e.g., what is called "natural
   evil"). We should, for example, distinguish between experiential
   evil (discomfort resulting from non-order and/or disorder on all
   levels), personal evil (antisocial behavior that causes suffering in
   others), punitive consequence (discomfort resulting from actions
   by God or rulers designed to punish or discourage personal evil
   and/or the perpetuation of disorder) and sin (ritual/moral impro-
   priety that damages relationship with deity). Most people use *sin*
   and *evil* interchangeably to refer to any or all of these.[1] This is
   unfortunate because the problem of evil is a larger discussion than
   the problem of sin that people face.

Beyond the larger theological and philosophical questions, a more
specific issue is raised when people try to integrate biblical and theological claims about sin and the fall with a scientific understanding
that posits humans before Adam and Eve or contemporary with them.
How would all of them have become subject to sin? After all, anthro-
pological evidence for violence in the earliest populations deemed
human would indicate that there was never a time when sinful (= at
least personal evil) behavior was not present. Consequently, such a
discussion must revolve around the question of accountability. In this
regard, Paul's statement in Romans 5:13 provides a critical insight: "To
be sure, sin was in the world before the law was given, but sin is not
charged against anyone's account where there is no law."

Starting then with accountability, we can identify *law* as that
which helps us to understand what is right and wrong. It can be
relative (a law against parking on a particular side of the street on a

particular day) and therefore not morally based, or it can be absolute, based on moral issues and inherently in accordance with the desires of God as revealed in the character of the law. In this discussion, we are interested only in the latter category. When a law is identified or when the desires or nature of God are made known, those who receive such information become accountable. By accountable, I mean that they can now be considered guilty of violation and are therefore subject to punishment by the one who established the law—in our discussion, God. There could well be natural consequences with or without accountability.

This reasoning suggests that even though any human population possibly preceding or coexisting with Adam and Eve may well have been engaged in activity that would be considered sin, they were not being held accountable for it: where there was no law or revelation, there was no sin (no consciousness of relationship, no immortality). In that scenario, the sin of Adam and Eve would be understood as bringing sin to the entire human race by bringing accountability. From Romans 5:13 we infer that, in Paul's view, sin comes into the world when accountability comes into the world. Any humans prior to Adam did not have a personal, conscious relationship to lose (though as God's creatures they were related to him), so nothing that they did could jeopardize relationship. They did have the potential for eventual relationship with God (having been given his image) but would not have to deal with the disorder introduced by sin, which is more than we have.[2]

As we then move from thinking about accountability to considering a doctrine of sin, it is important to distinguish between the various sources that inform our current doctrine. Augustine pushes beyond what Paul says, and Paul has moved beyond what Genesis says. In Old Testament theology there is no apparent necessity for asserting the fall, though they understand the reality of sin. Even in Paul, it is not original sin that pervades his writing but the need for the savior.[3]

AUGUSTINE AND IRENAEUS

The model of sin that is the foundation for most Protestant theology today was expounded by Augustine from his reading of Paul, not by Paul himself, so we have to tread carefully. Augustine's view of sin was premised from the start on his particular understanding of Adam, which he derived theologically rather than finding explicitly stated in the text.

> Augustine depicts Adam and Eve as very noble originally. He goes beyond and often against Genesis 2 and 3 to give them free will, full health, full knowledge, the chance for immortality by eating of the tree of life, the ability not to sin, an inclination to choose the good, and the ability to persist in this blessed state.[4]

We neither have the time nor is this the place to engage in a full-orbed treatment of Augustine's views of original sin. A few basic (and inevitably reductionistic) observations will have to suffice. Augustine's model is one in which sin is passed from generation to generation as we are born, though of course biology in general was not well understood in his time, and, more specifically, they were totally ignorant of genetics. The more we have learned about biology and genetics, the less likely Augustine's model has become. Furthermore, if his starting point (view of Adam) is debatable, the rest of his model is jeopardized. If Augustine's model has been undermined on both counts (starting point and mechanism), one might think that it would have collapsed under its own unwieldiness. The theory, however, has become so deeply entrenched in the history of theological thought and development that it has taken on a life of its own almost independent from its essential roots. Perhaps the time has come for the church to reconsider how original sin is formulated and understood.

The alternative that had been propounded by Irenaeus, even before Augustine, had more of a Pandora's box element to it. Sin/disorder was released into the world, where we all contract it like a contagion or pollution in the air.[5] One of the distinctions between the two models is that in the Augustinian model, the world is infected because we are infected, while in the Irenaean model we are infected from the world that got polluted because of that first act (disorder let loose and run amok).[6]

However we define original sin and its transmission, we have to be able to explain why Christ is not subject to it. Most have agreed that the virgin birth is central in arriving at an understanding, but it is less clear how it does so. In the Augustinian model, Jesus avoided original sin because he had no human father,[7] and thus sin was not passed to him.[8] This view has become increasingly problematic because the transmission of sin cannot logically be an issue of DNA. Only mystery remains since we cannot address the sources of Jesus' DNA. How was the father's side of DNA provided? Yet we also know that he was fully human as we all are. The Augustinian model, extrapolated to genetics as it must be when we apply the ancient theory to the modern understanding, cannot easily deliver.

Another critique of Augustine's model comes from the recognition that he was working from a Latin translation of Romans 5:12. This is what led him to believe that Paul was saying that all sinned "in Adam" whereas the Greek text has been purported to actually say "in this way death came to all people, because all sinned" (NIV), indicating that we all sin *because* Adam sinned. This is a good illustration of what a big difference a little word can make, and in this case the result is a huge and longstanding debate among theologians as well as exegetes.[9] All of this makes it very tricky to sort out what biblical and/or theological claims are actually being made and what claims would need to be reconciled with scientific models.

Perhaps a more fruitful path can be proposed (with a nod toward Irenaeus) in recognizing that the virgin birth distinguishes Jesus as God. The sin of wanting to be like God (as we have defined the nature of the fall) cannot be pollution to one who *is* God. The Son of God cannot be the source of disorder or be subject to disorder, for he is the very embodiment of order—wisdom personified (wisdom being the perception and pursuit of order). His divine nature therefore immunizes him from the effect of disorder and the fall. During his life he subdued non-order (calming storms, casting out demons, healing sickness), and in his death and resurrection he imposed order by defeating disorder.

In a pollution model, we know well that one person can pollute a stream and everyone downstream suffers; one company can pour in toxic waste and everyone gets cancer; one industry can pollute the air and everyone suffers. When one person makes his or her own interests the center, that person can create a toxic environment for everyone. In Genesis, the toxic environment involves what we might call "disorder pollution," but as in ecological pollution, all creation groans and disorder reigns. We are all born into that toxic environment, and we all suffer the consequences both universally and particularly, and therefore we are all in need of salvation. Though we continue to act out that disorder, the effects of sin are radical, not just behavioral. Mark Biddle describes the effects in sociological terms in which a system involves the infinite interactions of multitudes of individuals across generations.

> The actions of one reverberate throughout the system, upsetting the precarious balance of all those shaken by the wave of sin. The multitudes of choices and actions made by members of the system impinge upon all the individuals in the system, even across time, limiting the freedom of all to make fully free choices and, therefore, to act authentically.[10]

We are all subject to the disorder that has been introduced into the system since that first moment when our representatives decided that they desired to be the center of order. Its manifestation is corporate and cumulative.[11] Not only are we victims of such a condition in the world; we all contribute to it. Jesus was born into such a world (thus he is human in every respect and tempted as we all are), but he was immune to its effect and did not contribute to its disorder. He is the personification and, indeed, the incarnation of order.

Death Before the Fall

We have now laid the groundwork for considering the possibility that there was death before the fall. In chapter eight we examined information to support the idea that humankind was created mortal. There we concluded that Paul's statement about why we humans are all subject to death was that in sinning we had lost access to the antidote found in the tree of life. In chapter five (p. 57) we considered the idea that death and suffering would have been part of a non-ordered world rather than attached only to disorder. In that chapter we demonstrated how that would not be contradictory to the idea that creation was "good."

If we consider the model in which there were humans either preceding Adam and Eve or contemporary with Adam and Eve, we need to contemplate their vulnerability to suffering and death. If death and suffering can be feasibly inherent in a non-ordered world and be retained in a partially ordered world, then any pre-fall human population would be subject to them. If, as Paul asserts (Rom 5:13), sin is only charged when there is law or revelation, then this human population would have been in a state of innocence (not sinlessness) since they were not yet being held accountable, even though they *were* in the image of God. In this scenario we would expect to find predation, animal death, human death and violent behavior. Endowment with the image of God and the initiation of sacred space would provide the foundation for accountability through law and revelation. When Adam and Eve sinned, as representative priests for humanity, their sin brought disorder and accountability and made the antidote to death inaccessible. That disorder infects each one of us when we come into existence as human beings. Non-order is not being resolved according to the original plan (God teamed up with human vice-regents), and disorder brought the need for resolution through the work of Christ.

In response to people who inquire as to why God would create such a world where there is predation, suffering and death, and how that could be called "good," I would say we have to understand how all the pieces fit together. "Good" pertained to the *order* that was being formed in the midst of non-order. The *non-order,* then, was *not* good, though not evil either, but the plan for continued ordering involved a process by which all non-order would eventually be resolved. We know that because that *is* the eventual result in new creation (Rev 20). God's creating involved assigning a place in the ordered world. So, it would not be coherent to speak of God *creating* (in terms of ordering) a world of non-order. The material world would originally have been not yet ordered (Gen 1:2). Whenever God uses a process (and he often does), his intentions are revealed in the final result and may not be evident in the stages along the way.

Those who believe that there was no death or suffering before the fall have associated those consequences with disorder rather than with non-order. It is easy to see how that association might be made, but if the evidence fails to bear it out, we can conclude that association with non-order is defensible from a biblical and theological perspective and enjoys more support from history, biology and anthropology.

Jesus Is the Keystone of God's Plan to Resolve Disorder and Perfect Order

The teaching of Jesus offers little information about how we should understand Adam. The role of Jesus and his contrast to Adam, however, are addressed a few times by Paul and have an important place in the discussion. The Pauline material will be addressed in chapter nineteen in the excursus by N. T. Wright, but here we will take a look at the larger movement of God's plan and the roles that Jesus plays.

We currently live in an already/not yet situation in which a solution for disorder has been provided (the death of Jesus overcame sin and death), yet disorder still remains. Furthermore, the continuing process of bringing order can be understood through various phases that God initiated in the past as it waits for its final consummation in new creation.

In the interpretation that was presented earlier (chap. 3), the cosmology of Genesis 1 was constructed around the idea of bringing order into a non-ordered situation. This way of thinking about creation is commonplace in the ancient world and comports well with the text as it is presented in Genesis. The basis for this order was seen to be twofold: (1) the focus of this order was human beings made in the image of God, and (2) the center of order was where the presence of God was located. The cosmos became sacred space when God took up his residence in it, and his presence brought order. But he set up this ordered cosmos to function for people. This theological imagery concerns how God intends to relate to his people, and his presence inevitably brings order to our world.

Jesus has a very significant role in the continuing process of God bringing order to the cosmos. This is prominent in the Christology of Colossians 1:15-23. What observations could be made from this passage if we viewed it through the lens of the ideas proposed in this book? What new interpretive possibilities might emerge? How does Paul engage some of the issues of Genesis by elaborating or supplementing? With that perspective in mind we observe that

- Christ is the true image of the invisible God (harking back to Gen 1).

- He is the firstborn of all creation (placing him above Adam).

- In him all things were created (identifying him specifically as the Creator in every act of creation, including Gen 1).

- He created all things visible and invisible (the previous point identified *who* the Creator was/is; this one addresses *what* he creates; comprehensively includes both material and function/order in the human realm in that which is visible).

- He created all spiritual powers (expanding the range of creation to also include the spiritual realm).

- He is before all things (and therefore non-contingent).

- In him all things hold together. (Among the many ways that all things cohere in Christ, we might now include that he is the center and source of order—the role that belongs to God and that Adam and Eve aspired to in the fall.)

- He is the head of the church and the firstborn from the dead (bringing order, resolving disorder).

- The fullness of God dwells in him. (So he does not compete with God as center of order—he is the center as God always has been and he achieves that role as a human, attaining what Adam did not.)

- Through him all things are reconciled to God. (As Christ resolves the disorder of sin and the disorder brought by sin, he also provides for the eventual resolution of non-order in new creation.)

- We attain peace through his blood (related to "rest").

- Once people were alienated, but now they are reconciled. (Among the many accomplishments through the death of Christ, he brings order rather than disorder; life through death.)

To see the whole picture, we have to trace God's program and initiatives through history.

After order was all but eliminated by the flood (because of an advanced state of disorder), the geopolitical order known from the ancient world took shape (Gen 10, the Table of Nations representing the known world in the second millennium B.C.). But in Genesis 11, we find out that the impetus for that geopolitical order came about in an unusual way—through the building of a city featuring a prominent tower.

Most interpreters agree that the Tower of Babel should be understood as a ziggurat. Ziggurats were the famous towers that characterized all the major cities of ancient Mesopotamia. They were built adjacent to the temple and were part of sacred space. Modern readers are often confused about the tower, having assumed that the people building it intended to use it to ascend to heaven. In fact, however, all evidence points in the other direction. The ziggurats were provided to facilitate the deity's descent and were intended to invite him to do so. The idea was that the god would have a convenient means by which to descend to the temple so that he could receive the worship of his people.

The problem in Genesis 11, however, is seen in the motivation of the people. We have already described the Great Symbiosis (chap. 9) as the means by which people in the ancient world were inclined to think about their relationship to the gods. When Genesis 11:4 says that the people wanted to "make a name for [them]selves," the problem is not their pride (a common interpretation). The problem is the Great Symbiosis: they are constructing sacred space, but they are doing so for their own benefit—that their name might be exalted as a thriving, prosperous civilization. Making a name for oneself in the ancient world was a way to secure one's memory through successive generations. Sacred space should exalt and establish the name of God, but these people see it only as a way to improve their situation. God will presumably be flattered and pleased and therefore bring prosperity to the people.

Genesis 11 therefore recounts the initiative of people after the flood to re-establish sacred space. Sacred space had been lost in the aftermath of the fall, and, believing the Great Symbiosis, people wanted to get it back again. Unfortunately, they were motivated by all the wrong reasons. God is not pleased, and he disperses the people by confusing their languages. This brings non-order to their community and makes it impossible to complete their project.[1] At the same time, it becomes the basis for the geopolitical order that is described in Genesis 10.

We might ask why Genesis is arranged with the Table of Nations preceding the Tower of Babel account. Clearly the tower account comes first since Genesis 10 keeps referring to the various languages. I would identify two reasons for the sequence of the chapters. First, Genesis 10 is treated before Genesis 11 because it is the practice of the editor of Genesis to follow the less important lines (e.g., Cain, Ishmael, Esau) before returning to the line that is the focus of the plotline. So, Noah's sons are traced into history before returning to Shem and the line of Abraham.[2] Second, this arrangement most clearly juxtaposes Genesis 11 and Genesis 12. Genesis 11 (tower building) represents a human initiative to re-establish sacred space and God's disapproval of it. Genesis 12 (the covenant) represents God's initiative to re-establish sacred space because God is going to dwell again in the midst of people (Abraham's family, Israel), in the tabernacle and then the temple.

The intention of the covenant was that all the world would be blessed through Abraham and his family (Gen 12:1-3). That blessing occurs in numerous ways, but, most importantly, it is through Abraham and his family that God reveals himself to the world and re-establishes relationship with people through the mechanism of sacred space. Genesis does not finish that story; it only gets it started.

In Exodus it seems that the covenant is in disarray; the people of Israel are not in their land but are enslaved in Egypt. God's presence is nowhere to be seen. But as the book progresses, God's presence becomes increasingly evident from its first manifestation in the burning bush through the plagues, the pillar of cloud/fire and the theophany on Mount Sinai. The climax is reached at the end of the book as God comes down to dwell in the tabernacle that the Israelites have constructed according to his instructions.

Once God has taken up his residence again on earth, we see the temple as parallel to Eden. This can be seen in the visual imagery of the tabernacle but also in what the tabernacle makes possible. The presence of God again becomes the center of order and the source of life as it had been in Eden. The law establishes order for the people, and keeping it brings life. Life is available in relationship with God and being in his presence, just as it was in Eden. Deuteronomy 30:15-20 elaborates on this point:

> See, I set before you today life and prosperity, death and destruction. For I command you today to love the LORD your God, to walk in obedience to him, and to keep his commands, decrees and laws; then you will live and increase, and the LORD your God will bless you in the land you are entering to possess.
>
> But if your heart turns away and you are not obedient, and if you are drawn away to bow down to other gods and worship them, I declare to you this day that you will certainly be destroyed. You will not live long in the land you are crossing the Jordan to enter and possess.

This day I call the heavens and the earth as witnesses against you that I have set before you life and death, blessings and curses. Now choose life, so that you and your children may live and that you may love the LORD your God, listen to his voice, and hold fast to him. For the LORD is your life, and he will give you many years in the land he swore to give to your fathers, Abraham, Isaac and Jacob.

God's initiative to restore sacred space, then, began with the covenant—a relationship that would lead to more significant levels of relationship across the span of time. In the covenant relationship, God began revealing himself to Abraham and his family. Then he adopted Israel (the nation that came from Abraham) to be his people, and he took up his residence among them. They are to preserve the sanctity of this newly established sacred space both in the way that they live (the law, maintaining order in society) and in their rituals (where purity of sacred space is preserved). So, God's initiative provided for life and order in relationship with God through his abiding presence.

Unfortunately, however, the Israelites prove incapable of maintaining the law. The prophets Jeremiah and Ezekiel then begin to warn them that God is going to leave (e.g., Jer 7; Ezek 10), eventually leading to God's presence being compromised as the temple is destroyed and the exiled people lose the land. But these prophets also begin talking about a new covenant in which God will write his law on their hearts. In the ancient world, God writing on the entrails (usually in connection with divination) signified that he was revealing himself (Jer 31:31-33; NIV: "minds," v. 33).[3] This represents the same idea of Israel being a light to the nations in that they were intended to show the world what God was like.

As we know, the new covenant is accomplished through Jesus, but this is only one of the roles of Jesus relative to the unfolding plan of God's presence being restored. We learn in John 1:14 that "the Word became flesh and made his dwelling among us. We have seen his glory." This is the same language used with regard to the tabernacle. The incarnation thus plays a role in making God's presence available in the midst of his people. In this way, Jesus replaces the temple.[4] Jesus also brings reconciliation through his death (resolution of disorder) and thereby brings order and life by providing a mechanism for people to be in relationship with God.

When Jesus leaves, he tells the disciples that he will send a Comforter. At Pentecost, the elements of the Tower of Babel are revisited. God the Holy Spirit descends and takes up residence in a new sacred space—his people, who Paul later tells us are the temple (1 Cor 3:16; 6:19). Unlike the Tower of Babel, the disorder of languages is resolved when God descends in Acts 2, as everyone can understand in their own language (Acts 2:6). The new covenant therefore leads to further revelation, presence and relationship, both in the incarnation and in the church. These are initiatives of God through Christ. The church is testimony to God bringing order by resolving the disorder of sin. The church also represents order because it is the center of God's presence in the world. The church has received life and is the center of order in the world.

The final stage of God's plan is revealed in Revelation 21 in the presentation of new creation. Paul had already indicated that if anyone is in Christ, new creation has come (2 Cor 5:17). The full establishment of new creation, however, will have a higher level of order than that which characterized Eden, as well as a higher level of order than we now experience as his people.

The features of new creation are enumerated in Revelation 21:

- Revelation 21:1: no sea (recall that sea was the initial form that non-order took in Gen 1:2)

- Revelation 21:2: bride and groom (relationship formalized)

- Revelation 21:3: "God's dwelling place is now among the people, and he will dwell with them . . . and be their God" (presence)

- Revelation 21:4: no more death or mourning or pain (non-order resolved)

- Revelation 21:5: "seated on the throne" (recall that "rest" = reign—the basis of order)

- Revelation 21:22: no temple because the Lord Almighty and the Lamb are its temple (The idea of temple was that it marked the center of sacred space and that radiating out from it were zones of diminishing sacredness. With God replacing the temple, we might infer that there is no diminishment—that there is no center because it is all center.)

- Revelation 21:27: purity and life

This entire sequence of God's initiatives is focused on Jesus, the better Adam, who was able to attain that which Adam and Eve were unable to attain. Life and order are achieved through Christ. He fulfills the law (order founded on the presence of God); he fulfills the covenant (as the climax of God's program of revelation and reconciliation); and he fulfills creation (as he takes his place as the center of order and the source of life).

In this interpretation, the relationship between Adam and Jesus can be seen in stronger ways. Both are archetypal representatives and have a priestly role. Both are connected to the issues of life/death and order/disorder. These issues will be discussed more fully in the next chapter. In a final note, we can see that all of Paul's treatment of Adam pertains to the issues of sin, death and the theological archetypal roles of both Adam and Jesus. His patently theological comments do not address the issues of science (e.g., whether Adam was the first human or the only human at his time).[5] This will be discussed more fully in chapters twenty and twenty-one.

Paul's Use of Adam Is More Interested in the Effect of Sin on the Cosmos Than in the Effect of Sin on Humanity and Has Nothing to Say About Human Origins

Including an Excursus on Paul's Use of Adam by N. T. Wright

As we move more deeply into the relevant New Testament material, we continue our search for what the Bible, and Paul in particular, claims. We should not be distracted by the questions that emerge from our theological and scientific vantage point:

- Does Paul believe in a historical Adam?

- Is a historical Adam essential for a sound theological understanding of the fall and the need for salvation?

- What does Paul have to say about our discussions of human origins?

- How do Paul's statements support our traditional view of original sin?

- How did we all come to be sinners?

The modern questions and traditional readings can easily lead us off track if they are not focused on the actual case that Paul is building. It is important for us to set aside our modern questions and traditional interpretations and focus on what Paul is doing as he makes his points. For this we need the expertise of a New Testament scholar, and N. T. Wright has graciously agreed to handle this undertaking. In the following excursus he develops two important ideas:

- Paul's treatment of Adam has more to do with the kingdom of God in general, the whole creation project, than with salvation from sins.

- For Paul the parallels between the vocations (one might say functions) of Adam and Israel are more important than questions of human origins or the origin and transmission of sin.[1]

As a result, the fallen state of the cosmos redressed through Christ is the larger focus. The world can only be put right when people are put right. When people are saved by Christ, the entire creation project can get back on track. Read in this light, Paul has nothing to say about material human origins.

EXCURSUS ON PAUL'S USE OF ADAM

N. T. Wright, St. Mary's College, University of St. Andrews

Ever since the scientific revolutions of the eighteenth and nineteenth centuries, Christians have been in danger of focusing on the *existence* of Adam rather than the *vocation* of Adam. What's more, ever since the battle between Augustine and the Pelagians, we have tended to focus on questions of what we have called "original sin"—questions about how Adam's sin is somehow passed on to all his descendants— rather than on the role played by Adam's sin in the larger narrative of God and the world, and, within that, of God and Israel. This short excursus cannot be seen as even a full statement of preliminary considerations. It is only some initial reflections. But I hope it will be a pointer to some helpful further possibilities.

It is worth noting, at the start, that after the early chapters of Genesis Adam is hardly mentioned in the Old Testament. It is thus not so surprising that Adam is not a major topic of discussion in the postbiblical Second Temple texts, either. When Adam is mentioned in these later works, it is frequently in connection not with his sin and its effects but with the glorious dominion he was originally given over the world, and with the way in which that might be reclaimed. One of the Dead Sea Scrolls, *Pesher on Psalm 37* (4QpPs37), speaks of "the penitents of the desert [i.e., the Qumran sect itself] to whom all the glory of Adam shall belong, and to their descendants forever." This looks back not only to Genesis 1 and 2 but to Psalm 8, which echoes the creation story and speaks of God crowning his human creatures with "glory and honor" by "put[ting] everything under their feet" (Ps 8:5-6).

Where we do find mention of the sin of Adam is in two books written around the end of the first century A.D. These books are known as *4 Ezra* and *2 Baruch* (*4 Ezra* comprises most of the book called 2 Esdras in the Apocrypha), and they are struggling to make sense of the horrible events of A.D. 70, when the Romans destroyed Jerusalem and its temple. The writers are driven right back to the beginning since the only way they can make sense of the appalling national tragedy is to say that the whole human race, Israel included, has somehow been corrupted by a fatal disease from the very start. This, I think, may help us understand why Paul comes to a similar conclusion, in Romans in particular. He didn't start with a Jewish theory of "the fall of Adam," because such a theory did not exist. His reflections are prompted by a different apparent tragedy, but one that then turned to triumph: the crucifixion of Israel's Messiah and his resurrection from the dead. The problems of which Saul of Tarsus was aware in his early life—the problems, political and theological, caused by Roman oppression and by Jewish failure to keep Torah properly—were revealed, by the Messiah's cross, to be much deeper than he had imagined. If a crucified Messiah was the divine answer to the problem, the problem must have been far worse than he had thought.

But Paul is then able to develop the other "side" of the Adamic picture. Drawing (like some Jewish contemporaries) on Psalm 8, he sees the glory that the Creator intended to give to his human creatures—their dominion over the world—as being already fulfilled in Jesus, and now, remarkably, to be shared with those who are "in the Messiah." Both halves of this picture are important in Romans, where Adam is mentioned explicitly in Romans 5 but alluded to in various other places as well. Adam has been detected by many scholars, hiding under the argument of Romans 1:18-25 and Romans 7:7-12; the "old human being"(author's translation) of Romans 6:6 is almost certainly alluding back to the Adamic solidarity that has been expounded in Romans 5. And the human glory of which Paul speaks in Romans 8:17-30 seems to be an exploration of the "glory" of Psalm 8:5: when humans are glorified, creation itself will at last be brought back into proper order.

It is important to be clear about this wider context because the question generated by the scientific study of cosmic and human origins ("did Adam exist?" or "was there an original Adam?") has become muddled up with a *soteriological* question, as to whether an "original Adam" is necessary for a biblical doctrine of salvation. But this would-be biblical doctrine has often been presented in a shrunken and distorted way. It has often been supposed to work like this: (a) God demanded perfect obedience from Adam and Eve; (b) they broke his command; (c) Jesus has given God perfect obedience; (d) he therefore possesses a "righteousness" that is available to believers. There is no space here to explain why this is an inadequate and misleading version of what Paul says. What is more important for our present brief purposes is to note the very different (and deeply biblical) story about Adam that Paul tells. As in Genesis, where the new start in Genesis 12 represents the divine answer to the problem of Genesis 3–11, in Paul's exposition the divine answer to the problem of Adam (here at Rom 1:18–3:20) is the call of Abraham and the establishing of the covenant with him (here at Rom 4). For Paul, what God has done in and through

Jesus the Messiah and his faithful death is to be true to the covenant with Abraham, *and therefore to deal with the sin of Adam and its effects.* That is what Paul then sums up in Romans 5:12-21, and explains and expands more fully in Romans 6–8.

This is at the heart of the fresh way into the Paul-and-Adam discussion that I would propose (it requires, of course, much fuller treatment). First, Paul's exposition of Adam in these passages is explicitly in the service not of a traditional soteriology but of the kingdom of God. Second, there is a close parallel between the biblical vocation of Adam in Genesis and the biblical vocation of Israel, and when we explore this we may find fresh ways through to the heart of some contemporary puzzles.

Adam and the kingdom of God. First, then, Adam and the kingdom of God. Despite many generations in which Romans has been read simply as a book about "how we get saved," that is not the ultimate point, even of Romans 1–8 or Romans 5–8. The great climax of Romans 1–8 is the renewal of all creation, in Romans 8:17-26, where Jesus as Messiah, with a reference to Psalm 2, is given as his inheritance the uttermost parts of the world. For Paul it's clear: *the whole world is now God's holy land.* That's what Scripture prophesied, and that's what has been achieved in Jesus the Messiah. But this inheritance is shared with all Jesus' people; and the way this happens is ultimately through their resurrection. "Creation itself," declares Paul, "will be freed from its slavery to decay, to enjoy the freedom that comes when God's children are glorified" (Rom 8:21, author's translation). That doesn't mean that creation will *share* the glory, as some translations misleadingly suggest. Paul is working with Psalm 8 as well as Psalm 2, and in Psalm 8, exactly as in Genesis 1, humans are given glory and dominion over the world. Here is the problem to which Romans is the answer: not simply that we are sinful and need saving but that our sinfulness has meant that God's project for the whole creation (that it should be run by obedient humans) was aborted, put on hold. And when we are saved, as Paul spells out, that is in order that the whole-creation project can at last get back on track. When humans are redeemed, creation gives a sigh of relief and says, "Thank goodness! About time you humans got sorted out! Now we can be put to rights at last."

This is what Paul is really talking about in Romans 5:12-21. Out of many possible points, I here draw attention to Romans 5:17, 21. In Romans 5:17, Paul surprises us. "If, by the trespass of the one man, death reigned through that one man," he says, and we expect him to go on, "how much more will life reign through the one." But he doesn't. He says, "how much more will those who receive God's abundant provision of grace and of the gift of righteousness reign in life through the one man, Jesus Christ!" Adam's sin meant not only that he died but that he lost the "reign" over the world. God's creation was supposed to function through human stewardship, and instead it now produces thorns and thistles. Now humans are redeemed, in order to get God's creation-project back on track; and the word for all that is "reigning," "ruling," *basileuein* in Greek, in other words, "kingdom." Paul's Adam-theology is also his kingdom-theology, and the author of Genesis would have smiled in recognition. Romans 5:21 points, densely of course, in the same direction. Grace reigns "through righteousness" to the life of the age to come. God sets people right in order that through them he will set the world right. Justification by faith is God putting people right in advance, in order that through them God will put the world right.

We see the same from a different angle in 1 Corinthians 15:20-28. Again Paul is working with the Psalms, in this case Psalm 110 and again Psalm 8. His point is that Jesus is already enthroned, already king, already reigning. In other words, *he is at last where Adam was supposed to be.* There is at last an obedient human at the helm of the universe. Of course, this is part of Paul's now-and-not-yet theology; Jesus is already reigning, but one day the last enemies will be finally overcome, namely death itself. Paul is working very closely with Genesis 1–3 right across 1 Corinthians 15. And basic to his exposition of Genesis is this point: that God put his wonderful world into human hands; that the human hands messed up the project; and that the human hands of Jesus the Messiah have now picked it up, sorted it out and got it back on track. It won't do, therefore, simply to go to Paul and say, There you are, Paul believes in Adam; that proves a literalistic reading of Genesis. What this reading of the text exposes to view is the *failure* of the tradition to read either Paul or Genesis, because Paul's whole point is to pick up from Genesis the notion of *the vocation of Adam* and to show that it is fulfilled in the Messiah. Unless we put that in the middle, we are not being obedient to the authority of these central scriptural texts.

This sends me back to Genesis, then, encouraged by John Walton on the one hand and writers such as Richard Middleton and Greg Beale on the other, to look at the calling of Adam.[2] The notion of the "image" doesn't refer to a particular spiritual endowment, a secret "property" that humans possess somewhere in their genetic makeup, something that might be found by a scientific observation of humans as opposed to chimps. The image is a *vocation*, a calling. It is the call to be *an angled mirror*, reflecting God's wise order into the world and reflecting the praises of all creation back to the Creator. That is what it means to be the royal priesthood: looking after God's world is the royal bit, summing up creation's praise is the priestly bit. And the image is, of course, the final thing that is put into the temple (here I draw on John Walton's careful exposition of Genesis 1 and 2 as the creation of sacred space, and the seven days of Genesis 1 as the seven stages of temple building), so that the god can be present to his people through the image and that his people can worship him in that image. One of the great gains of biblical scholarship this last generation, not least because of our new understanding of first-century Judaism, is our realization that the temple was central to the Jewish worldview. This comes through in various places in Paul's letters. The temple was where heaven and earth met; when Paul says in Ephesians 1:10 that God's purpose was to sum up everything in heaven and on earth in the Messiah, we shouldn't be surprised that much of the rest of the letter is then about Jesus and the church as the true temple. But here is the problem: that we have seen the goal of it all as "humans being rescued so that they could have fellowship with God," but the Bible sees the goal of it all as "humans being rescued so that they could sum up the praises of all creation and look after that creation as God's wise stewards." Genesis, the Gospels, Romans and Revelation all insist that the problem goes like this: human sin has blocked God's purposes for the whole creation; but God hasn't gone back on his creational purpose, which was and is to work in his creation through human beings, his image-bearers. In his true image-bearer, Jesus the Messiah, he has rescued humans from their sin and death in order to reinscribe his original purposes, which include the extension of sacred space into all creation, until the earth is indeed full of God's knowledge and glory as the waters cover the sea. God will be present in and with his whole creation; the whole creation will be like a glorious extension of the tabernacle in the wilderness or the temple in Jerusalem. (This, by the way, is the foundation for what I see as a proper theology of the sacraments, though this is a topic for another occasion.)

Vocations of Adam and Israel. This is where I sense a strong parallel with the calling and vocation of the ancient people of Israel, and this is where we might glimpse some fresh light on Adam and the question of origins. Genesis itself makes a clear parallel between Adam and Abraham: "be fruitful and increase in number" (Gen 1:28) becomes "I will make you very fruitful; I will make nations of you" (Gen 17:6). Instead of the original paradise, with God present with his people, Israel is promised the land, and eventually given the temple as the place of God's presence. But the point is this: Israel, a small, strange nomadic people in an obscure part of the world, is chosen to be the promise-bearer: "through your offspring all nations on earth will be blessed" (Gen 22:18). Israel is to be a royal priesthood (Ex 19). Israel is to be the light of the nations (Is 42; 49). *Israel is chosen out of the rest* of the world in order to be God's strange means of rescuing the human race and so getting the creational project back on track. And God chooses Israel while knowing full well, in Paul's language, that Israel too is in Adam; the people who bear the solution are themselves part of the problem. That, in fact, is the clue to the hardest bits of Paul's theology, for instance the problem of the law. That's for another time. But watch closely. Israel is chosen to fulfill this divine purpose; Israel is placed in the holy land, the garden of God's delight; and Israel is warned that if they don't keep Torah they will be expelled, sent off into exile. It will look as though the whole project has been aborted. That is the horrible problem faced not only in the exile but in the so-called postexilic period. And it is that complex problem that the New Testament sees being dealt with, gloriously resolved, in Israel's Messiah, Jesus the Lord, and his death and resurrection. He has dealt with exile, and now the whole world is God's holy land, with Jesus and his people as the light of the world.

What might that tell us about the vocation of Adam, then? I do not know when Genesis reached its final form. Some still want to associate it with Moses; others insist it was at least edited during the exile. But whatever view you take about that, certainly the Jews of the Second Temple period would have no difficulty in decoding the story of Adam as an earlier version of their own story: placed in the garden; given a commission to look after it; being the place where God wanted to be at rest, to exercise his sovereign rule; warned about keeping the commandment; warned in particular that breaking it would mean death; breaking it and being exiled. It all sounds very, very familiar. And it leads me to my proposal: that just as God chose Israel from the rest of humankind for a special, strange, demanding vocation, so perhaps what Genesis is telling us is that *God chose one pair from the rest of early hominids for a special, strange, demanding vocation.* This pair (call them Adam and Eve if you like) were to be the representatives of the whole human race, the ones in whom God's purposes to make the whole world a place of delight and joy and order, eventually colonizing the whole creation, were to be taken forward. God the Creator put into their hands the fragile task of being his image-bearers. If they failed, they would bring the whole purpose for the wider creation, including all those other nonchosen hominids, down with them. They were supposed to be the life-bringers, and if they failed in their task, the death that was already endemic in the world as it was would engulf them as well. This, perhaps, is a way of reading the warning of Genesis 2: in the day you eat of it *you, too, will die.* Not that death, the decay and dissolution of plants, animals and hominids, wasn't a reality already; but you, Adam and Eve, are chosen to be the people through whom God's life-giving reflection will be imaged into the world, and if you choose to worship and serve the creation rather than the Creator, you will merely reflect death back to death, and will share that death yourself. I do not know whether this is exactly what Genesis meant, or what Paul meant. But the close and (to a Jewish reader) rather obvious parallel between the vocation of Israel and the vocation of Adam leads me in that direction. And already we should be able to see that the traditional Western picture of an Adam-and-Christ soteriological scheme represents a shrinkage of the original Pauline vision.

One might perhaps sum up the problem like this: It isn't just that Adam sinned, and that Israel sinned as well. The problem is that Israel was called to be God's means of rescuing the world, but Israel was part of the Adamic problem to which it was supposed to be providing the solution. In a similar way—not exactly parallel, but similar—Adam and Eve were chosen to take the Creator's purposes forward to a new dimension of life. But if they failed—if they abdicated their own image-bearing vocation, and followed the siren call of the elements of chaos still within creation—they would come to share the entropy that had so far been creation's lot. They did, and that's what happened.

Christology and the project of new creation. All this, of course, projects us forward toward a full and rich Christology. This will not be simply about Jesus as both divine and human; that's a given, but it's only a shorthand, a signpost. Look at Paul's language: Jesus is the beginning, the firstfruits, the true Image, the Temple in whom all God's fullness was pleased to dwell. He is Israel's Messiah, who fulfills Israel's obedience on the cross and thereby rescues both Israel and the whole human race. He does for Israel what Israel couldn't do for itself, and thereby does for humans what Israel was supposed to do for them, *and thereby launches God's project of new creation, the new world over which he already reigns as king.* This is the great narrative, the true Pauline Adam-and-Christ story, and we need to learn how to tell it and live it.

Here we stumble upon an interesting possibility. The biologists and philosophers have pointed toward the complex notion of altruism as something that might just be a signpost away from the closed continuum of selfish genes. So, too, in the Christian message we have the cross, not just as an act of altruism—*altruism* is after all a thin, bloodless word, a parody of the reality—but the supreme act of love. "The Son of God, who loved me and gave himself for me," wrote Paul (Gal 2:20). "Having loved his own who were in the world," wrote John, "he loved them to the end" (Jn 13:1). The cross is, and Jesus always said it was, the subversion of all human power-systems. The cross is the central thing that demonstrates the impossibility of the metaphysically inflated Evolution-with-a-capital-E. The weakness of God is stronger than human strength. And it leads, and Jesus said it would lead, to a life of following him that would itself be about taking up the cross and so finding life, about the meek inheriting the earth. That is how the Adamic vocation is to be fulfilled. If we can study Genesis and human origins without hearing *the call to be an image-bearing human being renewed in Jesus,* we are massively missing the point, perhaps pursuing our own dream of an otherworldly salvation that merely colludes with the forces of evil. That's what gnosticism always does.

Looking at Paul's picture of Adam from this point of view may be surprising to some. But it is not difficult to make oneself at home in it.

This is the greatest story ever told, and it will draw all our stories up into it. Yes, many humans, though not all, are deeply aware of problems in their own lives, of pains and fears and sorrows and deep-rooted puzzles, and that may well bring them to the foot of the cross. But the message ought never to be simply about me and my salvation. It ought to be about God and God's kingdom. That's what Jesus announced, and so should we. The full good news is that in Jesus, and through his death and resurrection, God has become king of the world. We look out at the world and see it in a terrible mess, and we are aware in our bones that we want to do something about it. But our own sin, our greed, our pride, our arrogance get in the way, and we rush off and try to do it in our own strength and (worse) our own way, like Moses trying to liberate Israel from Egypt by Egyptian means. He first needed liberating himself. We humans know in our bones that we are called to bring God's wise order into the world. That is our Adamic inheritance, just as much as the entail of evil. But for that to become a reality we need, ourselves, to be rescued from the same problem that afflicts the rest of the world. We are rescued by the blood of the Lamb in order to be a royal priesthood; and the way in which that works, according to the New Testament, is the same way it worked for Jesus: taking up the cross, a suffering but joyful witness. That, too, is part of Paul's picture of the redeemed Adam: we suffer with him, that we may (in line, remember, with Psalm 8) also share his glory. The distortions Western theology has introduced into Paul's Adam-theology are cognate with the distortions, or the downright ignoring, that have happened in relation to the kingdom of God. They belong together; and together they may give us a sense of how to talk wisely both about salvation and about origins.

It Is Not Essential That All People
Descended from Adam and Eve

This book has not been focusing on scientific issues because I am not a scientist, and those issues are complex.[1] Instead, I have focused on what the biblical claims are regarding biological human origins, and in that regard we have found no claims. At the same time, even very early interpreters undoubtedly considered Adam and Eve to be the progenitors of the entire human race.[2] Evidence has been presented that Genesis 2 talks about the *nature* of *all* people, not the unique *material origins* of Adam and Eve. Consequently, we do not find human origins stories in Genesis 2 that make scientific claims. That does not mean that modern scientific theories are therefore correct by default—it just means that we can consider scientific claims on their own merit rather than dismissing them because they contradict biblical claims.

GENETICS

Scientific consensus regarding genetics is most strongly represented in the information that has been developed from the mapping of the human genome and comparing it to other genomes. At its most basic level, the genome shows a history through the presence of fusions, breaks, mutations, retroviruses and pseudogenes. On this no one disagrees. The disagreement arises when we question whether this history actually happened or whether God created people with a genome that looks like it has a history. This is similar to the age-old question of whether Adam had a belly button.

If someone were to look at a dental x-ray of my mouth, they would see implants with titanium pegs, crowns, root canals, fillings, cracks in the enamel, etc. These would all stand as obvious evidence to a history, and in that way the evidence in my mouth is comparable to the human genome. With the genome, however, the history is passed on from generation to generation and can be compared with the genomes of other species. In such a comparison, remarkable similarities become evident that have indicated a material continuity between species, suggesting relatedness or similar histories. This is the understanding of common descent where genetic analysis provides evidence of a gradual development that would explain genetic diversity.[3]

The evidence for this shared history uncovered by comparative genomics is compelling and would be readily accepted were it not for the belief of some that, if such a history actually happened, it would contradict claims that are made in the Bible. Many who take the Bible seriously therefore insist that the history to which comparative genomics testifies in fact never happened.

To substantiate the position that this genetic history never happened, it is necessary to contend that God (1) created Adam de novo (distinct from any predecessors, using no biological process) with a complicated genome. This genome would contain parts that do not function as they do in other species, mutations that disable genes, etc. Furthermore, the genome just happens to look a lot like the genomes of related species with most of the same genetic history evident in them (same flaws in the same places). Or God (2) totally disrupted the genome, not only of humans but of all species (in very similar ways) as a response to the fall.

If the Bible makes such claims that the evidence of history in the genome needs to be denied in one of these ways, so be it. That an act of God could bring about a product that has marks of a history that never actually occurred has been attested in Jesus turning the water into wine. In terms of probability, the resurrection looks highly unlikely, yet we affirm its reality. At the same time, denying de novo human origins would not be a case of denying a miracle that the Bible affirms if the Bible does not affirm it. So, before we dismiss the evidence of a genetic history provided by the genome, let's take a hard look at the biblical claims to decide what stand we need to take as those who take the Bible seriously.

Two questions will be addressed in this chapter:

1. Does the Bible claim that Adam was the first human being ever to exist?

2. Does the Bible claim that all humans are descended from Adam and Eve?

Current scientific understanding maintains that there was no first human being because humanity is the result of an evolving population. The evidence of genetics also points to the idea that the genetic diversity that exists in humanity today cannot be traced back to two individuals—a single pair—but that such diversity requires a genetic source population of thousands. If the Bible claims otherwise, then we would have to take a stand against this emerging scientific consensus.

So far in this book, however, the analysis of the relationship of Genesis 1 and 2 has raised the possibility that the Adam and Eve account in Genesis 2 could have come after an en masse creation[4] of humanity in Genesis 1 (chap. 7), though Adam and Eve should be considered as having been included in that group. Paul does not demand that Adam and Eve are the first or only humans. When he speaks of Adam as the "first man," he is most interested in the archetypal role of Adam and in the theological issues surrounding sin (chap. 10). Finally, we should note that the two questions posed above are not concerned with whether Adam and Eve are real people in a real past—I have already affirmed that I believe they are. If Genesis 2 is not making claims about human origins or demanding that Adam and Eve are the first or only humans, does it make such claims elsewhere? We are especially interested in whether the Bible is making claims about human origins that have scientific ramifications and could therefore stand in contradiction to the scientific consensus of today.

Before we turn our attention to other biblical passages that have been thought to make claims about human origins, I want to note briefly some of the scientific conversations that are taking place that attempt to reconcile scientific conclusions and claims with biblical interpretation.

Mitochondrial Eve and Y-chromosomal Adam. There has been much interest in conclusions drawn by scientists to the effect that there is a single female, dubbed Mitochondrial Eve, from whom all current humans are descended. That is, she is the most recent common ancestor of all humans. Likewise, the Y-chromosome that is found only in males can be tracked back to a single source. But we can't get too excited about this, because the so-called Mitochondrial Eve (an African woman who lived about 180,000 years ago) and Y-chromosomal Adam (an African who is believed to have lived about 210,000 years ago) cannot be considered husband and wife! They are separated by 30,000 years. Furthermore, these two cannot succeed in lending support to the traditional Bible claims because to accept their existence means accepting many other premises of genetics that push in a different direction (e.g., the way in which the genome shows a history and suggests continuity and common descent). For example, the same sort of information that identifies them shows that they are both members of large populations. While all humans today may share single ancestors such as Mitochondrial Eve and Y-chromosomal Adam, they are not our only ancestors. I have no intention of arguing for or against the science. I only make the point that this information does not offer a way to integrate scientific findings with traditional biblical interpretation.

Size of the genetic source population. Population geneticists generally claim that the evolved human population was never less than 5,000 to 10,000 individuals. They estimate that the smallest number occurred at a population bottleneck about 150,000 years ago. These numbers are derived from computer models, and arguments can be mounted that the models may not have all the parameters set precisely enough to generate full confidence. True as that may be, we should not delude ourselves into thinking that with more precise models the number would go down to two. Population genetics at this stage does not offer a path to reconciliation with traditional biblical interpretation.

Adam and Eve among an initial population. In some models Adam and Eve are thought of as two of the members of a small population of humans and that through the course of time as generation followed generation, their descendants spread through the population and other lines died out such that by today everyone has genetic material from these two. This view attempts to place Adam and Eve in Genesis 1 among an en masse creation of humans and still retain the idea that Adam and Eve are the parents of us all. It affirms that Adam and Eve were (among) the first humans and that (through a complex process) we are all descended from Adam and Eve. Though it looks nothing like the traditional biblical interpretation, it makes similar affirmations while at the same time accommodating common descent and affirming that the history evident in the genome actually took place.

These all maintain aspects of traditional biblical interpretation while at the same time adopting some of the basic aspects of the current scientific consensus. They require selective acceptance of scientific findings and/or significantly adjusted biblical interpretation. We need to ask whether such complicated attempts at reconciliation are necessary, and so we return to the questions above: Does the Bible claim that Adam is the first human being to exist and that all are descended from him?

DOES ACTS 17:26 DEMAND "ONE MAN"?

Genesis 2 has already been discussed at length, as has the reference to Adam as the "first man" in 1 Corinthians 15. But the verse that many point to as the most persuasive on these issues is Acts 17:26: "From one man he made all the nations ["nations of mankind," *ethnos anthrōpōn*], that they should inhabit the whole earth; and he marked out their appointed times in history and the boundaries of their lands." This is found in Paul's speech to the philosophers on Mars Hill concerning the "unknown god." First, Paul presents the true God as noncontingent (Acts 17:24, "made the world and everything in it"), as transcendent (Acts 17:24, "does not live in temples built by human hands"), as not operating in the Great Symbiosis (Acts 17:25, has no needs) and as one on whom all people as his creatures are contingent (Acts 17:25, "gives everyone life and breath and everything else"). These statements all pertain to God's role as Creator.

In Acts 17:26, Paul's rhetoric transitions to a geopolitical, historical and societal focus. He indicates that nations, historical roles and territories are all dependent on God. I would contend that in this verse he is not talking about biology or about human origins. He is discussing national origins. God's "making" (*poieō*) of a nation is not a material act but an organizational one. We may well ask how and where in Scripture God makes the nations. The nations come into being through lines of descendants, and the Bible communicates that process very explicitly in Genesis 10, the so-called Table of Nations. There the lines of Noah's three sons are traced as a means of identifying the lineage of the seventy known countries and peoples in the author's time.[5] Genesis 10:32 concludes that from these three sons of Noah come all the nations: "These are the clans of Noah's sons, according to their lines of descent, within their nations. From these the nations [*ethnōn*] spread out over the earth after the flood." This is the only verse in the Old Testament that talks about the origins of the nations as a group and is therefore arguably the verse to which Paul refers. If that is so, the "one" that he refers to is Noah, not Adam.[6]

If human origins were the point, we might expect Paul to use the basic *anthrōpōn* rather than making the nations the focus. Furthermore, the concept of national identity fits better in this verse in connection with historical periods and territorial boundaries. Finally, he brackets this part of the speech with the conclusion "we are his offspring" (end of Acts 17:28), which parallels the beginning of Acts 17:26 ("from one man he made"). Between this and the focus on geopolitical entities, we can rightly question whether Paul was making a statement about material biological origins. Was he making a claim that argues against a wider range of genetic sources for humanity (polygenism)? That would be a dubious conclusion; Paul, of course, knew nothing about genetics. He is instead pointing to the remarkable work of God's formation of multiple national identities from the three sons of Noah.

MOTHER OF ALL LIVING

Genesis 3:20 is another verse from which some interpreters inferred a biblical claim that all humans trace their genetic heritage back to Adam and Eve. Here Adam gives his wife the name Eve (Hebrew *ḥawwāh* = life), indicating that she was "the mother of all the living."[7] Does this constitute a biblical claim that all humans are genetically descended from Eve? Several observations militate against that conclusion. First, the reference to the "living" in the explanation of her name is a word that can refer to all creatures, yet all animals are not biological descendants of Eve. Second, the expression "mother of all . . ." is not necessarily one that pertains to biology. Notice that in Genesis 4:20, Jabal "was the father of those who live in tents and raise livestock." In Genesis 4:21, Jubal "was the father of all who play stringed instruments and pipes." These usages show that this sort of expression has larger associations in mind than just biological descent.

GENEALOGIES

Another argument from the biblical text is that the genealogies consistently go back to Adam (Gen 5; 1 Chron 1; Lk 3:38), suggesting that he is the first human being. It would not be surprising if Israelites in Old Testament and New Testament times believed that Adam was the first human. The hermeneutical issue, however, is more subtle. Were they teaching that Adam was the first human being? Were they building theology on that concept? Or is God simply using their contemporary concepts as a framework for communication?

We have already used the examples of physiology and cosmic geography as examples of God using familiar ideas of the time rather than updating science. We noted that there is no new revelation in the Bible concerning the regular operations of the natural world. The allusion to physiology (for example) does not constitute revelation about physiology or a divine endorsement of a particular physiology.

We could make the same claim with regard to genealogy. Adam is the first significant person in their realm of knowledge (and he is indeed historically and theologically significant), and they drive all significant connections back to him. In Genesis, the genealogy offers the line from Adam (however he fits in) to Noah. In 1 Chronicles, the concern is about Jewish identity as the representatives of the kingdom of God. It is natural that Adam be viewed as the fountainhead of the people of God. That role does not depend on particular views of genetic ancestry or material continuity. His federal headship would easily serve as an appropriate basis for the genealogy to go back to him.[8] The genealogy in Luke 3 traces the lineage of Jesus back through genealogies to establish his place in history. It does not just go back to Adam; it goes back to God. This is a lineage through Joseph, so it is specifically *not* his biological lineage. Adam is the first significant human and the connection to God because of the very particular role that he had (again, federal headship gives an adequate connection, as does his priestly role).

In all these cases, while the Bible *could* be read as suggesting that Adam was the first human being, it is more debatable whether it is making a scientific claim that would controvert the possibility that modern humanity is descended from a pool of common ancestors as indicated by the genetic evidence. I would then conclude that any contention that the Bible is making a claim that Adam is the first human being or that all humans are descended from him is debatable.

Humans Could Be Viewed as Distinct Creatures and a Special Creation of God Even If There Was Material Continuity

In the last chapter, we discussed Adam and Eve's relationship to all of us who have come after them. In this chapter, we will begin by turning our attention to their relationship to what came before them. The modern scientific consensus affirms that there is material continuity between all species of life (technically designated phylogenetic continuity). Evolutionary models offer an explanation of how this gradual change over time from a common ancestor took place. It is one thing to believe that all species have a common ancestor, and it is quite another to explain what mechanisms drove the process of change. The former idea is almost universally affirmed among scientists; the latter is still under vigorous debate.

The fossil record, comparative anatomy and the genome likewise all point to common descent, but they offer no information about what factors drove the changes. In one sense, all of these offer snapshots at various stages, whereas evolutionary models attempt, in effect, to incorporate those snapshots into a video. Consequently, one could theoretically accept the concepts of phylogenetic continuity and common descent (based on the information from comparative genomics or the fossil record) yet be very skeptical of the current mechanisms proposed by evolutionary models (e.g., mutation, natural selection).

Evolution can be defined as an interpretation of the world around us that posits a material (phylogenetic) continuity among all species of creatures (biological and genetic, not spiritual) as the result of a process of change over time through various mechanisms known and unknown.[1] It is not inherently atheistic or deistic. It has plenty of room for the providence of God as well as the intimate involvement of God. It is beyond the scope of this book to discuss whether evolutionary models are correct or not. The more important question is whether the conclusions of common descent and material continuity are compatible with a faithful interpretation of the Bible.

Today many of those who are proponents of evolutionary models see those models as an alternative to the involvement of a Creator God, and some insist that such models show that the need for a Creator God is obsolete. Obviously, such conclusions cannot be accepted by Christians. Other scientists, however, accept the concept of common descent, and even some evolutionary models, but view God as one who is creating through a process that features change over time from a common ancestor. This approach is known as "evolutionary creation."[2] Therefore, to consider change over time, common descent, material continuity or even an evolutionary model is not a decision that automatically rules God out of the picture. These do not necessitate the conclusion that there is no God or that he was not active in creation. God can be viewed as Creator even in the context of such scientific conclusions.

At the same time, we would have to readily acknowledge that nothing in the biblical text suggests such an understanding of human origins. Since Genesis is an ancient document, we would not expect it to address these modern ideas. Nevertheless, we need to ask whether information based on the authoritative teaching of Scripture rules out

such a possibility. Could someone who takes the Bible seriously believe in common descent and material continuity?

The easiest, casual reading of the text (and one that has been believed for millennia), or one that did not have access to ancient Near
Eastern texts, would suggest a de novo creation of human beings. In a
fully de novo view, there is material discontinuity—no human or other
primate predecessors with whom humans shared a common ancestor.
In this view, God is directly involved in the special creation of Adam
and Eve distinct from other creatures and not derived from them in
any material way. That remains a very plausible interpretation, but,
again we ask, is such a view the actual claim of Scripture with the
weight of authority behind it such that failure to read this way constitutes rejection of biblical truths?

In previous chapters, I have offered what I believe to be a faithful
reading of the authoritative claims of Scripture in its own literary,
theological and cultural context that suggests that the Bible does not
need to be read as affirming a de novo view. Instead, I have suggested
that the Bible does not really offer any information about material
human origins. This would mean that the scientific claims of common
descent and material continuity would not be automatically ruled out.

It is important, nevertheless, to realize that the adoption of common
descent and material continuity does not eliminate the idea that
human beings are created by God and are uniquely spiritual beings
who possess the image of God. The image of God is not neurological
and not materially defined in terms of neuroscience or genetics; it has
no material component, though the image is embodied.

HUMAN DISTINCTIVENESS IS SPIRITUAL

We can discuss spiritual uniqueness in three basic categories. First,
based on the discussion in chapter twelve, we can see that Adam and
Eve are distinguished from any other humans that may have existed
in their time by having been designated as priests serving representa-

tively in sacred space. This is presented as a role given to them by God, a role that is spiritual in nature. Note that in similar ways Abraham is not materially distinct from any others of his time, but he is selected by God and assigned a spiritual role.

Second, it is the Christian belief that humans have a spiritual nature of some sort. There is still much discussion (and perhaps even increasing disagreement) over how that spiritual part of us needs to be described and understood, but we believe that we are more than biological specimens; we are more than carbon-based life forms. Neuroscience can provide explanations about how we came to *realize* that we are more than biological specimens but not how we came to *be* more. Whether we call this the soul or spirit and whether we are dualists or monists or something else, as Christians we believe that there is some part of us, in fact, the most important part of us, that survives the death of the body. This is not something that can evolve; it is not possessed by those other creatures in a line of common descent. It represents a spiritual discontinuity even if one concludes that there is material continuity. It is granted by God (we don't know how or when) as a direct, special creative act of God, and it differentiates us from every other creature.

The third aspect of our human spiritual uniqueness is found in the image of God that we have been given. The image of God is not the same thing as our spiritual nature, but like our spiritual nature it is not something that just develops in the human species over time. One of the most common ways to define the image of God is to start with the proposition that the image of God distinguishes us from all creatures, and with this I would agree. I would, however, disagree with then drawing the conclusion that anything that distinguishes us from other creatures tells us what the image of God is. Fortunately, such theories focus on mental capacities rather than the presence of opposable thumbs. Even so, the image of God must be seen as more than the sum total of capacities whose developments can be traced by neuroscience. The image of God is, by definition, who we are as human beings. It is not the mark of humanity; it is how humans are marked. It is not what makes us human, but, as humans, we have the image of God. I believe that the image of God is something that is a direct, spiritually defined gift of God to humans. For those who believe that humans are biologically a product of change over time through common descent, the image of God would be given by God to humans at a particular time in that history. It would not be detectable in the fossil record or in the genome. So now we must take a closer look at what the image of God is.

IMAGE OF GOD

The image of God has been the topic of numerous dissertations and monographs in a variety of disciplines (e.g., exegetical treatments of Genesis, theology, philosophy, art history, neuroscience/psychology), so this treatment will be embarrassingly brief. I have only space enough to survey the aspects of the image of God that these studies (as well as my own) have identified. This will entail a brief presentation of four aspects: function, identity, substitution and relationship. These are not mutually exclusive alternatives, and I would propose that each of them is true.

Function. The understanding of the image of God as an assigned role with an inherent function has long been part of the discussion. Most recently, it has been championed by J. Richard Middleton.[3] In this view, humanity corporately functions as God's vice-regents—stewards who are charged with subduing and ruling as articulated in the very context in which the image is granted (Gen 1:26-30). As a corporate designation, it differentiates humanity from all other creatures and species. Those capacities that can be discussed neurologically (self-awareness, God-awareness, etc.) may well be understood as allowing us to carry out this task, but they would not themselves define the image of God. All humans have a role to play in this aspect of our corporate identity, regardless of how well they function mentally or physically.

Identity. This aspect of the image of God expresses our core identity: this is who we are.[4] We should recall that naming is an act of creation in the ancient Near East. It then follows that when God designates humankind as his image, that is what humankind becomes. The image becomes interwoven in our destiny and our nature. Like any name in the Old Testament, it takes on reality over time in any number of possible ways. This identity is assigned by our Creator; it is not something we could take on our own for ourselves, and it is not something that can just develop in us. Just as naming is an act of creation in the ancient world, so this giving of identity is a spiritual act of special creation.

Substitution. When a king in the ancient world had an image of himself placed by the gate in a city he had conquered or at the border of a land that he claimed, the image proclaimed the king's presence there. It was a substitute, but it was more than just a stand-in. In its aesthetics, it communicated important ideals about the king and about kingship.[5] The images of the gods in the temples did the same on a larger scale because the images of the gods had been inaugurated by a ritual that endowed the image with the divine essence. In this way, the material nature and existence of the image faded almost into nonsignificance (though the very best materials had been used). It had become a fit repository for the divine essence, and that was the most important thing about it. The image did not just contain the divine essence; it was transformed into something spiritual in nature.[6]

It is interesting that in Genesis, God's image, humanity, is crafted from the very meanest of materials, thus emphasizing in contrast the proportionally heightened value of the divine image. Yet, as in the case of images in the ancient world, we, as his image, stand in as God's substitutes. We represent his presence in sacred space. His essence makes us spiritual beings and constitutes discontinuity from any other creature. Just as images were revered as divine creations in the ancient world, we are considered to be the works of God in the truest possible sense.

Divine-human relationship. In each of the previous categories, the premise of the category implied some level of relationship between God and his people. In this last category, more specificity can be provided to suggest that the relationship is best expressed in filial terms.[7] In the biblical text this can be most easily observed when Adam begets Seth "in his own likeness, in his own image" in Genesis 5:1-3. This same idea can be identified in the ancient Near East, where the image is considered to be born in heaven even though it is made on earth.

Summary of image. The image of God provides yet another piece of evidence from the biblical text concerning the spiritual discontinuity that is characteristic of humans in contradistinction to other creatures. The four categories for understanding the image of God presented above are not mutually exclusive—all four can be accepted as each gives insight into the descriptor. When we consider the image in these four categories, we can affirm that all human beings must be considered as participating in the divine image. It is something that is more corporate than individual. Furthermore, it is clear from the occurrences throughout the biblical text that the image was not lost when Adam and Eve were sent from the garden, though it was marred. The functions that were entrusted to us in Genesis 1 are still our responsibilities, though our ability to carry out those functions may be hampered in a variety of ways by our current condition.

Even as we have seen many points of contact between Genesis and the ancient Near East, we should not neglect to notice the places where the Israelites were departing from the standard ways of thinking in the ancient world. People (God's images) were placed in sacred space just as the images of the Babylonian gods were placed in sacred space in their temples to mediate God's presence and God's revelation. But images were excluded in worship in Israel—we are the only images God allows.

CONCLUSION

In this chapter, we have not proffered a conclusion regarding material continuity. Instead we have observed that comparative genomics indicates that there is a history, so we have to decide whether the Bible claims that such a history never took place, because God created humans de novo. To the extent that we become aware of viable interpretations of the biblical text that do not require de novo, we can consider other options for understanding God's creation of humans. Not only can we see that God the Creator is in any of these models; we can also recognize that there are numerous points of spiritual discontinuity where we recognize special creative work of God that cannot be explained by any understanding of natural change over time or identified in the human genome, even if there is a higher level of material continuity than traditionally accepted. Humans are the special, direct creation of God in certain ways—that is not in question. The uncertainty lies in how much of that special creation falls into the material category.

Conclusion and Summary

In the preceding chapters, we have examined the biblical claims concerning Adam and Eve, the garden, the serpent, and the fall. Our investigation has focused on the text of Genesis as an ancient Near Eastern document. We have been particularly interested in determining the extent to which the biblical claims may or may not conflict with the claims made in the current scientific consensus about human origins. We have studiously avoided imposing scientific or ancient Near Eastern claims on the Bible. Instead we have sought to assess the biblical claims independently and only then to compare to what we find in other ancient Near Eastern literature and to the evidence suggested by scientific findings. We expect Genesis to be characterized in part by perspectives that are found in the literature of the ancient Near East because God was communicating into an ancient Near Eastern culture: ancient Israel. We also expect Genesis, read properly, to be compatible with the truths about our world that scientists uncover because both the world and the Word emanate from God.

The first several chapters of this book summarized the interpretation I have previously offered of Genesis 1. These focused on the idea that the origins story that Genesis 1 tells has more to do with order, functions and roles than with the material cosmos. The order that God established inaugurated sacred space in the cosmos. God intended to enter into the place that he had prepared for people in his image and to be in relationship with them there.

Genesis 2 then tells of the establishment of a terrestrial center of sacred space in what is identified as a garden, where Adam and Eve are commissioned as priests to serve in sacred space mediating revelation of God and access to God. Adam and Eve are presented as archetypes in their formation: they embody all people, and the affirmations of the forming accounts are affirmations made of everyone, not uniquely of them. All humans are made of dust; womankind is from the side of mankind. Adam and Eve are also established as priestly representatives through whom life and wisdom can be achieved as people are drawn into relationship with God. Unfortunately, they failed to achieve these benefits because they opted to position themselves as the center of order (and, in so doing, becoming like God) in place of God.

A number of these elements in Genesis find similarities with ancient Near Eastern literature, while others are entirely unique in the ancient world. Proper interpretation will recognize both. We should note, however, that the Israelites often show marked dissimilarity from the surrounding cultures even when they share concepts with the ancient world. So, for example, even though ancient Near Eastern literature considers the creation of humanity to involve a large group of humans, the underlying reasons are far different from what would exist in the biblical text if en masse creation of humanity were to be seen from Genesis 1. In the ancient Near East creation narratives, many humans are created at once because many gods were intending to use many humans to supply their needs. The purposes of the gods would not be well served if only a few humans were created. In contrast, if Genesis 1 allows en masse creation of humans (as I have argued), it is not for the same reason. The God of the Bible has no needs, and the function of humans is presented in very different terms. Likewise, the roles and functions of human beings as presented in the Bible cannot be confirmed through science because science is incapable of discussing final causes.

When we shift our attention to the archetypal roles, the fact that ancient Near Eastern texts also feature an archetypal view of human origins helps us to recognize that this way of thinking would not be unusual for Israelites in their cultural context. At the same time, we find that the message to be found in the archetypal presentation in Genesis is of a totally different sort from what is found in the ancient Near East. The messages associated with the archetypal representation in Genesis are as follows:

- Humankind was created with mortal bodies.

- Humankind was provisioned by God (garden).

- Humankind was given the role of serving in sacred space (implies relationship with God).

- Humankind was divided into male and female and so would seek out new family relationship.

These points constitute the main teaching of Genesis 2. They convey important ideas about the nature of God, the nature of humanity, and both horizontal and vertical relationships.

Once the forming accounts are recognized as archetypal, they cease to be meaningful in terms of chronology or history of material human origins, even given my continued assertion that Adam and Eve are historical persons. If the accounts of their forming are archetypal in nature rather than material, those forming accounts are important not as events of material creation but as ideas about the nature of humanity. Nevertheless, I have identified in the text evidences that the Israelites as well as the New Testament authors believed Adam and Eve to be real people who lived in a real past. The question to be asked, however, is whether this belief is simply cultural and therefore not binding. The hermeneutical principle that I use to make that determination is whether the text hangs theology on the belief. For example, in the ancient world they believed that the heart was the center of intellect and emotion, and the text affirms that belief. But no theology is built on it in the biblical text. Therefore, once that is recognized as simply a cultural way of thinking in the ancient world rather than the inspired, authoritative revelation of God, I can safely set aside that belief.

The question, then, is whether theological teachings are derived from the historicity of Adam and Eve. On this question we can draw a distinction between the theology connected to the doctrine of Scripture and that connected to other doctrines (e.g., sin). If we simply say that inerrancy demands that we accept a historical Adam because he is mentioned in the genealogies, we are failing to distinguish between that which the Old Testament authors may have incidentally believed and that which the Bible affirms as its authoritative teaching. Where might God be accommodating their current thinking? To return to the example of thinking with the heart, one could not claim that inerrancy demands that we believe that the heart is physiologically the center of our intellect. Inerrancy pertains to that which the text affirms, and we have concluded that physiology is not affirmed by the text; instead the ancient views of physiology were accommodated. If someone were to claim that the historicity of Adam is theologically mandated because of inerrancy, they would have to make the case that historical Adam is part of the authoritative message that the text propounds. This case can be made, but other faithful interpreters may well develop an interpretation that comes to a different conclusion. Historical Adam is only tied into inerrancy to the extent that it can be demonstrated not just that the biblical authors considered him historical but that the biblical teaching incorporated that understanding into its authoritative message. If someone were to contend that belief in a historical Adam was cultural, not affirmed in the theological or revelatory intent of the text but rather part of the framework of communication, then inerrancy would not apply, just as believing that Melchizedek had no parents would not be an issue of inerrancy. I raise this distinction theoretically because I do affirm the historicity of Adam. But I do not consider interpreters who are trying to be faithful to Scripture to be denying inerrancy if they arrive at a different conclusion.

It is evident that this distinction between the affirmation of the text and the accommodation of the text is not just a modern issue from the fact that it is addressed as soon as scientific sophistication began to raise questions about biblical interpretation. John Calvin, for example, addressed the hermeneutical issue in the introduction to his commentary on Genesis when he discussed Moses' accommodation to the audience of his time with regard to scientific elements:

> Moses wrote in a popular style things which, without instruction, all ordinary persons, endued with common sense, are able to understand; but astronomers investigate with great labor whatever the sagacity of the human mind can comprehend. Nevertheless, this study is not to be reprobated, nor this science to be condemned, because some frantic persons are wont boldly to reject whatever is unknown to them. . . .
>
> Nor did Moses truly wish to withdraw us from this pursuit in omitting such things as are peculiar to the art [e.g., the scientific details]; but because he was ordained a teacher as well of the unlearned and the rude as well as of the learned, he could not otherwise fulfill his office than by descending to this grosser method of instruction. Had he spoken of things generally unknown, the uneducated might have pleaded in excuse that such subjects were beyond their capacity. Lastly, since the spirit of God here opens a common school for all, it is not surprising that he should chiefly choose those subjects which would be intelligible to all.[1]

The method and perspective that Calvin laid out for the solar system can be just as easily applied to human origins.

We must then consider whether theological assertions other than inerrancy are intertwined with the historicity of Adam. The primary (and some would contend the only) theological discussion in the Bible that relies on a historical Adam is the theology of the fall—particularly the idea that sin (or at least accountability for sin) entered the cosmos at a specific moment due to a specific act and that through that act we all became subject to sin and its consequence, death. Thus *the historicity of Adam finds its primary significance in the discussion of the origins of sin rather than in the origins of humanity.* This is tacitly affirmed in the pastoral response provided by Philip Ryken in *Four Views on the Historical Adam.* His response contends that "we cannot understand the world or our faith without a real, historical Adam."[2] Though Ryken gives brief attention to the idea that Adam is presented as a real person in the text, the bulk of his argument concerns sin (or, even further removed, sociological [no. 3] or missional [no. 5] issues):

1. The historical Adam explains humanity's sinful nature.

2. The historical Adam accounts for the presence of evil in the world.

3. The historical Adam (with the historical Eve) clarifies the biblical position on sexual identity and family relationships.

4. The historical Adam assures us that we are justified before God.

5. The historical Adam advances the missionary work of the church.

6. The historical Adam secures our hope in the resurrection of the body and the life everlasting.

All these points could be discussed at great length, and some are undoubtedly a matter of interpretation for which other bona fide explanations could be offered. Regardless, it illustrates the true focus of the historical Adam question. Even if we accept without question all these points, we could still maintain that no theology is built on the scientific implications commonly associated with Adam and Eve: that they must (theologically speaking!) be created de novo, as the only people at the beginning of humanity and those from whom we are all descended. Throughout this book, I have offered biblical support for the possibility that humanity was created en masse in Genesis 1, that the presence of other people is assumed in Genesis 4 and that Genesis 2 does not intend to offer an account of fully de novo material human origins. If the evidence should prove persuasive that (1) no theology is dependent on or derived from the traditional assertions of de novo creation or Adam and Eve as the first two humans, who were alone in the world and the direct progenitors of the entire human race, and if (2) sound, faithful, exegetical analysis offers plausible alternative interpretations, then we would have no reason to be committed to those traditional beliefs as the only acceptable interpretation. In such a case, inerrancy and the text would not demand them from us, and we would hold them by our preference. In short, there may be a wider range of possibilities for a biblical and theological understanding of human origins than previously recognized. If it turns out (as I believe it does) that science offers evidence to the contrary, we are free to consider its claims. In other words, if neither exegesis nor theology intractably demands those conclusions that argue against the modern scientific consensus premised on common descent, we have no compelling reason to contest the science. That does not mean that all questions can now easily be answered. But progress can be made.

Some readers will feel some reticence about adopting new interpretations of the biblical text. How dare we disregard two millennia of church history? Are we better than the church fathers? Would God leave us without sound interpretation for so long? These sorts of questions show a commendable impulse to caution. As we address these concerns, however, we might recall that opponents of the Reformers would have raised similar objections. Furthermore, it will be noted that in this work the suggested innovations are primarily exegetical rather than theological.

This question concerning the place of theological tradition is an important one and has been dealt with in works that are dedicated to that study.[3] Here I will only offer seven brief observations for readers to consider.

- The church fathers often disagree deeply with one another. This means that they cannot all be right, and there was never total unanimity.

- The church fathers regularly make statements and hold positions that no one today accepts. We are not bound to their thinking.

- The thinking and writing of the church fathers was driven by the needs of their time, whether Gnosticism, Stoicism, Arianism, the numerous heresies that regularly arose or the theological debates that dominated. They were not simply dealing with text, and they rarely were attempting to get back to what the authors of Scripture intended to say.

- The church fathers were primarily driven by Christology. This gave them very little reason to think about the text in its ancient context. Theologically it was important for them to focus on clarifying this important aspect of Christian doctrine. Unfortunately, the resulting attention to Christology tended to overbalance their theology and their hermeneutics—an inclination that remains at times today.

- Through many periods of church history, writers and thinkers were not familiar with the biblical languages. They were not therefore in a position to do close reading of a Hebrew text.

- The church fathers had no access to the ancient world. They were lacking the resources that have been recovered today through archaeological excavation. Over a million cuneiform texts now offer us unparalleled access to important information about the ancient world in which the Old Testament was written.

- Some of the ideas that are presented in this work actually were considered by some interpreters in the early history of the church, so they are not as new as we might think.

These comments do not suggest that we neglect or ignore the history of interpretation, only that we recognize that a history of faithful interpretation continues and that as the textual evidence dictates, we may still find occasion to take our departure from some traditionally held ideas.

We can contend that Adam and Eve are theologically and historically significant even if they were not the first humans. We can contend that Adam and Eve are appropriately positioned as fountainheads of humanity even if we are not all their direct descendants. We can contend that humanity has a distinct place in the created order, unique among species, even if Adam and Eve are not de novo creations.

The most significant issue that we have been examining is whether the Bible and science make mutually exclusive claims about human origins. The current scientific consensus is that humans share a common ancestor with other species based on the evidence of material (phylogenetic) continuity. Our close reading of the biblical text and theological studies has indicated that they would allow for such material continuity and common ancestry.

I am not in an advantageous position to suggest a hypothetical scenario that accounts for both the biblical and scientific data, and such has not been my intention. This book represents a much more limited endeavor: to determine what the Bible and theology require with regard to human origins so that we can conclude which scientific proposals we may be obliged to reject. The analysis offered in these pages suggests that a careful reading of Genesis as an ancient Near Eastern document results in exegetical conclusions and theological affirmations that do not inherently conflict with common descent or conclusions drawn from and implications derived from the history that is observable in the human genome (see chap. 20). Acceptance of the principle of common descent or the idea that the history attested to by the genome actually happened is not the same as accepting the theory of evolution as it exists today, though it would clear the way for some theory of evolution to be compatible with the Bible. The rest would call for science to make its best case.

In conclusion, we might ask why all of this is important. I therefore will close with four reasons why this conversation needs to move forward: creation care, ministry, evangelism and considering the future.

CREATION CARE

Who we believe we are as a race has significant influence on how we interact with the world around us. It is interesting that both militant atheists and fundamentalist Christians might agree in a full exploitation of the environment: atheists, because one's own self-interests are all that matter, and Christians, who believe that the earth is doomed for destruction anyway so there is no need to exercise care. Yet, at the same time, atheists could be concerned about earth-keeping because they take the long view on human existence. Christians should care about the environment because we have come to understand that God has appointed us as caretakers of his world. As his vice-regents, we have been charged with subduing and ruling, but that leaves no room for exploitation or abuse. We have the responsibility to maintain the space that is ultimately sacred and ultimately his.

MINISTRY

Many Christians who work in the various fields of science find themselves in treacherous waters. If they are bold in making their faith known in the workplace, they can be easily marginalized by their colleagues and bosses because of the supposed ways in which faith is thought to undermine one's ability to function in a scientifically oriented world. They may find themselves not taken seriously, and their careers might suffer because of their faith commitments.

When these people come to the church expecting to find support and encouragement as they face the struggles of their workplace, too often they find that the church is suspicious of them. And worse, if they have come to accept some of the tenets of the scientific consensus that the church has traditionally disparaged, they are also marginalized in the church. The message is loud and clear: leave your scientific conclusions at the door.

We are not doing a good job of ministering to these brothers and sisters. We have communicated that their commitment to Christ is subverted, their service to the church is unwanted and their very salvation is suspect. We have to do better in providing safe contexts for people in the sciences, and we would do well to learn from them. At times, however, they are confused, and it would be appropriate for the church to help them work through these difficult issues—not by making them choose (Bible or science) but by charting a path of convergence and compatibility.

EVANGELISM

Many non-Christians opposed to the gospel and to Christianity habitually ridicule the church for what they paint as a naive commitment to an ancient mythology. Some of the traditional opposition that some Christians have mounted concerning the age of the earth or human origins has become fodder for those who seek an excuse to reject the teachings of Christ. But not all are antagonistic; some sit on the sidelines and watch. They are intrigued by Christianity, particularly when they have met Christians who impress them. Despite their curiosity and intrigue, they have heard that to accept Christianity means to abandon their brains. They have heard from both the secular world and the Christian world that to accept Christ means to reject certain scientific conclusions—a step they cannot take. They have been told that to become a Christian means to believe the Bible; to believe the Bible means to jettison science that they find convincing. So they remain outside looking in.

The church has to do a better job of presenting an unencumbered gospel. Given the conclusions reached in these pages, we can easily alleviate the concerns of those inquiring about Christianity when they ask whether the Bible requires them to believe that the earth is young or that no evolutionary model is acceptable by a Christian. The gospel is clear—believe in the Lord Jesus Christ and you will be saved.

CONSIDERING THE FUTURE

Finally, and perhaps most importantly, whenever we misrepresent what the Bible says by positioning it as being in conflict with science, we force people to make a choice. Certainly we make a choice when we affirm that God is the Creator. But when we tell the young people reared in a Christian faith that there is a war between science and faith and that if they accept certain scientific conclusions, they will be abandoning the Bible, they often believe us. Then, when they are confronted with a very persuasive presentation of an old earth or a case for common ancestry from the genomic record, they decide that the Bible must go. It is not because they no longer believe in Jesus but because they have been taught that believing in an old earth or believing some form of evolutionary theory is not compatible with believing the Bible. They have heard their revered pastors tell them that people who believe in evolution cannot be Christians. In repeated surveys of those who have become disillusioned with the church, this is listed as one of the primary reasons.

We cannot claim that the Bible/science debate is the only culprit responsible for people leaving the church, but it is one of the most commonly mentioned ones. What if we could tell them that their scientific conclusions did not make a difference and that they could still believe the Bible, could still be in relationship with Christ, could still be members in good standing in the church? Wouldn't that make a difference? There is no need to lose our young people to this debate. It does not matter whether you as a reader are sympathetic to scientific conclusions or not. It does not matter whether you find the exegetical and theological conclusions in this book persuasive or not. If we can think beyond ourselves and accept the fact that a vital Christian faith need not have exactly the same interpretive profile that we believe, we might see that the church is bigger than any of us. Certainly there are beliefs (or, more often, unbeliefs) that place one outside this big tent we call the church. But there is room for a variety of beliefs as long as they derive from sound exegesis, sound theology and sound herme-neutics. We have tried to demonstrate that Genesis 1 is concerned with God's ordering of sacred space with the goal of being in relationship with us. We have tried to demonstrate further that the Adam account is more concerned with the entry of disorder into the world than with giving an account of human origins. These are conclusions that derive from a faithful reading of Scripture and offer legitimate alternatives even if they do not convince all readers.

Think, then, of our children and grandchildren. When they come home from college having accepted some scientific understanding about human origins that we do not find persuasive, are we going to denounce them, disinherit them and drive them from the doors of our homes and churches? Or are we going to suggest to them that there may be a way to interpret Scripture faithfully that will allow them to hold on to both science and faith? Can we believe that such a path does not represent a compromise that dilutes the faith but rather one that opens new doors to understanding that the next generation may find essential even though we find ourselves paralyzed on the threshold? Let us pray together that we can chart a path of faithfulness and stop the hemorrhaging.

Notes

INTRODUCTION

[1]Peter C. Bouteneff, *Beginnings: Ancient Christian Readings of the Biblical Creation Narratives* (Grand Rapids: Baker, 2008), pp. ix-x. His focus is on the Greek patristic literature.

[2]And its inerrancy rightly understood.

PROPOSITION 1: GENESIS IS AN ANCIENT DOCUMENT

[1]Significant portions of this chapter are adapted from John H. Walton and D. Brent Sandy, *The Lost World of Scripture: Ancient Literary Culture and Biblical Authority* (Downers Grove, IL: InterVarsity Press, 2013).

[2]Illocutions are the focus of the speech-act, e.g., promise, command, blessing or instruction. The illocution identifies what the communicator is doing with his or her words.

[3]For definitions of terms such as this, consult the glossary, p. 240.

[4]Even Jerome recognized this distinction. He notes, "Many things in Sacred Scripture . . . are said in accordance with the opinion of the time in which the events took place, rather than in accordance with the actual truth of the matter." Jerome, *Commentary on Jeremiah,* 28:10-11, trans. Michael Graves, Ancient Christian Texts (Downers Grove, IL: InterVarsity Press, 2012), p. 173. I am grateful to Michael Graves for this reference.

[5]A technique illustrated in K. Lawson Younger Jr., *Ancient Conquest Accounts: A Study in Ancient Near Eastern and Biblical History Writing* (Sheffield: JSOT Press, 1990); and John H. Walton, *The Lost World of Genesis One: Ancient Cosmology and the Origins Debate* (Downers Grove, IL: InterVarsity Press, 2009).

[6]See discussion in Theo M. M. A. C. Bell, "Humanity Is a Microcosm: Adam and Eve in Luther's Lectures on Genesis (1534–1545)," in *Out of Paradise: Eve and Adam and Their Interpreters,* ed. Bob Becking and Susan Hennecke (Sheffield: Sheffield Phoenix, 2010), pp. 67-89.

PROPOSITION 2: IN THE ANCIENT WORLD AND THE OLD TESTAMENT, CREATING FOCUSES ON ESTABLISHING ORDER BY ASSIGNING ROLES AND FUNCTIONS

[1]One of the ways we know this is because if he actually created in Genesis 1:1, it would mean that he created it *tōhû* (the condition in Gen 1:2), yet Isaiah 45:18 clearly says he did not create it *tōhû*. NIV's rendering, "he did not create it to be empty," unfortunately has to add the words "to be," which are neither represented in the Hebrew text nor implied by the syntax of the Hebrew text.

[2]For more information see John H. Walton, "Principles for Productive Word Study," in *New International Dictionary of Old Testament Theology and Exegesis*, ed. Willem A. VanGemeren (Grand Rapids: Zondervan, 1997), 1:161-71.

[3]Combinations are important because sometimes words have meaning in combination that conveys more than their meanings individually (e.g., "assault and battery").

[4]*The Context of Scripture*, ed. William W. Hallo and K. Lawson Younger Jr. (Leiden: Brill, 2003), 1:111.

[5]These are only a few of the many examples. For more a comprehensive listing and detailed analysis, see John H. Walton, *Genesis 1 as Ancient Cosmology* (Winona Lake, IN: Eisenbrauns, 2011), pp. 23-62.

[6]Ibid., pp. 127-39; idem, *The Lost World of Genesis One: Ancient Cosmology and the Origins Debate* (Downers Grove, IL: InterVarsity Press, 2009), pp. 36-43.

[7]This was noted by Augustine in his discussion of Isaiah 45:7 in *The Catholic and Manichean Ways of Life*, Fathers of the Church Patristic Series 56 (Washington, D.C.: Catholic University of America Press, 1966), pp. 71-72. Concerning *bārā'* he states, "To 'create' means to order and arrange."

[8]Though not in the technically philosophical categories developed by Aristotle.

[9]Note that even in our preschool instruction in church we don't hesitate to say that "God made each and every one of us."

[10]Note that here the function, "governing," 1:16, is the focus. The Israelites can use *'āśâ* here even though they do not consider the moon an object.

[11]The thrust of the conversation in the patristic literature (e.g., Athanasius) was ontological and dealt with non-contingency. I am grateful to Jonathan Walton for pointing this out to me.

[12]Walton, *Genesis 1 as Ancient Cosmology.*

PROPOSITION 3: GENESIS 1 IS AN ACCOUNT OF FUNCTIONAL ORIGINS, NOT MATERIAL ORIGINS

[1]See my discussion of the term in John H. Walton, *The Lost World of Genesis One: Ancient Cosmology and the Origins Debate* (Downers Grove, IL: InterVarsity Press, 2009), pp. 55-57; idem, *Ancient Near Eastern Thought and the Old Testament: Introducing the Conceptual World of the Hebrew Bible* (Grand Rapids: Baker Academic, 2006), pp. 168-70.

[2]The Hebrew word is *šĕḥāqîm*; note particularly its usage in Job 37:18, 21. Full discussion can be found in John H. Walton, *Genesis 1 as Ancient Cosmology* (Winona Lake, IN: Eisenbrauns, 2011), pp. 155-61; or idem, *Job*, NIV Application Commentary (Grand Rapids: Zondervan, 2012), pp. 371-73.

[3]If one retains the view that *rāqîaʿ* refers to the solid sky, there is still a problem with seeing Genesis 1 as a material origins account. Perhaps the Israelites thought of the solid sky in material terms, but since we do not believe that there actually is a material solid sky, we end up insisting that God created something that does not in reality exist.

[4]The reading of Genesis 1 labeled the framework hypothesis recognizes the ways in which days one through three find parallels to days four through six (one/four; two/five; three/six). I agree that this literary structuring is intentional and meaningful. Many who adopt the framework hypothesis, however, are content to stop there. They maintain that the seven-day structure is only literary and move on. I believe that in addition to the literary structuring, the element of ordering the cosmos is needed to grasp the full intentions of the account.

[5]Hints of a similar view may be inferred from Job 9:7 and Psalm 8:3; 147:7; see further discussion in John H. Walton, Victor H. Matthews and Mark W. Chavalas, *IVP Bible Background Commentary: Old Testament* (Downers Grove, IL: InterVarsity Press, 2000), loc. cit.

[6]See discussion in Walton, *Genesis 1 as Ancient Cosmology*, pp. 173-74.

[7]In a work known as the *Exploits of Ninurta* the text says, "Let the mountains increase the fecundity of quadrupeds for you."

[8]It is true that as herdsmen they actually saw the birth process of sheep and cattle and would have recognized its similarity to human births, but we must remember that their perspective does not represent the logic of science. This is another evidence that they are not discussing the actual, physical birth process.

[9]There is an ancient Near Eastern piece that we call *Enki and World Order* that describes the Sumerian god Enki bringing order to the cosmos. See

http://etcsl.orinst.ox.ac.uk/cgi-bin/etcsl.cgi?text=t.1.1.3#. Note that I am not suggesting that the two accounts have much in common in the details (they don't), and I am certainly not suggesting that the Bible borrowed from this Sumerian myth. I only suggest that both accounts ultimately are concerned with the establishment of order by the command of the pertinent deity.

[10]Others could be identified when we move to the larger canon.

[11]These do not give license for us to exploit—we are caretakers in God's place. The Hebrew verb translated "subdue" (*kbš*) refers to bringing someone or something under control. The Hebrew word translated "rule" (*rdh*) differs from the one used in Genesis 1:16-18. It refers essentially to exercising authority that has been granted or acknowledged. For more discussion see John H. Walton, *Genesis,* NIV Application Commentary (Grand Rapids: Zondervan, 2001), p. 132 for the Hebrew and pp. 139-45 for some practical observations.

[12]That the image of God is marred by the fall and restored in Christ highlights the fact that our ability to be vice-regents in God's program is hampered when we go our own way. That does not change our identity. The image of God will be discussed in more detail in chap. 21.

[13]See complete discussion with texts cited in Walton, *Genesis 1 as Ancient Cosmology,* pp. 46-68.

[14]See Walton, *Genesis 1 as Ancient Cosmology.*

[15]Miriam Lichtheim, *Ancient Egyptian Literature* (Berkeley: University of California Press, 1973), 1:106.

[16]This analogy was first suggested to me by Leith Anderson.

[17]I have developed many other examples of this sort of distinction that cannot be elaborated here. Among them, the origins of an organization (home) versus the origins of the building that houses them (house); the origins of a local church (home) versus the origins of the building they meet in (house); the origins of a country (home) versus the origins of the terrain and topography where they live (house); the origins of a college with its mission, faculty, curriculum and students (home) versus the origins of its campus buildings (house). One could also consider how a neighborhood is described—by its buildings and streets (house) or by the people who live there (home). Taking a slightly different slant, one could talk about the physical features of a laptop (polymers, soldering on the motherboard)—a material discussion—or about the software and applications—order and function.

[18]Passages in both Old and New Testaments confirm this. In the Old Tes-

tament, statements that God spreads out the earth (Ps 136:6; Is 42:5; 44:24) or that he laid the foundations of the earth (Job 38:4; Ps 24:2; 102:25; 104:5; Is 48:13; Zech 12:1) indicate that he is the builder of the house. In the New Testament we see similar affirmations in John 1:3: "Through him all things were made; without him nothing was made that has been made." Colossians 1:16 similarly states that "for in him all things were created: things in heaven and on earth, visible and invisible." At the same time Paul specifically delineates "thrones or powers or rulers or authorities"—items pertaining to order and function. Hebrews 1:2 identifies Christ as the one through whom God made the "universe," though it is noteworthy that the text refers to the *aiōnas* rather than to the *kosmos,* therefore showing a functional orientation, not just a material one (same in Heb 11:3). *Aiōnas* generally refers to the world in terms of time and history rather than in terms of spatiality and materiality.

Proposition 4: In Genesis 1, God Orders the Cosmos as Sacred Space

[1]It is true that the Hebrew employs the verb *yšb*, which often merely means to sit or to dwell. Nevertheless, the context here and in a number of other contexts indicates clearly that it is a seat of power and authority from which one rules, e.g., Numbers 21:34; 1 Samuel 4:4; 2 Samuel 6:2; throughout 1 Kings 1–2; 15:18; 22:10; Psalm 7:7; 9:7; 22:3; 29:10; 55:19; 68:16; and many others.

[2]This does not mean that our work on those six days is only self-serving.

[3]Extensive evidence for the ancient Near Eastern connections (cosmology and temple, rest and temple, etc.) can be found in John H. Walton, *Genesis 1 as Ancient Cosmology* (Winona Lake, IN: Eisenbrauns, 2011), pp. 100-119, 178-92.

[4]Notice the two sets of seven days in 1 Kings 8:65, and in 2 Chronicles 7:9 the seven days of dedication (*ḥănukka*) of the altar having been celebrated (*ʿāśâ*). Note also the seven-day sanctification of the altar in Exodus 29:35-37. For thorough discussion see Victor Hurowitz, *I Have Built You an Exalted House: Temple Building in the Bible in Light of Mesopotamian and Northwest Semitic Writings,* Journal for the Study of the Old Testament Supplement 115 (Sheffield: Sheffield Academic Press, 1992), pp. 260-61, 266-84, esp. 275-76. Such inaugurations are connected variably to the feast of Passover and Unleavened Bread, to Sukkoth/Booths or to Hanukkah—all festivals connected to seven days.

[5]Note that in Exodus many chapters are spent talking about the material construction; then a seven-day ceremony inaugurates it as sacred space.

[6]A further nuance can be identified here. In chapter seven I am going to consider the possibility that there may have been a period of time between the seven-day account and the garden account. If that view is accepted, sacred space would have a two-phase process. In Genesis 1 God orders the cosmos to be sacred space and rests (*šbt*) by ceasing his ordering work. His presence would then be in the cosmos and presumably acting in some ways in relationship with people in his image. The garden story would be the next phase during which God's presence actually took up residence (*nwḥ*) in Eden, the designated center of sacred space. This would be the stage in which a designated priesthood was established. The understanding that God's presence is established in phases can be supported in general by the long process from creation to Babel to covenant to temple to incarnation to Pentecost to new creation (for full discussion see chap. 18, "Jesus Is the Keystone"). This understanding is more particularly illustrated by the way that God's presence was realized in stages through the covenant (Abram inaugurating sacred space by building altars in Gen 12) and the steps that led from the burning bush, through the plagues, the pillar of cloud and his appearance on Mount Sinai, eventually coming to a climax in the tabernacle (Ex 40), where he took up his dwelling place in the center of sacred space. The tabernacle/temple is the culmination of a long process whereby sacred space became focused in temple. While we can identify a general theological continuity and coherence regarding the presence of God and sacred space, the imagery also shows some fluidity.

Proposition 5: When God Establishes Functional Order It Is "Good"

[1]See the similar conclusions by I. Provan, *Seriously Dangerous Religion* (Waco: Baylor University Press, 2014), p. 283.

[2]The only explanations that we have to offer for these exclusions are that the absence of the phrase in day two may be due to a copyist's error somewhere in the transmission of the text and that the isolation of the *tannînim* in day five may be more Masoretic interpretation than factual detail of the Hebrew text. Nevertheless, these should only be a last resort, and I am reluctant to go this direction.

[3]Observed by Ronald E. Osborn, *Death Before the Fall: Biblical Literalism and the Problem of Animal Suffering* (Downers Grove, IL: InterVarsity Press, 2014), p. 29.

PROPOSITION 6: *ʾādām* IS USED IN GENESIS 1–5 IN A VARIETY OF WAYS

[1]Many of the data in this chapter are derived from Richard S. Hess, "Splitting the Adam: The Usage of *ʾādām* in Genesis i–v," in *Studies in the Pentateuch*, ed. J. A. Emerton, Supplement to Vetus Testamentum 41 (Leiden: Brill, 1990), pp. 1-15.

[2]In Hebrew, when there is an attached preposition, the only determination of whether it has a definite article is in the vowel pointing that the Masoretes assigned in reflection of their received tradition.

[3]An archetype differs from a prototype in that the latter is simply the first in a series and does not imply representation; it is only a model.

PROPOSITION 7: THE SECOND CREATION ACCOUNT (GEN 2:4-24) CAN BE VIEWED AS A SEQUEL RATHER THAN AS A RECAPITULATION OF DAY SIX IN THE FIRST ACCOUNT (GEN 1:1–2:3)

[1]Some translations render Genesis 2:19 as "Now the LORD God *had* formed out of the ground all the wild animals" (NIV, emphasis added), but all admit that the Hebrew constructions used in the verse are not the usual means by which the past perfect is conveyed.

[2]Such a view is known and was widely circulated as early as the seventeenth century in the work of Isaac La Peyrère, discussed at length in Willem J. van Asselt, "Adam and Eve as Latecomers: The Pre-Adamite Speculations of Isaac La Peyrère (1596–16/6)," in *Out of Paradise. Eve and Adam and Their Interpreters*, ed. Bob Becking and Susan Hennecke (Sheffield: Sheffield Phoenix, 2010), pp. 90-107. La Peyrère saw evidence not only in Genesis 4 but in Romans 5:14 in Paul's reference to those "who did not sin by breaking a command [that is, not like the transgression of Adam], as did Adam."

[3]I am not persuaded by the current scholarly theories that accept the premise that Genesis 1 and 2 represent competing origins stories and that they are inherently contradictory. I believe that sense can be made of them as sequel accounts.

[4]This was also suggested by La Peyrère; see Asselt, "Adam and Eve as Late-comers," p. 96. La Peyrère saw Adam and Eve as the first Jews, a view that I am not inclined to accept.

[5]Discussion and examples can be found in Bernard F. Batto, "Paradise Re-examined," in *In the Beginning: Essays on Creation Motifs in the Ancient Near East and the Bible*, ed. Bernard F. Batto (Winona Lake, IN: Eisenbrauns,

2013), pp. 54-85, originally published in *The Biblical Canon in Comparative Perspective*, ed. K. Lawson Younger Jr., William W. Hallo and Bernard F. Batto, Scripture in Context 4 (Lewiston, NY: Mellen, 1991), pp. 33-66; and Gonzalo Rubio, "Time Before Time: Primeval Narratives in Early Mesopotamian Literature," in *Time and History in the Ancient Near East: Proceedings of the 56th Rencontre Assyriologique Internationale at Barcelona 26-30 July 2010*, ed. Lluís Feliu, G. del Olmo Lete, J. Llop and A. Millet Albà (Winona Lake, IN: Eisenbrauns, 2013), pp. 3-17.

[6]Translations from Rubio, "Time Before Time," p. 7.

[7]See Batto, "Paradise Reexamined," p. 70. Batto is interacting with Thorkild Jacobsen, "The Eridu Genesis," *Journal of Biblical Literature* 100 (1981): 513-29, translation on p. 516n7.

[8]Jean-Jacques Glassner, *Mesopotamian Chronicles*, Society of Biblical Literature Writings from the Ancient World 19 (Atlanta: Society of Biblical Literature, 2004), p. 147.

[9]Discussion of the motif can be found in F. A. M. Wiggermann, "Agriculture as Civilization: Sages, Farmers, and Barbarians," in *The Oxford Handbook of Cuneiform Culture*, ed. Karen Radner and Eleanor Robson (Oxford: Oxford University Press, 2011), pp. 663-89. See also Daniel DeWitt Lowery, *Toward a Poetics of Genesis 1–11: Reading Genesis 4:17-22 in Its Near Eastern Context* (Winona Lake, IN: Eisenbrauns, 2013), pp. 140-52.

PROPOSITION 8: "FORMING FROM DUST" AND "BUILDING FROM RIB" ARE ARCHETYPAL CLAIMS AND NOT CLAIMS OF MATERIAL ORIGINS

[1]Note that *de novo* is not the same as *ex nihilo*. The former could use ingredients but not any process that we view as "natural." It would reflect an origin of humans from that which is not human. *Ex nihilo* uses no ingredients—a claim that is never made for human origins in the Bible.

[2]Evolutionary theory offers an explanatory model for thinking about material continuity, but accepting material continuity would not necessarily be the same as accepting evolutionary theory as the explanatory model.

[3]Three times in Genesis 2, once in narrative (2 Kings 19:25), seven times in Psalms and the remaining thirty-one in the Prophets, with sixteen being in Isaiah 43–46.

[4]Think of the impact on our understanding of Genesis 2 if we read "God planned the human from the dust of the earth."

[5]Not being used in a material sense because the Israelites certainly did not

consider light to be material in nature.

[6]Also noted on p. 7 of Bob Becking, "Once in a Garden: Some Remarks on the Construction of the Identity of Woman and Man in Genesis 2–3," in *Out of Paradise: Eve and Adam and Their Interpreters*, ed. Bob Becking and Susan Hennecke (Sheffield: Sheffield Phoenix, 2010), pp. 1-13. Examples from the ancient Near Eastern literature will be documented and discussed in chap. 9.

[7]Mark E. Biddle, *Missing the Mark: Sin and Its Consequences in Biblical Theology* (Nashville: Abingdon, 2005), p. 11; Terence E. Fretheim, *God and the World in the Old Testament* (Nashville: Abingdon, 2005), p. 77; and I. Provan, *Seriously Dangerous Religion* (Waco: Baylor University Press, 2014), pp. 280-81. See also Terje Stordalen, *Echoes of Eden: Genesis 2–3 and Symbolism of the Eden Garden in Biblical Hebrew Literature* (Leuven: Peeters, 2000), p. 291. Stordalen also argues that not only has the tree of life been allowed, but Adam and Eve have been eating from it. He effectively refutes the grammatical case that some have made against this from Genesis 3:22 (*Echoes of Eden*, pp. 230-32). See also Peter C. Bouteneff, *Beginnings: Ancient Christian Readings of the Biblical Creation Narratives* (Grand Rapids: Baker, 2008), p. 6.

[8]This conclusion is actually represented early on in church history. The Antiochenes in the fourth century were already proposing two ways to think about mortality, referring to Adam's pre-fall condition as a "natural," not "punitive," mortality. For discussion see George Kalantzis, "*Creatio ex Terrae*: Immortality and the Fall in Theodore, Chrysostom, and Theodoret," *Studia Patristica* 67 (2013): 403-13.

[9]A difference without a distinction is that in Genesis 2:7 *yṣr* is a verbal form whereas here the root is used in one of its noun forms. Nouns and verbs from the same root do not automatically or always share the same semantic footprint, but in this case usage shows that they do.

[10]Some would see evidence in Job 15:7 that there is an early understanding that the first man was born, though I am not inclined to read this verse as making this sort of statement.

[11]One of the Amoraim, considered the second great generation of rabbinic interpreters, third to fourth century A.D.

[12]It is not always legitimate to examine nouns and their related verb forms together because they can take different directions of meaning, but in this case both remain in the same semantic range and can be evaluated as a single group.

[13]Michael V. Fox, *Proverbs 10–31*, Anchor Bible (New Haven, CT: Yale University Press, 2009), p. 513.

[14]M. Oeming, *"tardēmâ,"* *Theological Dictionary of the Old Testament,* ed. G. Johannes Botterweck, Helmer Ringgren and Heinz-Josef Fabry, trans. David E. Green and Douglas W. Stott (Grand Rapids: Eerdmans, 2004), 13:338.

[15]Andrew Louth, with Marco Conti, eds., *Genesis 1–11,* Ancient Christian Commentary on Scripture, Old Testament 1 (Downers Grove, IL: InterVarsity Press, 2001), pp. 66-67.

[16]This also makes much better sense of Matthew 19:5-6//Mark 10:7-8, 1 Corinthians 6:16-17 and especially Ephesians 5:31, where Paul is talking about being members of one body. Ontology is more central to this discussion than sex is. Genesis 2:24 may therefore have less to say about the institution of marriage and the nature of marriage than has been commonly thought.

PROPOSITION 9: FORMING OF HUMANS IN ANCIENT NEAR EASTERN ACCOUNTS IS ARCHETYPAL, SO IT WOULD NOT BE UNUSUAL FOR ISRAELITES TO THINK IN THOSE TERMS

[1]This chapter is adapted from material first published in John H. Walton, *Genesis 1 as Ancient Cosmology* (Winona Lake, IN: Eisenbrauns, 2011).

[2]*The Context of Scripture,* ed. William W. Hallo and K. Lawson Younger Jr. (Leiden: Brill, 2003), 1:157. This text is also called *Praise of the Pickax;* see Richard J. Clifford, *Creation Accounts in the Ancient Near East and in the Bible,* Catholic Biblical Quarterly Monograph Series (Washington, D.C.: Catholic Biblical Association, 1994), p. 31.

[3]Hallo and Younger, *Context of Scripture,* 1:511.

[4]Clifford, *Creation Accounts,* pp. 29-30.

[5]W. G. Lambert, *Babylonian Creation Myths* (Winona Lake, IN: Eisenbrauns, 2013), pp. 330-45; Hallo and Younger, *Context of Scripture,* 1:159.

[6]The reading proposed by Lambert, *Babylonian Creation Myths,* p. 505. This remains a controversial issue.

[7]Lambert, *Babylonian Creation Myths,* pp. 350-60; Clifford, *Creation Accounts,* pp. 50-51. Benjamin R. Foster, *Before the Muses: An Anthology of Akkadian Literature,* 3rd ed. (Bethesda, MD: CDL Press, 2005), pp. 491-93, merges the Sumerian and Akkadian versions into a single translation.

[8]See discussion in Lambert, *Babylonian Creation Myths,* p. 511.

[9]Ibid., pp. 366-75.

[10]See the translation and notes of Foster, *Before the Muses,* pp. 236-37.

[11]Hallo and Younger, *Context of Scripture,* 1:130. For discussion of various details, see Tzvi Abusch, "Ghost and God: Some Observations on a Babylonian

Understanding of Human Nature," in *Self, Soul, and Body in Religious Experience,* ed. Albert I. Baumgarten, Jan Assmann and Guy G. Stroumsa (Leiden: Brill, 1998), pp. 363-83; and Bernard F. Batto, "Creation Theology in Genesis," in *Creation in the Biblical Traditions,* ed. Richard J. Clifford and John J. Collins, Catholic Biblical Quarterly Monograph Series (Washington, D.C.: Catholic Biblical Association, 1992). In *Atraḫasis,* both flesh and blood are used, whereas in *Enuma Elish* and *KAR 4,* only the blood is mentioned. Only in *Atraḫasis* is a combination of common and divine materials clearly used. There is no indication in *KAR 4* that the two slain deities are rebels. The bilingual version of *Enki and Ninmaḫ* suggests that some kind of mixture may also occur there. See W. G. Lambert, "The Relationship of Sumerian and Babylonian Myth as Seen in Accounts of Creation," in *La Circulation des biens, des personnes et des idées dans le Proche-Orient ancien: Actes de la XXXVIIe Rencontre assyriologique internationale, Paris, 8-10 juillet 1991,* ed. Dominique Charpin and Francis Joannès (Paris: Editions Recherche sur la civilisations, 1992), pp. 129-35.

[12]The Assyrian version is explicit about the number.

[13]Lambert, *Babylonian Creation Myths;* Hallo and Younger, *Context of Scripture,* 1:111.

[14]Clifford, *Creation Accounts,* pp. 69-71.

[15]James P. Allen, *Genesis in Egypt: The Philosophy of Ancient Egyptian Creation Accounts,* Yale Egyptological Studies (New Haven, CT: Yale University Press, 1988); Ewa Wasilewska, *Creation Stories of the Middle East* (London: Jessica Kingsley, 2000); and James K. Hoffmeier, "Some Thoughts on Genesis 1 and 2 and Egyptian Cosmology," *Journal of the Ancient Near Eastern Society* 15 (1983): 29-39.

[16]Hallo and Younger, *Context of Scripture,* 1:8.

[17]Ibid., 1:17; see also 1:9. This source of the life of human beings is also referred to in passing in spell 80.

[18]Ibid., 1:35.

[19]Translation from Leonard H. Lesko, "Ancient Egyptian Cosmogonies and Cosmology," in *Religion in Ancient Egypt: God, Myths, and Personal Practice,* ed. Byron E. Shafer (Ithaca, NY: Cornell University Press, 1991), p. 103.

[20]Hoffmeier, "Some Thoughts on Genesis 1 and 2," p. 37; P. O'Rourke, "Khnum," in *Oxford Encyclopedia of Ancient Egypt,* ed. Donald B. Redford (Oxford University Press, 2001), 2:231; Siegfried Morenz, *Egyptian Religion,* trans. Ann E. Keep (Ithaca, NY: Cornell University Press, 1973), pp. 183-84; and

Ronald Simkins, *Creator and Creation: Nature in the Worldview of Ancient Israel* (Peabody, MA: Hendrickson, 1994), p. 70. See also a reference to similar ingredients (clay and straw) in *Amenemope* 25:13-14. Translation found in Lichtheim, *Ancient Egyptian Literature* (Berkeley: University of Califormia Press, 1976), 2:160.

[21]In Atraḫasis 1.64-66, the junior gods burn their tools. *COS* 1.130 (p.450).

[22]For instance, in *KAR* 4.

[23]See Jan Assmann, *The Search for God in Ancient Egypt*, trans. David Lorton (Ithaca, NY: Cornell University Press, 2001), pp. 3-6; he cites a hymn to Re that portrays the king as representing the gods by judging humankind and as representing humans by satisfying the gods. See the additional texts that Assmann refers to on pp. 174-77 (*Coffin Texts* spell 1130).

[24]The most comprehensive analysis was carried out by Edward Mason Curtis, "Man as the Image of God in Genesis in Light of Ancient Near Eastern Parallels" (PhD diss. [supervised by Jeffrey H. Tigay], University of Pennsylvania, 1984), ProQuest AAI8422896. Other important studies include W. Randall Garr, *In His Own Image and Likeness*, Culture and History of the Ancient Near East 15 (Leiden: Brill, 2003); and Zainab Bahrani, *The Graven Image: Representation in Babylonia and Assyria* (Philadelphia: University of Pennsylvania Press, 2003). See also Walton, *Genesis 1 as Ancient Cosmology*, pp. 78-85.

[25]Assmann, *Search for God*, p. 173.

[26]Karel van der Toorn, *Family Religion in Babylonia, Syria and Israel: Continuity and Changes in the Forms of Religious Life* (Leiden: Brill, 1996), p. 96; cf. Clifford, *Creation Accounts*, pp. 8-9.

Proposition 11: Though Some of the Biblical Interest in Adam and Eve Is Archetypal, They Are Real People Who Existed in a Real Past

[1]John W. Hilber, *Cultic Prophecy in the Psalms*, Beiheft zur Zeitschrift für die alttestamentliche Wissenschaft 352 (Berlin: Walter de Gruyter, 2005), pp. 76-88.

[2]The biblical text makes it clear that David's sons served as priests (2 Sam 8:18), though translations often obscure this point. Although the tribe of Levi had been exclusively assigned all the duties related to the sanctuary, there is no text that prohibits non-Levites from performing other priestly tasks. It is just that as time went on, priestly tasks not related to the sanctuary were gradually

eliminated (see 2 Kings 23:8). The existence of priestly duties carried out within the family context is indicated in post-Sinai contexts (Judg 6:24-26; 13:19; 1 Sam 20:29), and in the general culture of the ancient Near East the oldest son frequently had priestly duties in the veneration of ancestors. Saul had been reprimanded for his involvement in a priestly function, but that may have been because it violated the charter (1 Sam 10:25) that delineated his role with respect to Samuel's role. David's priestly prerogatives may have been attached to the traditional roles in Jerusalem. The existence of such a royal priestly tradition is recognized in David's participation in the ceremony of installing the ark (2 Sam 6:14).

[3]*Assumption of Moses* 6:1; Josephus, *Antiquities* 16.163.

[4]Paul Kobelski, *Melchizedek and Melchireša*, Catholic Biblical Quarterly Monograph Series 10 (Washington, D.C.: Catholic Biblical Association, 1981); and C. Marvin Pate, *Communities of the Last Days: The Dead Sea Scrolls and the New Testament* (Downers Grove, IL: InterVarsity Press, 2000), pp. 121, 209.

[5]Richard Longenecker, "The Melchizedek Argument of Hebrews: A Study in the Development and Circumstantial Expression of the New Testament Thought," in *Unity and Diversity in New Testament Theology: Essays in Honor of George E. Ladd*, ed. Robert A. Guelich (Grand Rapids: Eerdmans, 1978), pp. 161-85.

[6]The paragraphs about the Jewish traditions are adapted from John H. Walton, *Genesis*, NIV Application Commentary (Grand Rapids: Zondervan, 2001), pp. 426-27.

[7]John H. Walton, "Genealogies," in *Dictionary of Old Testament: Historical Books*, ed. Bill T. Arnold and Hugh G. M. Williamson (Downers Grove, IL: InterVarsity Press, 2005), pp. 309-16; Mark W. Chavalas, "Genealogical History as 'Charter': A Study of Old Babylonian Period Historiography and the Old Testament," in *Faith, Tradition and History: Old Testament Historiography in Its Near Eastern Context*, ed. A. R. Millard, James K. Hoffmeier and David W. Baker (Winona Lake, IN: Eisenbrauns, 1994), pp. 103-28.

[8]For example, a document known as the *Genealogy of the Hammurabi Dynasty* has the purpose of providing a list of the spirits of the dead for a memorial service that will recognize the ancestors and thereby counteract any threat they may present (Chavalas, "Genealogical History as 'Charter,'" p. 121).

[9]Genesis and 1 Chronicles are descending lists (starting at the beginning and moving forward through time). Luke is ascending (starting with the present and moving backward in time).

[10]In some of the antediluvian king lists we find the name Dumuzi, a character

later known as a god. There is still discussion, however, regarding whether
he began as a human king. Even if he did not, however, this is a king list, not
a genealogy and therefore not determinative.

[11]In a Seleucid period text (second century B.C.) there is a list of scholars that
begins with legendary/mythological beings known as the *apkallu*. But this
is not a genealogy. See Alan Lenzi, *Secrecy and the Gods: Secret Knowledge
in Ancient Mesopotamia and Biblical Israel*, State Archives of Assyria Studies
19 (Helsinki: Neo-Assyrian Text Corpus Project, 2008), pp. 106-9.

[12]Toponyms, names that pertain to places and, by extension, the people
groups who live there, are frequent in the Table of Nations in Genesis 10 as
well as in the *Genealogy of the Hammurabi Dynasty*.

[13]At the same time, there are lists that start with gods (as Gen 5 also does).
Some Egyptologists believe that the Turin Canon starts with gods and moves
to demigods before it begins discussing kings. See discussion in Dexter E.
Callender Jr., *Adam in Myth and History: Ancient Israelite Perspectives on the
Primal Human*, Harvard Semitic Studies 48 (Winona Lake, IN: Eisenbrauns,
2000), pp. 33-34. But it should be noted that this is a king list rather than a
genealogy.

Proposition 12: Adam Is Assigned as Priest in Sacred Space, with Eve to Help

[1]For further discussion see John H. Walton, *Genesis*, NIV Application Commentary (Grand Rapids: Zondervan, 2001), pp. 180-83.

[2]For full discussion see ibid., pp. 172-74, 185-87, from which the discussion
here is adapted.

[3]This direction is also chosen by commentators Gordon J. Wenham, *Genesis
1–15*, Word Biblical Commentary 1 (Waco, TX: Word, 1987), p. 67; and John
Sailhamer, *Genesis Unbound: A Provocative New Look at the Creation Account*
(Colorado Springs, CO: Dawson Media, 1996), p. 45. Dexter E. Callender Jr.,
*Adam in Myth and History: Ancient Israelite Perspectives on the Primal
Human*, Harvard Semitic Studies 48 (Winona Lake, IN: Eisenbrauns, 2000),
pp. 59-65, favors the royal role based on the imagery in Mesopotamia of the
king as gardener, but it must be recalled that the king also had priestly functions. Callender also makes the observation that the purpose for these activities is for the garden's sake, not for the humans' own sustenance (p. 55).

[4]This implies the existence of non-order such as that represented by chaos
creatures.

[5]J. Martin Plumley, "The Cosmology of Ancient Egypt," in *Ancient Cosmologies,* ed. Carmen Blacker and Michael Loewe (London: Allen & Unwin, 1975), p. 36.

[6]For an understanding of Israelite rituals in this light, see Frank H. Gorman Jr., *The Ideology of Ritual: Space, Time, and Status in the Priestly Theology,* Journal for the Study of the Old Testament: Supplement 91 (Sheffield: JSOT Press, 1990), pp. 28-29.

[7]Eric Hornung, *Conceptions of God in Ancient Egypt: The One and the Many,* trans. John Baines (Ithaca, NY: Cornell University Press, 1982), p. 183.

[8]See James C. VanderKam, "Adam's Incense Offering (*Jubilees* 3:27)," in *Meghillot: Studies in the Dead Sea Scrolls V–VI: A Festschrift for Devorah Dimant,* ed. Moshe Bar-Asher and Emanuel Tov (Jerusalem: Bialik Institute, 2007), pp. 141-56.

[9]Gary A. Anderson, *The Genesis of Perfection: Adam and Eve in Jewish and Christian Interpretation* (Louisville, KY: Westminster John Knox, 2001), p. 122.

[10]A remarkable Hittite document from the mid-second millennium B.C. contains instructions for priests and other temple personnel. This document offers detailed information about the roles of priests that includes those here delineated. Jared L. Miller, *Royal Hittite Instructions and Related Administrative Texts,* Society of Biblical Literature Writings from the Ancient World 31 (Atlanta: Society of Biblical Literature, 2013), pp. 244-65.

[11]See pp. 105-9.

[12]Notice similarly that in Exodus 18:14 Jethro observes that it is not good for Moses to be alone in judging the cases that the people bring. It is too big a job for one person. There a whole group is selected and trained. Here, at this stage, only one additional representative is appointed.

[13]Shamhat is likely a cult prostitute according to A. R. George, *The Babylonian Gilgamesh Epic: Introduction, Critical Edition and Cuneiform Texts* (Oxford: Oxford University Press, 2003), 1:148. The text only identifies her as a prostitute *par excellence,* but she takes Enkidu back to the shrine of Ishtar, presumably her home.

[14]For discussion of the role of women in sacred space, see Phyllis Bird, "The Place of Women in the Israelite Cultus," in *Ancient Israelite Religion: Essays in Honor of Frank Moore Cross,* ed. Patrick D. Miller Jr., Paul D. Hanson and S. Dean McBride (Philadelphia: Fortress, 1987), pp. 397-419, esp. the summary on pp. 405-8.

[15]Hennie J. Marsman, *Women in Ugarit and Israel: Their Social and Religious Position in the Context of the Ancient Near East* (Leiden: Brill, 2003), pp. 490-91.

These roles nearly disappeared after the Old Babylonian period (first half of the second millennium B.C.). The same diminishing of women in priestly roles is evident in the same period in Egypt (Middle Kingdom). Scholars propose that in Egypt the role of women priestesses declined with the professionalization of the priesthood.

[16]Ibid., pp. 544-47.

[17]Notice that this designation occurs *before* permanent sacred space is established, indicating that ritual performance is not the main role of priests.

[18]I would contend that this also represents the main task of the Aaronid and Levitical priests in the tabernacle and temple. That is *how* they serve and keep sacred space just as Adam and Eve do.

[19]This uses the Akkadian cognate to Hebrew *lqḥ, leqû.*

[20]A. R. George, *The Babylonian Gilgamesh Epic: Introduction, Critical Edition and Cuneiform Texts* (Oxford: Oxford University Press, 2003), 1:716-17.

[21]Tablet X, lines 76-90.

[22]Uses the causative stem of the verb that is cognate with the Hebrew verb *yšb.*

[23]The identity of two of the rivers of Eden as the Tigris and Euphrates would not detract from this view. Significant bodies of water are part of cosmic space.

[24]George, *Babylonian Gilgamesh Epic*, 1:152.

PROPOSITION 13: THE GARDEN IS AN ANCIENT NEAR EASTERN MOTIF FOR SACRED SPACE, AND THE TREES INDICATE GOD AS THE SOURCE OF LIFE AND WISDOM

[1]A country's flag is a symbol, but it is also something real.

[2]This against Terje Stordalen, *Echoes of Eden: Genesis 2–3 and Symbolism of the Eden Garden in Biblical Hebrew Literature* (Leuven: Peeters, 2000), p. 298, who explicitly makes the point that Yahweh does not dwell in the garden. On a fine point, I would agree. I have elsewhere made the point that the garden is not Eden but adjoins Eden. Eden is where the presence of God is, and, as is typically the case, that sacred space of divine presence has a garden adjacent to it. See John H. Walton, *Genesis*, NIV Application Commentary (Grand Rapids: Zondervan, 2001), pp. 167-68.

[3]Note particularly the construction of a garden area in Nineveh by Sennacherib. See full discussion and the proposal that this is actually the famous "hanging gardens of Babylon" in Stephanie Dalley, *The Mystery of the Hanging Garden of Babylon: An Elusive World Wonder Traced* (Oxford: Oxford University Press, 2013).

[4]That there could be a time lapse between designating the cosmos as sacred space (Gen 1) and actually establishing the terrestrial center and putting people there (Gen 2) would be illustrated by the time lapse that exists between God designating Canaan as the covenant land grant to Abraham and the actual inhabitation of that land centuries later at the time of Joshua.

[5]Carol L. Meyers, *The Tabernacle Menorah: A Synthetic Study of a Symbol from the Biblical Cult*, American Schools of Oriental Research Dissertation 2 (Missoula, MT: Scholars Press, 1976); Detlef Jericke, "Königsgarten und Gottes Garten: Aspekte der Königsideologie in Genesis 2 und 3," in *Exegese vor Ort: Festschrift für Peter Welten*, ed. Christl Maier, Rüdiger Liwak and Klaus-Peter Jörns (Leipzig: Evangelische Verlagsanstalt, 2001), pp. 161-76, draws out the similarities between the Garden of Eden and the royal gardens of the ancient Near East and considers them cosmic gardens (pp. 172-74); Lawrence E. Stager, "Jerusalem as Eden," *Biblical Archaeology Review* 26, no. 3 (2000): 41, lists biblical occurrences of waters flowing from the temple; Manfred Dietrich, "Das biblische Paradies und der babylonische Tempelgarten: Überlegungen zur Lage des Gartens Eden," in *Das biblische Weltbild und seine altorientalischen Kontexte*, ed. Bernd Janowski and Beate Ego (Tübingen: Mohr Siebeck, 2001), pp. 281-323, esp. pp. 290-93; Elizabeth Bloch-Smith, "Solomon's Temple: The Politics of Ritual Space," in *Sacred Time, Sacred Place: Archaeology and the Religion of Israel*, ed. Barry M. Gittlen (Winona Lake, IN: Eisenbrauns, 2002), pp. 83-94; Victor Hurowitz, "Yhwh's Exalted House—Aspects of the Design and Symbolism of Solomon's Temple," in *Temple and Worship in Biblical Israel: Proceedings of the Oxford Old Testament Seminar*, ed. John Day (New York; London: Continuum; T & T Clark, 2005), pp. 63-110; Gordon J. Wenham, "Sanctuary Symbolism in the Garden of Eden Story," in *"I Studied Inscriptions from Before the Flood": Ancient Near Eastern, Literary, and Linguistic Approaches to Genesis 1–11*, ed. Richard S. Hess and David Toshio Tsumura, Sources for Biblical and Theological Study 4 (Winona Lake, IN: Eisenbrauns, 1994), pp. 399-404, reprinted from *Proceedings of the Ninth World Congress of Jewish Studies, Division A: The Period of the Bible* (Jerusalem: World Union of Jewish Studies, 1986), pp. 19-25; and Moshe Weinfeld, "Gen. 7:11, 8:1-2 Against the Background of Ancient Near Eastern Tradition," *Die Welt des Orients* 9 (1978): 242-48.

[6]Bloch-Smith, "Solomon's Temple," p. 88.

[7]Hurowitz, "Yhwh's Exalted House," p. 87.

[8]It should be noted that there are many other points on which *Jubilees* offers a very different interpretation than that presented in this book, so I am not sug-

gesting that if an interpretation is found in *Jubilees* it is right. This simply shows that the interpretation of Eden as sacred space is an ancient idea, not a modern one.

[9]Gary A. Anderson, *The Genesis of Perfection: Adam and Eve in Jewish and Christian Imagination* (Louisville, KY: Westminster John Knox, 2001), pp. 55-58, 79-80. For example, Ephrem considered the tree of wisdom to be like the veil of the temple and the tree of life to be the holy of holies. See Ephrem the Syrian, *Hymns on Paradise,* intro. and trans. Sebastian Brock (Crestwood, NY: St. Vladimir's Seminary Press, 1990), p. 57 (Paradise Hymn 3.13).

[10]See Kathryn L. Gleason, "Gardens," in *Oxford Encyclopedia of Archaeology in the Near East,* ed. Eric M. Meyers (New York: Oxford University Press, 1997), 2:383; Renate Germer, "Gardens," in *Oxford Encyclopedia of Ancient Egypt,* ed. Donald B. Redford (Oxford: Oxford University Press, 2001), 2:5; and Othmar Keel, *The Symbolism of the Biblical World: Ancient Near Eastern Iconography and the Book of Psalms,* trans. Timothy J. Hallett (New York: Seabury, 1978), p. 135. It should be noted that temples and palaces often shared adjoining space (Elizabeth Bloch-Smith, "'Who Is the King of Glory?': Solomon's Temple and Its Symbolism," in *Scripture and Other Artifacts: Essays on the Bible and Archaeology in Honor of Philip J. King,* ed. Michael D. Coogan, J. Cheryl Exum and Lawrence E. Stager [Louisville, KY: Westminster John Knox, 1994], p. 26).

[11]Stager, "Jerusalem as Eden," p. 43.

[12]Alix Wilkinson, "Symbolism and Design in Ancient Egyptian Gardens," *Garden History* 22 (1994): 1-17.

[13]See a translation on the Oxford website for Sumerian literature at http://etcsl.orinst.ox.ac.uk/cgi-bin/etcsl.cgi?text=t.1.1.1#. For analysis of this and other relevant texts, see Bernard F. Batto, "Paradise Reexamined," in *In the Beginning: Essays on Creation Motifs in the Ancient Near East and the Bible,* ed. Bernard F. Batto (Winona Lake, IN: Eisenbrauns, 2013), pp. 54-85, originally published in *The Biblical Canon in Comparative Perspective,* ed. K. Lawson Younger Jr., William W. Hallo and Bernard F. Batto, Scripture in Context 4 (Lewiston, NY: Mellen, 1991), pp. 33-66.

[14]Stordalen, *Echoes of Eden,* pp. 144-46.

[15]See Batto, "Paradise Reexamined," pp. 59-62.

[16]Stordalen, *Echoes of Eden,* pp. 153-55.

[17]For defense of this equation see Walton, *Genesis,* pp. 170-72.

[18]The primary manuscript of this tale was found at Amarna (therefore fourteenth century B.C.). This means that the tale was known in the region in the

Late Bronze period—the period of Israel's entry into the land. The earliest known manuscript evidence is in Sumerian and dates to the Old Babylonian period. Full listing of the extant manuscripts is found in Shlomo Izre'el, *Adapa and the South Wind: Language Has the Power of Life and Death* (Winona Lake, IN: Eisenbrauns, 2001), pp. 5-7. Translation is in *The Context of Scripture*, ed. William W. Hallo and K. Lawson Younger Jr. (Leiden: Brill, 2003) vol. 1, p. 449.

[19]Izre'el indicates that even though Adapa is presented in the text as a "single human being," he "definitely symbolizes humanity or, rather, the essence of being human" (*Adapa*, pp. 120-23).

[20]Adapa B68; Izre'el, *Adapa*, pp. 20-21. For discussion see Tryggve N. D. Mettinger, *The Eden Narrative: A Literary and Religio-historical Study of Genesis 2–3* (Winona Lake, IN: Eisenbrauns, 2007), pp. 104-7.

[21]Differences include plot, setting and characters. Though food is included in both, they are very different sorts of food. There is no tempter or temptation. For more detailed discussion of these, see Mettinger, *Eden Narrative*, p. 108.

[22]Translation of the Sumerian in CT 16.46 by Daniel Bodi, used with permission.

[23]Known in Akkadian as the *kiškanu* tree. See discussion in Ake W. Sjöberg, "Eve and the Chameleon," in *In the Shelter of Elyon: Essays on Ancient Palestinian Life and Literature*, ed. W. Boyd Barrick and John R. Spencer, Journal for the Study of the Old Testament Supplement 31 (Sheffield: JSOT Press, 1984), pp. 217-25; and Mariana Giovino, *The Assyrian Sacred Tree: A History of Interpretations*, Orbis biblicus et orientalis 230 (Göttingen: Vandenhoeck & Ruprecht, 2007), pp. 12-20, 197-201.

[24]As a cosmological feature, one thinks also of the "primeval hillock" represented in all Egyptian temples as the mound that first emerged from the waters.

[25]This tree has prominence throughout the ancient Near East in the Old Testament period, from an early-second-millennium Sumerian epic, *Lugalbanda and Anzud*, to the later mid-first-millennium *Story of Erra and Ishum* (*meshu* tree). In the *Gilgamesh Epic* it is known as the *ḫuluppu* tree, and it is featured prominently in neo-Assyrian palace reliefs. For thorough discussion (though with idiosyncratic interpretation), see Simo Parpola, "The Assyrian Tree of Life: Tracing the Origins of Jewish Monotheism and Greek Philosophy," *Journal of Near Eastern Studies* 52 (1993): 161-208.

[26]See discussion in Daniel Bodi, "Ezekiel," in *Zondervan Illustrated Bible Backgrounds Commentary: Old Testament*, ed. John H. Walton (Grand Rapids: Zondervan, 2009), 4:472-73; Matthias Henze, *The Madness of Nebuchadnezzar: The Ancient Near Eastern Origins & Early History of Interpretation*

of Daniel 4 (Leiden: Brill, 1999), pp. 77-80; and Daniel I. Block, *The Book of Ezekiel, Chapters 25–48* (Grand Rapids: Eerdmans, 1998), pp. 187-89.

[27]Gilgamesh tablet XI, lines 281-307. See n. 20 in previous chapter; see also A. R. George, *The Babylonian Gilgamesh Epic: Introduction, Critical Edition and Cuneiform Texts* (Oxford: Oxford University Press, 2003), 1:721-23. See also his discussion concerning the realities of Dilmun (= Bahrain), 1:524. Note there also his consideration that the text of *Gilgamesh* actually refers to a particular coral that has the appearance of a plant and is fabled to have medicinal value.

[28]Herman L. J. Vanstiphout, *Epics of Sumerian Kings: The Matter of Aratta,* Society of Biblical Literature Writings from the Ancient World 20 (Atlanta: Society of Biblical Literature, 2003), p. 119.

[29]Another example is a plant of birth in the tale of Etana, a plant that will allow Etana's barren wife to bear children.

[30]By using this language I am not abandoning the idea that God is the source, merely recognizing that literary shaping is in the realm of the human aspects of Scripture.

[31]Giovino, *Assyrian Sacred Tree.*

[32]Parpola, "Assyrian Tree of Life," p. 161.

[33]Giovino, however, is not convinced it is a real tree at all but thinks it could be a cult object representing a tree (*Assyrian Sacred Tree,* conclusions on p. 201).

[34]Othmar Keel and Christoph Uehlinger, *Gods, Goddesses, and Images of God in Ancient Israel,* trans. Thomas H. Trapp (Minneapolis: Augsburg Fortress, 1998).

[35]Barbara Nevling Porter, *Trees, Kings, and Politics: Studies in Assyrian Iconography,* Orbis biblicus et orientalis 197 (Göttingen: Vandenhoeck & Ruprecht, 2003), pp. 11-20. Giovino, *Assyrian Sacred Trees,* p. 104, in contrast, is reticent since the palm flower clusters are too large to be represented as they are on the reliefs.

[36]Stordalen, *Echoes of Eden,* p. 290. In fig. 14 on p. 490 he also shows an interesting Assyrian seal that shows a divine figure with a drawn bow protecting a tree from a horned serpent that is reared up.

[37]Parpola, "Assyrian Tree of Life," p. 173.

[38]Some have favored the term *sacramental*; see Stordalen, *Echoes of Eden,* pp. 291-92.

[39]For the location of Dilmun, see George, *Babylonian Gilgamesh Epic,* vol. 1, pp. 519-20; he says that "mouth of the rivers" refers to any place where river

waters rise to the surface from the Apsu (p. 521). If this is true, the mouth of the waters is equivalent to Apsu, and the phrase refers to the domain of the god Ea. The Springs of Bahrain were considered the mouth of the rivers in antiquity.

[40]Stordalen argues for peripheral (*Echoes of Eden*, pp. 297-99). See also Umberto Cassuto, *Commentary on the Book of Genesis, Part 1: From Adam to Noah*, trans. Israel Abrahams (Jerusalem: Magnes, 1961), p. 118, where he argues that the garden is not situated in the world. Ephrem, along with Gregory of Nyssa, contended that the garden was outside time and space. He viewed the garden as a conical canopy to the earth with the underside of the cone being the solid sky of the cosmos (Ephrem the Syrian, *Hymns on Paradise*, p. 54).

[41]Ziony Zevit, *What Really Happened in the Garden of Eden?* (New Haven, CT: Yale University Press, 2013), pp. 108-11.

PROPOSITION 14: THE SERPENT WOULD HAVE BEEN VIEWED AS A CHAOS CREATURE FROM THE NON-ORDERED REALM, PROMOTING DISORDER

[1]Thorkild Jacobsen, "Mesopotamian Gods and Pantheons," in *Toward the Image of Tammuz and Other Essays on Mesopotamian History and Culture*, ed. William L. Moran (Cambridge, MA: Harvard University Press, 1971), p. 24; Jeremy Black and Anthony Green, *Gods, Demons and Symbols of Ancient Mesopotamia* (Austin: University of Texas Press, 1992), p. 139; see also W. G. Lambert, "Trees, Snakes and Gods in Ancient Syria and Anatolia," *Bulletin of the School of Oriental and African Studies* 48 (1985): 435-51.

[2]Nicole B. Hansen, "Snakes," in *Oxford Encyclopedia of Ancient Egypt*, ed. Donald B. Redford (Oxford: Oxford University Press, 2001), 3:297.

[3]John H. Walton, "Genesis," in *The Zondervan Illustrated Bible Backgrounds Commentary: Old Testament* (Grand Rapids: Zondervan, 2009), pp. 35-36.

[4]All Pyramid Text citations refer to utterance numbers and are taken from Raymond O. Faulkner, *The Ancient Egyptian Pyramid Texts* (Oxford: Oxford University Press, 1969).

[5]*Bašmu* is sometimes portrayed as having two front legs (Joan Goodnick Westenholz, *Dragons, Monsters and Fabulous Beasts* [Jerusalem: Bible Lands Museum, 2004], p. 190). See a picture of the seal of Gudea showing Ningishzida introducing him to Enki, in Black and Green, *Gods, Demons and Symbols*, p. 139.

[6]"May your poison fangs be in the earth, your ribs in the hole" (no. 230); "spittle in the dust" (no. 237).

[7]*The Context of Scripture,* ed. William W. Hallo and K. Lawson Younger Jr. (Leiden: Brill, 2003), 1:108 (line 8). This is a stock description also found in the *Gilgamesh Epic* and *Nergal and Ereshkigal.*

[8]Ancient Egyptian texts list thirty-seven types of snakes along with the symptoms of bites and believed remedies. See Hansen, "Snakes," 3:296. Cf. Heinz-Josef Fabry, "*nahaš*," *Theological Dictionary of the Old Testament* (Grand Rapids, Eerdmans, 1998), 9:359.

[9]Faulkner, *Ancient Egyptian Pyramid Texts.*

[10]Full discussion in James H. Charlesworth, *The Good and Evil Serpent: How a Universal Symbol Became Christianized* (New Haven, CT: Yale University Press, 2010).

[11]See full discussion in John H. Walton, *Job,* NIV Application Commentary (Grand Rapids: Zondervan, 2012), pp. 74-86.

[12]Michael V. Fox, *Proverbs 1-9,* Anchor Bible (New Haven, CT: Yale University Press, 2000), pp. 35-36. Note that the Greek translation of the Septuagint used a Greek term that means "most intelligent" (*phronimōtatos*).

[13]Ziony Zevit, *What Really Happened in the Garden of Eden?* (New Haven, CT: Yale University Press, 2013), p. 163.

[14]Ibid.

[15]In the Bible such composite creatures are identified as cherubim and seraphim, though they are not chaos creatures per se. Chaos creatures would be ones such as Leviathan and Rahab. For extensive treatment of such creatures, see Westenholz, *Dragons, Monsters and Fabulous Beasts.*

[16]For discussion of these see John H. Walton, "Demons in Mesopotamia and Israel: Exploring the Category of Non-Divine but Supernatural Entities," in *Windows to the Ancient World of the Hebrew Bible: Essays in Honor of Samuel Greengus,* ed. Bill T. Arnold, Nancy Erickson and John H. Walton (Winona Lake, IN: Eisenbrauns, 2014), pp. 229-46.

[17]Charlesworth, *Good and Evil Serpent,* p. 438; note, however, that he rejects the idea that the serpent in Genesis 3 should be considered a chaos creature, p. 294.

[18]It is interesting that many interpreters insist that since Revelation identifies the serpent as Satan that we have to accept that as biblical truth (not just an associative picture); yet I have encountered few who view the serpent as a dragon based on the information from the same verses in Revelation (though Augustine did view the serpent that way in his *Sermon*

36. Augustine, *Sermons*, trans. Edmund Hill, The Works of Saint Augustine: A Translation for the 21st Century III/2 [Brooklyn, NY: New City Press, 1990], p. 281).

[19]This would also offer a ready explanation of the serpent speaking without leading to an anatomical analysis of the larynxes of serpent species.

[20]Richard E. Averbeck, "Ancient Near Eastern Mythography as It Relates to Historiography in the Hebrew Bible: Genesis 3 and the Cosmic Battle," in *The Future of Biblical Archaeology: Reassessing Methodologies and Assumptions*, ed James Karl Hoffmeier and Alan R. Millard (Grand Rapids: Eerdmans, 2004), pp. 328-56, esp. 352-53.

[21]See grammatical, syntactical discussion in John H. Walton, *Genesis*, NIV Application Commentary (Grand Rapids: Zondervan, 2001), pp. 204-5.

[22]Zevit, *What Really Happened in the Garden of Eden?*, pp. 202-3.

[23]See this suggestion in Ronald Veenker, "Do Deities Deceive?," in *Windows to the Ancient World of the Hebrew Bible: Essays in Honor of Samuel Greengus*, ed. Bill T. Arnold, Nancy Erickson and John H. Walton (Winona Lake, IN: Eisenbrauns, 2014), pp. 201-14.

[24]Walton, *Genesis*, pp. 174-75; Zevit, *What Really Happened in the Garden of Eden?*, pp. 124-26.

[25]For further discussion of the anachronism embedded in some of our genre labels, see John H. Walton and D. Brent Sandy, *Lost World of Scripture: Ancient Literary Culture and Biblical Authority* (Downers Grove, IL: InterVarsity Press, 2013), pp. 199-215.

[26]This use of imagination and imagery is even evident in John 1 as Jesus is described as the *logos*, "word." John 1 is not mythological in genre, nor is Jesus a character of mythology. But the form of thinking being expressed is dependent on image.

[27]Not to be confused with the term that exists already as a technical description of a movement in modern poetry from the early twentieth century.

[28]Lutherans might even say that the trees are sacramental, representing mystical realities.

[29]Those familiar with anthropology will recognize this as an attempt to think in emic categories (indigenous criteria) rather than etic ones (our categories superimposed on another culture).

[30]Nicolas Wyatt, "The Mythic Mind," in *The Mythic Mind: Essays on Cosmology and Religion in Ugaritic and Old Testament Literature* (London: Equinox, 2005), p. 160, refers to this as the "narrative-paradigmatic polarity."

PROPOSITION 15: ADAM AND EVE CHOSE TO MAKE THEMSELVES THE CENTER OF ORDER AND SOURCE OF WISDOM, THEREBY ADMITTING DISORDER INTO THE COSMOS

[1]Mark E. Biddle, *Missing the Mark: Sin and Its Consequences in Biblical Theology* (Nashville: Abingdon, 2005), pp. vii-viii.

[2]Gary A. Anderson, *Sin: A History* (New Haven, CT: Yale University Press, 2009).

[3]Ibid., pp. 27-28.

[4]See discussion in Alex Luc, "חטא (ḥṭʾ)," in *New International Dictionary of Old Testament Theology and Exegesis*, ed. Willem A. VanGemeren (Grand Rapids: Zondervan, 1997), 2:87-93.

[5]This latter, however, uses the Hiphil form of the verb, where other occurrences indicate misdirection. It is the Qal forms that mean "to sin."

[6]So in English, *awful* does not mean "inspiring," and *sinister* does not mean "left-handed."

[7]Similar observations could be made about the Greek terminology.

[8]See for example Mark J. Boda, *A Severe Mercy: Sin and Its Remedy in the Old Testament* (Winona Lake, IN: Eisenbrauns, 2009), p. 515; Luc, "חטא (ḥṭʾ)," p. 89. This concept is represented in the later development of the theological concept of "spiritual death" first introduced by Origen (though there is no textual reason to think that the punishment was spiritual death rather than physical death).

[9]Biddle, *Missing the Mark,* pp. xii-xiii.

[10]Salvation is certainly an important trajectory, but that can be understood as what God has done to vouchsafe our access to his presence. Relationship in his presence is the objective; salvation is the instrument by which it is achieved.

[11]For that matter, neither does the New Testament. As Ziony Zevit points out, the prophets had ample opportunity to relate Israel's sin to the sin in the garden, and they never do so (*What Really Happened in the Garden of Eden?* [New Haven, CT: Yale University Press, 2013], pp. 19-22). When Isaiah 43:27 makes reference to Israel's first father who sinned, it is talking about Jacob, not Adam.

[12]Translation from James H. Charlesworth, *The Old Testament Pseudepigrapha* (Garden City, NY: Doubleday, 1983), 1:541. The work is dated to about A.D. 100. Note that this portion also affirms human participation in the sin. See also *2 Baruch* 48:42-43. The expression "the fall" was popularized by the early church fathers but is little evidenced in the Greek fathers. Even as late as the fourth century (Gregory of Nyssa) it is not being used as a technical noun

representing a theological construct. It was earlier in the Latin fathers where the concept took on more prominence. I am grateful to my colleague George Kalantzis for this historical information.

[13]I. Provan sees it as inherently a denial that God is good in *Seriously Dangerous Religion* (Waco: Baylor University Press, 2014), p. 174.

[14]This is similar to the idea expressed in Romans 8:17, that we are coheirs with Christ. It would not be appropriate for us to think of ourselves as autonomous heirs *instead of* Christ; we join him as heirs and are heirs through him. In the same way it was not appropriate for people to think of attaining wisdom apart from God. The only acceptable wisdom is found in participation with God.

[15]James Gaffney, *Sin Reconsidered* (New York: Paulist Press, 1983), pp. 48-49.

[16]F. A. M. Wiggermann, "Agriculture as Civilization: Sages, Farmers, and Barbarians," in *The Oxford Handbook of Cuneiform Culture*, ed. Karen Radner and Eleanor Robson (Oxford: Oxford University Press, 2011), p. 674.

[17]More detail is given about the ancient Near Eastern situation in John H. Walton, *Ancient Near Eastern Thought and the Old Testament: Introducing the Conceptual World of the Hebrew Bible* (Grand Rapids: Baker Academic, 2006).

[18]Developed at length in Karel van der Toorn, *Sin and Sanction in Israel and Mesopotamia: A Comparative Study* (Assen: Van Gorcum, 1985).

[19]Much of Protestant understanding of sin is more indebted to Augustine even than to Paul. For more about Augustine and the fall, see Willemien Otten, "The Long Shadow of Human Sin: Augustine on Adam, Eve and the Fall," in *Out of Paradise: Eve and Adam and Their Interpreters*, ed. Bob Becking and Susan Hennecke (Sheffield: Sheffield Phoenix, 2010), pp. 29-49. Augustine was heavily influenced by neoplatonism, asceticism and the desire to refute Gnosticism, Pelagianism and Donatism.

[20]See further discussion in Walton, *Ancient Near Eastern Thought*, pp. 210-14.

PROPOSITION 16: WE CURRENTLY LIVE IN A WORLD WITH NON-ORDER, ORDER AND DISORDER

[1]For further discussion see John H. Walton, "The Ancient Near Eastern Background of the Spirit of the Lord in the Old Testament," in *Presence, Power and Promise: The Role of the Spirit of God in the Old Testament*, ed. David G. Firth and Paul D. Wegner (Downers Grove, IL: InterVarsity Press, 2011), pp. 38-67, esp. pp. 39-44.

[2]Mark Smith, *On the Primaeval Ocean: Carlsberg Papyri 5*, CNI Publications 26 (Copenhagen: Museum Tusculanum Press, University of Copenhagen, 2002),

pp. 53-63; see also p. 194. In earlier texts, the air god Shu uses a blast from his mouth in creation.

[3]See further discussion in John H. Walton, *Genesis 1 as Ancient Cosmology* (Winona Lake, IN: Eisenbrauns, 2011), pp. 37-62.

[4]Mark Harris, *The Nature of Creation: Examining the Bible and Science* (Durham, NC: Acumen, 2013), p. 147. He contends that "suffering and death are not unmitigated evils; there are subtleties to account for"—note the praise to God for providing prey for carnivorous animals (Job 38:39-41; Ps 104:21; 147:9).

[5]Of course we acknowledge that sin *can* cause some of these. Someone can experience disease because of sin (e.g., STDs), and natural disasters can be indirectly linked to irresponsible behavior by humans (whether oil spills, defoliation or greenhouse gases).

PROPOSITION 17: ALL PEOPLE ARE SUBJECT TO SIN AND DEATH BECAUSE OF THE DISORDER IN THE WORLD, NOT BECAUSE OF GENETICS

[1]I am grateful to Jonathan Walton for these helpful categories.

[2]I am grateful to Jonathan Walton for this insight.

[3]Mark Harris, *The Nature of Creation: Examining the Bible and Science* (Durham, NC: Acumen, 2013), pp. 145-46.

[4]Patricia A. Williams, *Doing Without Adam and Eve: Sociobiology and Original Sin* (Minneapolis: Fortress, 2001), p. 42. This synopsis draws widely from a number of Augustine's works, including his early work *On Genesis Against the Manichees* and his *Confessions* (books 11 and 12), but mainly reflected in his *Literal Commentary on Genesis* and finally refined in book 11 of his *City of God*. Selected excerpts from the church fathers are conveniently gathered in Andrew Louth, with Marco Conti, eds., *Genesis 1–11*, Ancient Christian Commentary on Scripture (Downers Grove, IL: InterVarsity Press, 2001).

[5]This is not to imply that the creation is no longer "good" or that relationship with God is no longer possible. For helpful clarification and distinctions see I. Provan, *Seriously Dangerous Religion* (Waco: Baylor University Press, 2014), pp. 134-37.

[6]Note that though this formulation is based on Irenaeus's model; he did not frame it this way.

[7]In Augustine's time it was thought that women were simply incubators—men were the ones who provided the seed.

[8]But to do this Augustine had to include the immaculate conception of Mary

as a necessary element so that sin was not passed down. It is interesting that Protestants reject the immaculate conception of Mary yet still accept Augustine's formulation of the transmission of sin.

[9]See discussion in Williams, *Doing Without Adam and Eve*, pp. 40-47, and in any technical commentary on Romans.

[10]Mark E. Biddle, *Missing the Mark: Sin and Its Consequences in Biblical Theology* (Nashville: Abingdon, 2005), p. xiii.

[11]Ibid., p. xvii.

PROPOSITION 18: JESUS IS THE KEYSTONE OF GOD'S PLAN TO RESOLVE DISORDER AND PERFECT ORDER

[1]As we can see, there is also then a "lost world of the Tower of Babel."

[2]As a side note, this may indicate that the tower builders were in Shem's line.

[3]See full discussion in John H. Walton, *Ancient Near Eastern Thought and the Old Testament: Introducing the Conceptual World of the Hebrew Bible* (Grand Rapids: Baker Academic, 2006), pp. 257-58.

[4]Nicholas Perrin, *Jesus the Temple* (Grand Rapids: Baker, 2010). Note, for example, John 2:19-21.

[5]Notice that in 1 Corinthians 15:45-47, Paul's reference to Adam as the first man is paralleled by mention of Jesus as the last and then as the second. Biologically speaking, Jesus is neither the second nor the last, so we understand that Paul's reference is theological in nature, not biological.

PROPOSITION 19: PAUL'S USE OF ADAM IS MORE INTERESTED IN THE EFFECT OF SIN ON THE COSMOS THAN IN THE EFFECT OF SIN ON HUMANITY, AND HAS NOTHING TO SAY ABOUT HUMAN ORIGINS

[1]The parallels identified between the vocations of Adam and Israel do not result in a view that Adam is nothing more than a glyph for Israel, symbolically telling the story of the exile. This is one of the major points of disagreement I have with the position in Peter Enns, *The Evolution of Adam: What the Bible Does and Doesn't Say About Human Origins* (Grand Rapids: Brazos, 2012).

[2]John H. Walton, *The Lost World of Genesis One: Ancient Cosmology and the Origins Debate* (Downers Grove, IL: InterVarsity Press, 2009); J. Richard Middleton, *The Liberating Image: The Imago Dei in Genesis 1* (Grand Rapids: Brazos, 2005); and G. K. Beale, *The Temple and the Church's Mission: A Biblical Theology of the Dwelling Place of God* (Downers Grove, IL: InterVarsity Press, 2004).

PROPOSITION 20: IT IS NOT ESSENTIAL THAT ALL PEOPLE DESCENDED FROM ADAM AND EVE

[1]For those who are more scientifically minded and want to gain an understanding of the way that genetics relates to this information, see Denis Alexander, *Language of Genetics: A Primer* (Conshohocken, PA: Templeton, 2011); Francis Collins, *The Language of God* (New York: Free Press, 2007); and Graeme Finlay, *Human Evolution: Genes, Genealogies and Phylogenies*, (Cambridge: Cambridge University Press, 2013).

[2]E.g., second-century B.C. Tobit 8:6, "those two were parents of all humans."

[3]This would be so whether or not the current theories on evolutionary theory are on the right track.

[4]Yet to be discussed is whether that "creation" is de novo or involved a longer process (God is creating in either scenario).

[5]For fuller discussion see John H. Walton, *Genesis*, NIV Application Commentary (Grand Rapids: Zondervan, 2001), pp. 367-69.

[6]Even with regard to Noah, this verse makes limited claims. Paul is making the point that in our common humanity we all have a thirst for God, and, indeed, we are *all his* offspring (obviously not a biological/genetic statement). Our commonality does not require a genetic relationship to Noah any more than it requires a genetic relationship to God. Furthermore, even if this verse addresses genetic diversity, it makes no statement about material origins.

[7]Contra NIV, which says she "would become" the mother. If Hebrew wanted to say that, there is a different verbal construction.

[8]The concept of federal headship was popularized during the Reformation by Johannes Cocceius and John Calvin. On the basis of Romans 5, it identifies Adam as the "federal" head of humanity and sees his fountainhead role as more covenantal than biological. In the same way, Christ became the federal head under the covenant of grace.

PROPOSITION 21: HUMANS COULD BE VIEWED AS DISTINCT CREATURES AND A SPECIAL CREATION OF GOD EVEN IF THERE WAS MATERIAL CONTINUITY

[1]By this I am acknowledging that some of the standard mechanisms that have long been part of evolutionary theory, such as natural or random selection and mutation, may well be inadequate to carry the weight. Scientists have long recognized this, and other models are constantly being put forward.

[2]See www.biologos.org for many resources explaining this approach.

[3]J. Richard Middleton, *The Liberating Image: The Imago Dei in Genesis 1* (Grand Rapids: Brazos, 2005).

[4]Ryan Peterson, "The Imago Dei as Human Identity: A Theological Interpretation" (PhD diss., Wheaton College, 2010).

[5]Zainab Bahrani, *The Graven Image: Representation in Babylonia and Assyria* (Philadelphia: University of Pennsylvania Press, 2003); and Edward Mason Curtis, "Man as the Image of God in Genesis in Light of Ancient Near Eastern Parallels" (PhD diss., University of Pennsylvania, 1984), ProQuest AAI8422896.

[6]Christopher Walker and Michael B. Dick, *The Induction of the Cult Image in Ancient Mesopotamia: The Mesopotamian mīs pî Ritual*, State Archives of Assyria Literary Texts 1 (Helsinki: Neo-Assyrian Text Corpus Project, 2001), with specific discussion on pp. 6-8. Additional discussion of cult images in Michael B. Dick, "Prophetic Parodies of Making the Cult Image," in *Born in Heaven, Made on Earth: The Making of the Cult Image in the Ancient Near East*, ed. Michael B. Dick (Winona Lake, IN: Eisenbrauns, 1999), pp. 1-53; and Angelika Berlejung, "Washing the Mouth: The Consecration of Divine Images in Mesopotamia," in *The Image and the Book: Iconic Cults, Aniconism, and the Rise of Book Religion in Israel and the Ancient Near East*, ed. Karel van der Toorn (Leuven: Peeters, 1997), pp. 45-72.

[7]Catherine Leigh Beckerleg, "The 'Image of God' in Eden: The Creation of Mankind in Genesis 2:5–3:24 in Light of the *mīs pî pīt pî* and *wpt-r* Rituals of Mesopotamia and Ancient Egypt" (PhD diss., Harvard University, 2009), ProQuest 3385433.

CONCLUSION AND SUMMARY

[1]John Calvin, *Genesis*, trans. John King (Grand Rapids: Baker, 1979 printing), pp. 86-87.

[2]Philip Ryken, "We Cannot Understand the World or Our Faith Without a Real, Historical Adam," in Matthew Barrett and Ardel B. Caneday, eds., *Four Views on the Historical Adam* (Grand Rapids: Zondervan, 2013), pp. 267-79.

[3]Many are cited throughout the foregoing chapters, but I would mention particularly Peter C. Bouteneff, *Beginnings: Ancient Christian Readings of the Biblical Creation Narratives* (Grand Rapids: Baker, 2008).

Glossary

archetype—In a literary sense, an archetype refers to a recurrent symbol or motif, even a type of character. Fictional characters often serve as archetypes of good or evil, heroism or treachery, etc. In this book I am using the term in a narrower sense. An archetype here refers to a representative of a group in whom all others in the group are embodied. As a result, all members of the group are included and participate with their representative.

cognitive environment—This refers to what is sometimes called a worldview. It refers to the sum total of how people of a particular time or culture thought about themselves, their society, their world and their God(s). Israel would have had a cognitive environment very similar to that of the broader ancient Near East (certainly much more in common with that cognitive environment than with our modern one), yet at the same time, God's revelation was constantly introducing innovative concepts, mostly about himself, into their cognitive environment.

common ancestry—This stands as the main conclusion of evolutionary theory, maintaining that all life has developed from the first elementary forms of life.

comparative genomics—This is the process of comparing the genetic makeup of various species and subspecies to identify similarities and differences. Such comparison often provides the basis for reconstructing the history of development of species.

de novo—This descriptive term refers to an understanding of human origins that sees Adam and Eve as having been made through a direct, material act of God distinct from any predecessors, and using no biological process. It features material discontinuity from any other species, including *homo*-types, in the process God used (even though there are obvious genetic similarities). Some would see room for God to use genetic material from previously existing species but insist that he is involved to produce something material that cannot be explained naturally. For some, this could be as slight as a tweak in the DNA at the final stage. "Fully de novo" refers to the view that no prior genetic material was involved.

epistemology—This is the branch of metaphysics dealing with knowledge—its sources and its nature. It answers questions like, how do we come to know something with confidence? Scientific experimentation and theorization serve as a foundation of epistemology for many today. For others, faith in revelation constitutes the focal point of their epistemology.

evolution—In its most basic, nonmetaphysical sense, evolution refers to a concept of change over time with modification. More specifically, it is an interpretation of the world around us that posits a material (phylogenetic) continuity among all species of creatures (biological and genetic, not spiritual) as the result of a process of change over time through various mechanisms known and unknown. It is not inherently atheistic or deistic.

ex nihilo—This is the concept of creating material objects using no prior existing matter.

exegesis/exegete/exegetical—This describes analysis of text at every level.

federal representative—This is a concept popularized by Calvinism, though its roots go back to Irenaeus and Augustine. Adam is viewed as one who represents all those who are bound together by covenant or something similar. Adam is viewed as the federal head of humanity as is Christ in related ways. The concept is used in explaining original sin and the imputation of righteousness.

Great Symbiosis—The foundation of religion in Mesopotamia is that humanity has been created to serve the gods by meeting their needs for food (sacrifices), housing (temples) and clothing, and generally by giving them worship and privacy so that those gods can do the work of running the cosmos. On the other side of the symbiosis, the gods will safeguard their investment by protecting their worshipers and providing for them. Humans thus find dignity in the role that they have in this symbiosis to aid the gods (through their rituals) in running the cosmos.

Hasmoneans—In the second century B.C. the family of Mattathias and Judah Maccabee, from the clan known as the Hasmoneans, led a revolt against the Seleucid overlords who ruled Israel. They established Jewish independence that lasted for about eighty years.

intertextuality—This term refers to how texts are related to other texts. The most obvious form of intertextuality is quotation of another text. But any level of use or allusion qualifies.

Masoretes—These Jewish scholars preserved the Hebrew Bible from generation to generation; their roots go back to the third century A.D., and their work continued into the 10th century. Their expertise in scribal arts was used in the meticulous transmission of the traditional text. Their innovations are found in the systems they devised to incorporate metatextual information (such as vowel pointings and cantillation indicators) into the written text without interfering with the traditional consonantal text. Their manuscripts provide the most complete testimony to the Old Testament text.

naturalism—This is a philosophical commitment to the idea that all we observe can be explained by investigation of cause and effect applying natural laws. This philosophy does not leave room for a God who is involved with his creation and acting in it. Natural science, in contrast, does not deny the existence of God or supernatural cause.

ontology—This is the branch of metaphysics that explores existence in general (what does it mean when we say something exists?) or the existence of something more particular (the ontology of genders or of sin).

soteriology—This is the doctrine of salvation.

steady-state universe—This theory was developed in the 1930s in opposition to the expanding universe or the Big Bang cosmology. In the steady-state theory, new galaxies and stars were being formed within the expanding universe so that it always looked the same wherever one might be positioned in the universe.

Targum Neofiti—The Targums are expansive Aramaic translations/paraphrases of biblical texts. This Targum, containing almost the entire Pentateuch, is preserved in a sixteenth-century copy of what is thought to originate in the first several centuries A.D.

Further Reading

Books

Alexander, Denis. *Creation or Evolution: Do We Have to Choose?* Oxford: Monarch, 2008.

———. *Language of Genetics: A Primer.* Conshohocken, PA: Templeton, 2011.

Anderson, Gary A. *The Genesis of Perfection: Adam and Eve in Jewish and Christian Interpretation.* Louisville, KY: Westminster John Knox, 2001.

———. *Sin: A History.* New Haven, CT: Yale University Press, 2009.

Barrett, Matthew, and Ardel B. Caneday, eds. *Four Views on the Historical Adam.* Grand Rapids: Zondervan, 2013.

Becking, Bob, and Susan Hennecke. *Out of Paradise: Eve and Adam and Their Interpreters.* Sheffield: Sheffield Phoenix, 2010.

Biddle, Mark E. *Missing the Mark: Sin and Its Consequences in Biblical Theology.* Nashville: Abingdon, 2005.

Boda, Mark J. *A Severe Mercy: Sin and Its Remedy in the Old Testament.* Winona Lake, IN: Eisenbrauns, 2009.

Bouteneff, Peter C. *Beginnings: Ancient Christian Readings of the Biblical Creation Narratives.* Grand Rapids: Baker, 2008.

Callender, Dexter E., Jr. *Adam in Myth and History: Ancient Israelite Perspectives on the Primal Human.* Harvard Semitic Studies 48. Winona Lake, IN: Eisenbrauns, 2000.

Charlesworth, James H. *The Good and Evil Serpent: How a Universal Symbol Became Christianized.* New Haven, CT: Yale University Press, 2010.

Collins, C. John. *Did Adam and Eve Really Exist? Who They Were and Why You Should Care.* Wheaton, IL: Crossway, 2011.

Collins, Francis S. *The Language of God: A Scientist Presents Evidence for Belief.* New York: Free Press, 2007.

Crowther, Kathleen M. *Adam and Eve in the Protestant Reformation*. Cambridge: Cambridge University Press, 2010.

Enns, Peter. *The Evolution of Adam: What the Bible Does and Doesn't Say About Human Origins*. Grand Rapids: Brazos, 2012.

Falk, Darrel R. *Coming to Peace with Science: Bridging the Worlds Between Faith and Biology*. Downers Grove, IL: InterVarsity Press, 2004.

Finlay, Graeme. *Human Evolution: Genes, Genealogies and Phylogenies*. Cambridge: Cambridge University Press, 2013.

Fowler, Thomas B., and Daniel Kuebler. *The Evolution Controversy: A Survey of Competing Theories*. Grand Rapids: Baker Academic, 2007.

Giovino, Mariana. *The Assyrian Sacred Tree: A History of Interpretations*. Orbis biblicus et orientalis 230. Göttingen: Vandenhoeck & Ruprecht, 2007.

Haarsma, Deborah B., and Loren D. Haarsma. *Origins: Christian Perspectives on Creation, Evolution, and Intelligent Design*. Grand Rapids: Faith Alive Christian Resources, 2011.

Harris, Mark. *The Nature of Creation: Examining the Bible and Science*. Durham, NC: Acumen, 2013.

Izre'el, Shlomo. *Adapa and the South Wind: Language Has the Power of Life and Death*. Winona Lake, IN: Eisenbrauns, 2001.

Joines, Karen. *Serpent Symbolism in the Old Testament: A Linguistic, Archaeological and Literary Study*. Haddonfield, NJ: Haddonfield House, 1974.

Mettinger, Tryggve N. D. *The Eden Narrative: A Literary and Religio-historical Study of Genesis 2–3*. Winona Lake, IN: Eisenbrauns, 2007.

Meyers, Carol L. *The Tabernacle Menorah: A Synthetic Study of a Symbol from the Biblical Cult*. American Schools of Oriental Research Dissertations 2. Missoula, MT: Scholars Press, 1976.

Osborn, Ronald E. *Death Before the Fall: Biblical Literalism and the Problem of Animal Suffering*. Downers Grove, IL: InterVarsity Press, 2014.

Plantinga, Cornelius. *Not the Way It's Supposed to Be: A Breviary of Sin*. Grand Rapids: Eerdmans, 1995.

Provan, Iain. *Seriously Dangerous Religion*. Waco, Texas: Baylor University Press, 2014.

Rana, Fazale, and Hugh Ross. *Who Was Adam?: A Creation Model Approach to the Origin of Man.* Colorado Springs, CO: NavPress, 2005.

Stordalen, Terje. *Echoes of Eden: Genesis 2–3 and Symbolism of the Eden Garden in Biblical Hebrew Literature.* Leuven: Peeters, 2000.

Walton, John H. *Ancient Near Eastern Thought and the Old Testament: Introducing the Conceptual World of the Hebrew Bible.* Grand Rapids: Baker Academic, 2006.

———. *Genesis.* NIV Application Commentary. Grand Rapids: Zondervan, 2001.

———. *Genesis 1 as Ancient Cosmology.* Winona Lake, IN: Eisenbrauns, 2011.

———. *The Lost World of Genesis One: Ancient Cosmology and the Origins Debate.* Downers Grove, IL: InterVarsity Press, 2009.

Williams, Patricia A. *Doing Without Adam and Eve: Sociobiology and Original Sin.* Minneapolis: Fortress, 2001.

Zevit, Ziony. *What Really Happened in the Garden of Eden?* New Haven, CT: Yale University Press, 2013.

Articles

Averbeck, Richard E. "Ancient Near Eastern Mythography as It Relates to Historiography in the Hebrew Bible: Genesis 3 and the Cosmic Battle." In *The Future of Biblical Archaeology: Reassessing Methodologies and Assumptions,* edited by James K. Hoffmeier and Alan R. Millard, pp. 328-56. Grand Rapids: Eerdmans, 2004.

Batto, Bernard F. "Paradise Reexamined." In *In the Beginning: Essays on Creation Motifs in the Ancient Near East and the Bible,* edited by Bernard F. Batto, pp. 54-85. Winona Lake, IN: Eisenbrauns, 2013. Originally published in *The Biblical Canon in Comparative Perspective,* edited by K. Lawson Younger Jr., William W. Hallo and Bernard F. Batto, Scripture in Context 4 (Lewiston, NY: Mellen, 1991), pp. 33-66.

Bloch-Smith, Elizabeth. "Solomon's Temple: The Politics of Ritual Space." In *Sacred Time, Sacred Place: Archaeology and the Religion of Israel,* edited by Barry M. Gittlen, pp. 83-94. Winona Lake, IN: Eisenbrauns, 2002.

Feinman, Peter. "Where Is Eden? An Analysis of Some of the Mesopotamian Motifs in Primeval J." In *Creation and Chaos: A Reconsideration
of Hermann Gunkel's* Chaoskampf *Hypothesis,* edited by JoAnn
Scurlock and Richard H. Beal, pp. 172-89. Winona Lake, IN: Eisenbrauns, 2013.

Gleason, Kathryn L. "Gardens." In *Oxford Encyclopedia of Archaeology in
the Near East,* edited by Eric Meyers, 2:383. New York: Oxford University Press, 1997.

Hurowitz, Victor. "Yhwh's Exalted House—Aspects of the Design and
Symbolism of Solomon's Temple." In *Temple and Worship in Biblical
Israel: Proceedings of the Oxford Old Testament Seminar,* edited by John
Day, pp. 63-110. New York: Continuum, 2005.

Parpola, Simo. "The Assyrian Tree of Life: Tracing the Origins of Jewish
Monotheism and Greek Philosophy." *Journal of Near Eastern Studies* 52
(1993): 161-208.

Stager, Lawrence E. "Jerusalem as Eden." *Biblical Archaeology Review* 26,
no. 3 (2000): 38-43.

Tuell, Steven S. "The Rivers of Paradise: Ezekiel 47.1-12 and Genesis 2.10-
14." In *God Who Creates: Essays in Honor of W. Sibley Towner,* edited
by William P. Brown and S. Dean McBride, pp. 171-89. Grand Rapids:
Eerdmans, 2000.

Venema, Dennis R. "Genesis and the Genome: Genomics Evidence for
Human-Ape Common Ancestry and Ancestral Hominid Population
Sizes." *Perspectives on Science and Christian Faith* 62 (2010): 166-78.

Weinfeld, Moshe. "Gen. 7:11, 8:1-2 Against the Background of Ancient
Near Eastern Tradition." *Die Welt des Orients* 9 (1978): 242-48.

Wenham, Gordon J. "Sanctuary Symbolism in the Garden of Eden Story."
In *"I Studied Inscriptions from Before the Flood": Ancient Near Eastern,
Literary, and Linguistic Approaches to Genesis 1–11,* edited by Richard
S. Hess and David Toshio Tsumura, pp. 399-404. Sources for Biblical
and Theological Study 4. Winona Lake, IN: Eisenbrauns, 1994.
Reprinted from *Proceedings of the Ninth World Congress of Jewish
Studies, Division A: The Period of the Bible* (Jerusalem: World Union of
Jewish Studies, 1986), pp. 19-25.

Wyatt, Nicolas. "The Mythic Mind." In *The Mythic Mind: Essays on Cosmology and Religion in Ugaritic and Old Testament Literature,* pp. 151-88. London: Equinox, 2005.

Many articles on these issues can be found on the website www.biologos .org.

AUTHOR INDEX

Subject Index

SCRIPTURE INDEX

Finding the Textbook You Need

The IVP Academic Textbook Selector
is an online tool for instantly finding the IVP books
suitable for over 250 courses across 24 disciplines.

---

ivpacademic.com
